The French
Revolution

The
French
Revolution

The Beginning of Modern Democracy

Walter Grab

BRACKEN BOOKS

LONDON

First published in 1989 in Germany by Parkland Verlag as
Die Franzosische Revolution 1789, Aufbruch in die moderne Demokratie

This edition first published 1989 by Bracken Books
an imprint of Bestseller Publications Ltd.
Princess House, 50 Eastcastle Street
London W1N 7AP, England

ISBN 1 85170 248 2

Translation by Terry Bond in co-operation with First Edition

Printed and bound in Yugoslavia

49.95

Contents

Introduction   7
The Revolution as the crowning of the Enlightenment

1. The Old Regime during the Reign of Louis XVI, 1774–1788   17
The feudal system in France – Economic and financial crises, the status of the French monarchy,
aristocracy, clergy, bourgeoisie, peasantry and lower classes – The military – The provinces – The
political and legal systems, and the Constitution

2. The Beginning of the Bourgeois Revolution   33
August 1788 – The peasant uprising of 1789 – The States-General – The rights of the Third Estate –
The Tennis-Court Oath – Unrest in Paris – Necker's dismissal – The electoral assemblies – The
storming of the Bastille – The march on Versailles

3. The Work of the Constituent National Assembly   59
The founding of the National Assembly – The Declaration of Human Rights – The destruction of
the old order – The expropriation of church property – The *assignats* – New ideals – The death of
Mirabeau – The flight of the king in June 1791

4. Revolutionary Escalation, 1791–1792   81
Who supported the war? – The onset of war – The Constitution of 3 September – The king's Veto
– The offensive of the allied monarchs

5. The Conflict of Interests between the Girondins and the Montagnards   103
The storming of the Tuileries and the fall of the monarchy – The National Convention – The
king's execution – The revolutionary tribunals – The uprising in the Vendée

6. Jacobin Rule 1793–1794   137
Agrarian reform – The murder of Marat – The Revolutionary Government – The *levée en masse* –
The storming of the Convention – The Terror – The Civil War – Dechristianization and the revol-
utionary calendar – The *Indulgents* – Robespierre's fall from power

7. Thermidor and the Directory 1794–1799   175
The White Terror – Peace with Prussia – The Constitution of the Year III – Babeuf and the Conspiracy of Equals – The war of aggression – Napoleon's Egyptian campaign – The coup of 18
brumaire

8. Napoleon Bonaparte as Heir and Destroyer of the Revolution   201
The Jacobin legacy – Economic reform – Peace with England – Reconciliation with the *émigrés* and the Church – The Civil Code – War with England – Napoleon becomes Consul for life – Napoleon as Emperor

Chronological Table of Events   223

List of illustrations   228

Selected Bibliography   235

Index of place names   236

Index of names   237

The Revolution as the Crowning of the Enlightenment

The French Revolution at the end of the eighteenth century is no closed chapter of history, but an event of great significance for our time. It initiated a process of renewal in all spheres of life, which affected not only France, but the culture and civilization of the whole of mankind.

For the first time ever, the French Revolution offered a glimpse of a social order in which all men would be politically free and equal in the eyes of the law, an order in which no-one would be subject to the authority of another, but in which each individual would determine his own destiny. For the first time ever, the radical spokesmen of the Revolution placed the abolition of all social privilege on the political agenda. For the first time ever, they demanded that the concepts of liberal parliamentary democracy and the welfare state should form the basis for organizing government. The ideals of the French Revolution are just as relevant and valid today as they were two hundred years ago: economic and religious freedom and the right of free speech; political equality; the knowledge that one's life and

Colourful fan from the first years of the Revolution, symbolizing the union of the monarchy, the clergy and the people. At the top of the freedom tree, which is surrounded by two churchflags, the red Jacobin cap has been placed. The group of 'sansculottes' carry pikes – the lance-like weapon used by the militant crowds – or rifles with bayonettes from which some of them have hung their caps. The monk is clearly trying to address the crowd.

property are secure; the separation of powers; constitutional guarantees to protect the rights of political, national and religious minorities; the legal right to resist state tyranny; the right to a government which must submit itself to the democratic process; the inalienable sovereignty of the people, and the right to national self-determination. These concepts still impassion the underprivileged and humiliated today, and are a source of inspiration and confidence to the people of every land.

At the head of the Revolution stood a group of determined and courageous members of the bourgeoisie. France's bourgeoisie, which in the course of several generations had amassed a great deal of capital, was well aware of its economic strength and was demanding the right to participate in the political decision-making process. Its revolutionaries succeeded in overthrowing the class-based absolutist order, abolishing the traditional supremacy of the aristocracy, and becoming the leading force in national politics.

The French Revolution was, however, not the first ever bourgeois uprising. Indeed, more than two hundred years before, in the 1660s, the bourgeoisie of the affluent maritime and trading towns of the Netherlands rose up against their oppression by the mighty Spanish Empire. Supported by the masses and after an 80-year long struggle for freedom, the proud and self-confident bourgeoisie of Amsterdam, Rotterdam, the Hague and other Dutch towns succeeded in defeating Spain's superior forces and in winning national independence. The Dutch justified their revolt against the Spanish Crown by linking it with the teachings of the Church reformer Calvin, who declared resistance to despotic and cruel governments to be perfectly legitimate. They wanted to retain their medieval privileges and regarded their bourgeois revolution as the throwing off of the Catholic yoke which had been forced upon them by Spanish foreign rule.

In the mid-seventeenth century a second bourgeois revolution took place. The lower house of the English Parliament revolted against King Charles I, who was attempting to set himself up as an absolutist ruler, thereby violating the traditional rights enjoyed by those citizens represented in the House. The English revolutionaries, under the command of Oliver Cromwell, were backed up by the rural and urban lower classes, and the parliamentary forces

triumphed over Charles' army. Like the Dutch before them, the English insurgents drew their spiritual weaponry from the Old Testament and fought under the ideological standard of religion. They believed the purpose of their struggle to be the defence of their laws, hallowed by tradition, against the tyranny of a monarch who had become a despot. Charles I was sentenced to death by Parliament and beheaded, primarily because he had encroached upon the vested rights of the bourgeoisie.

The religious element, however, played no significant part in the third bourgeois revolution, the revolt in the 1760s of the thirteen English colonies on the East Coast of North America. Indeed, the Philadelphia Congress, which in 1776 declared independence from its English motherland and founded the United States, justified the uprising by citing the English king's violation of the traditional rights enjoyed by the Colonies.

It was, in fact, a common feature of the three earlier bourgeois revolutions – in the Netherlands, in England and in North America – that their political spokesman had taken their bearings from the past, from allegedly better days gone by. They had regarded their struggles as attempts to restore legal rights which were fast being eroded by tyrannical rule and were only enjoyed by quite specific classes and in quite specific spheres. For this reason, these successful bourgeois upheavals, although they resulted in significant shifts in power within their own borders, influenced the thinking of only a few scholars abroad.

France's great revolution, however, was altogether different. It was the first to be aimed at the wholesale defeat of the old order and the establishment of a totally new legal and governmental system based on the principles of reason. The force and appeal of its call for universal liberation broke through national boundaries and opened the door to a new age in the history of mankind.

The French revolutionaries were driven by the hope and longing for a happy future, free of conflict. They purposely broke with tradition and the past in order to create a society founded on freedom and social justice. In doing so, they worked on the principle that man was capable of establishing a natural society, that is to say, a society in harmony with his own true nature. They were just as convinced of the need and ability to change the existing social order

The philosopher Jean-Jacques Rousseau (1712–1778), born in Geneva, demanded in *The Social Contract* (1762) that a democratic State should be created, which would guarantee equal rights to all citizens. His theory on the State exercised a great influence over the French revolutionaries. His remains were buried in the Pantheon in Paris by the Jacobins.

and ways of life, as they were of the concept that people would act in their own interests as soon as they were able to recognize and understand them. They aspired to a social order based on the material and spiritual development of man's talents and abilities. The unhindered development of each individual was regarded as a prerequisite for the development of a harmonious social system guided by reason, which would be based on sound moral principles and would overcome the distinction between morality and politics which had always existed.

Enlightenment and revolution grew out of the same roots, namely the emancipation of the bourgeoisie from a social order based on the privileges of the estates of the realm. The thinkers of the Enlightenment were not the authors of the Revolution, but they did articulate social demands which were then transformed by the revolutionaries into political demands and were, to some extent, realized. The most important ideological weapon employed by the revolutionaries was taken from Rousseau's arsenal of teachings, which proclaimed the innate equality of all men. It was Rousseau who developed the concept of '*Volonté Générale*', the general will, superior to that of the individual, which takes into account only the interests of the whole. According to Rousseau, man could only live freely and happily in a state in which each individual subordinated his private, egoistic interests to those of the whole, to the '*Volonté Générale*'. Rousseau was, in fact, calling for nothing other than the moral conscience carried in the breast of every human being to form the basis of the political system.

Rousseau's *Social Contract* stressed the need for political equality for all men, something which amounted to the abolition of all historical class distinctions and the vestiges of feudalism. According to Rousseau's teachings on the state, from which we have taken the theoretical conception of modern democracy, the social and legal features of an order based on privilege were an affront to the true nature of mankind. He demanded the transformation of all political and social structures. The social order which he dreamed of would no longer be divided into classes, but would represent a voluntary coalition of equal and rationally thinking individuals.

Long before the Revolution, the thinkers of the Enlightenment had recognized that the social function of religion was to consolidate the existing balance of power and that the Church was the most steadfast mainstay of the class-based order. The intellectual spokesmen of the bourgeoisie therefore fought against the Church's legitimation of those claiming to rule with the grace of God, opposed the Church's teachings on the earthly vale of tears, and disputed God's alleged requirement for all to subjugate themselves to the tyranny of the monarch. Whilst the forces of religion postponed the equality desired by so many until the afterlife, the philosophy of the Enlightenment was that men had a claim to equal rights *in this world*. This philosophy ripped away the veil of superstition which the ruling powers had attempted to transform into something mysterious and mystical, and declared that kings and aristocrats had obtained power through acts of force, conquest and oppression and had joined forces with the Church in order to find an ideological anchor for their rule. The thinkers of Enlightenment demonstrated that tyranny and religion went hand in hand: wherever the first oppresses, the other is at hand with the word of God to portray the ruler as a divinely designated authority and the wretchedness of the people as a divine test. They no longer had any respect for the Church, for in their eyes it had sanctioned the powerlessness of the common man.

In place of divine justice, the thinkers of the Enlightenment talked of the good sense of the bourgeois citizen, who would put aside his own interests and those of his class, recognize his role as the representative of a mankind wracked by suffering, and identify with those classes which had been oppressed under the old class-based system and which enjoyed no political rights.

The revolutionaries who translated the theories of the Enlightenment into political and social reality replaced the religious ideology of feudalism with a new bourgeois ideology: that of the nation. They destroyed Europe's traditionalistic order and released the continent from the Middle Ages by establishing France as a secular nation-state. They threw off the tutelage of the aristocratic and ecclesiastical powers and achieved an historical alliance between universal ideals and national opinion.

Through their attempts to remove the discrepancies between ethics and politics, might and right, the revolutionaries tore down the walls which divided the classes and replaced the omnipotence of the king with national sovereignty. Patriotic revolutionaries linked the concept of the nation with a call for the population to contribute to the process of law-giving and to take an active and purposeful part in shaping its own destiny. In the new nation-state, both the divine right of kings and all class division based on the privileges of birth were eliminated. In their place could be found a system under which political leaders had to submit themselves to the democratic process, and a parliament elected by a sovereign people and with the authority to take decisions on any matter.

The revolutionaries' achievements are not diminished by their mistaken belief that they would be able to put an end to *every* form of oppression and domination of one man by another, and thus bring about universal emancipation from social and political tyranny. They believed that the abolition of the 'unreasoned' feudal system would be sufficient to produce a 'virtuous' social order which would adopt as its guiding principle not selfish profit, but achievement and public well-being. In the event, however, these noble hopes remained unfulfilled. Nevertheless, they provided the bourgeois revolutionaries with their optimism and their readiness to make sacrifices and were the source of their inspiration during the struggle.

It would be wholly wrong to say that the Revolution was merely a consequence of the Enlightenment. Rather, it was economic factors which made the upsurge of revolution amongst the bourgeoisie necessary, even inevitable. Economically, the tradi-

Title page for the first edition (published 1762) of Rousseau's treatise on the State, *The Social Contract or The Basic Rules for the General State Law*. The basic theories of this work were adopted by the French Revolution's Constitution in 1791 and 1793.

DU
CONTRACT SOCIAL;
OU,
PRINCIPES
DU
DROIT POLITIQUE.

PAR J. J. ROUSSEAU,
CITOYEN DE GENEVE.

Dicamus leges. —— fœderis æquas
Æneid. XI

À AMSTERDAM,
Chez MARC MICHEL REY.
MDCCLXII.

Overleaf: The declaration of the rights of man of 26 August 1789 which were inserted as an Introduction to the 1791 Constitution.

tional class system rested on two main pillars: feudal land-ownership and the fact that statute-labourers were tied to a particular piece of land, being unable to leave the land which they worked without the permission of the lord of the manor. This system took no account of dynamic changes in social and economic relations. It permitted little social mobility and condemned the vassals to everlasting powerlessness in the field of politics. In the decades before the Revolution the beginnings of a capitalist system based on competition had been developing at the very heart of the class-based society. This new economic system required investments to be calculable and profitable, something which was only possible within the framework of a bourgeois constitutional state. Improved methods of production and increased maritime trade strengthened the self-confidence and boldness of the bourgeoisie, who increasingly perceived the privileged status enjoyed by the clergy and the aristocracy as unnecessary, because it was not in any way based on economic performance. The needs of the developing market economy made it imperative for the bourgeoisie to be equal in the eyes of the law, but this equality was not attainable in a class-based system. A meritocracy made up of citizens with political rights and based on confidence in the legal system was a vital necessity for the bourgeoisie. It

DECLARATION OF THE RIGHTS OF MAN AND CITIZENS

26th August 1789

The representatives of the French people, having been installed as a National Assembly, and being of the opinion that ignorance and oblivion of, and contempt for human rights are the sole causes of public misery and the corruptness of governments, have resolved to set forth the natural, inalienable and sacred rights of man in a solemn declaration, that this declaration might permanently remain before all members of society and constantly remind them of their rights and duties, that the actions of both the law-givers and those who exercise power might at any moment be checked against the ultimate goal of each political institution and might thus earn more respect, that the rights of the citizen, henceforth founded upon simple and indisputable principles, might serve to safeguard the Constitution and public well-being. Consequently, the National Assembly hereby recognises and proclaims the following human and civil rights and commends them to the protection of the Allmighty.

Article 1.
Men are born free and with equal rights.
Social distinctions shall be justifiable only for the benefit of the common good.

Article 2.
The objective of every political union is to safeguard the natural and inalienable rights of man. These are the rights of freedom and security, the right to own property and to resist oppression.

Article 3.
All sovereignty has its ultimate origins in the nation. No organisation, no individual shall exercise sovereignty unless that sovereignty is drawn expressly from the nation.

Article 4.
Freedom consists of the ability to take any action which does not harm another. Thus the exercise of each individual's natural rights is restricted only by such limitations as safeguard the ability of other members of society to enjoy equal rights. These limitations may only be laid down by the law.

Article 5.
Only the law has the right to forbid actions which are detrimental to society. No act which is not forbidden by law may be prevented, and no man shall be forced to do what it does not command.

Article 6.
The law is an expression of the common good, and all citizens are entitled, either personally or through their representatives, to play a part in shaping it. It shall treat all men equally, whether in protecting or punishing them. Since all citizens are equal in its eyes, they shall find equal admission to all positions, posts and offices according to ability and without any distinction other than their own qualities and talents.

Article 7.
No man shall be accused, arrested or detained other than in such cases and in such forms as the law provides. Those who follow, issue, carry out, or require to be carried out, any arbitrary order shall be punished. Furthermore, any citizen summoned or apprehended under the law, shall immediately respond. By resisting, he renders himself liable to prosecution.

Article 8.
The law shall impose only such penalties as are manifestly absolutely necessary, and no man shall be punished on the basis of any law which had not been enacted, promulgated and legally applied at the time of his offence.

Article 9.
Since every individual is considered innocent until proven guilty, and assuming that arrest is deemed unavoidable, any force over and above that necessary to secure his person shall be strictly forbidden by law.

Article 10.
No man shall be persecuted on account of his views, even those of a religious nature, as long as the expression of those views does not threaten the legally established public order.

Article 11.
The free communication of thoughts and views is one of the most precious of all human rights. Every citizen shall be free to write, say and publish whatever he wishes, but shall be held responsible for any abuse of that freedom as stipulated by the law.

Article 12.
The rights of man and citizens can only be safeguarded with the help of armed forces. These forces shall be deployed for the benefit of all and not to the particular advantage of those to whom they are entrusted.

Article 13.
This being unavoidable, a universal tax shall be levied to cover the cost of maintaining the armed forces and of their administration. It shall be evenly levied on all citizens in consideration of their financial circumstances.

Article 14.
All citizens shall be entitled, either personally or through their representatives, to assess the need for such a public tax, to approve it freely, to verify its use and to determine its level, its nature, the manner of its collection and its duration.

Article 15.
Society has the right to demand of any public official that he give an account of his administration.

Article 16.
A society in which such rights are not guaranteed and in which the separation of powers is not defined, has no constitution.

Article 17.
Since the right to own property is an inviolable and sacred right, no man may be deprived of his property except in the case of clearly and legally proven public need and unless such action is accompanied by just compensation in advance.

Duvergier, *Lois, I,* P. 38.
French translation, p. 303ff.

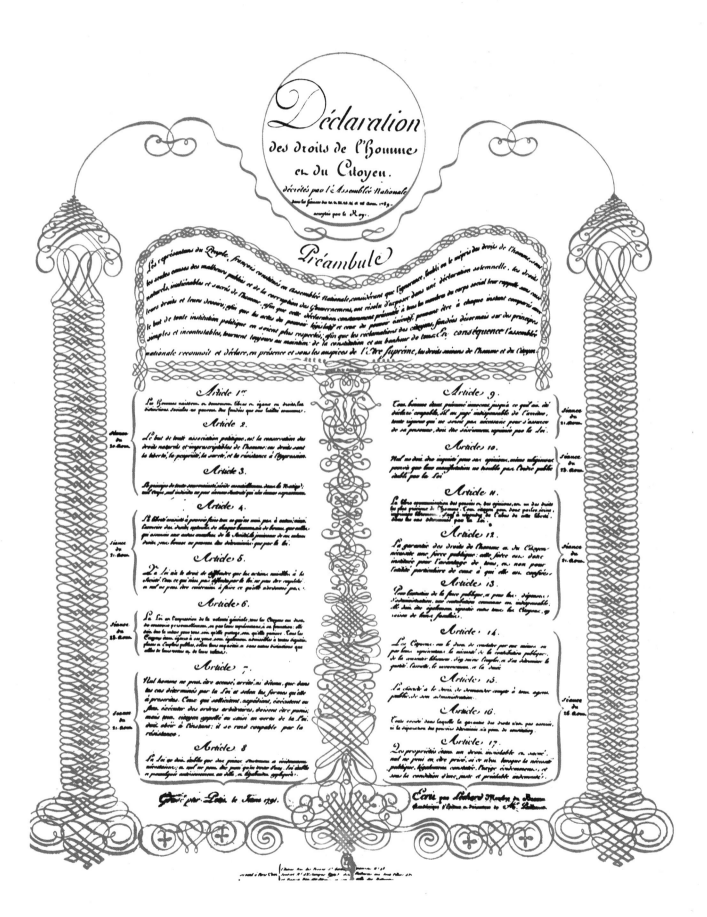

AUX GRANDS HOMMES LA PATRIE RECONNAISSANTE

could, however, only be brought about through revolutionary action designed to snap the chains of privilege. The mounting tensions between the old regime, propped up as it was by tradition and religion, and the bourgeoisie, whose economic spur was competition and individual profit, could, in the end, only be discharged through revolution.

In one revolutionary storm, the bourgeoisie swept away the spiritual, political and economic foundations of the old regime. In its own interest, however, it held fire on one particular privilege: that of ownership. The revolutionaries declared the right of ownership to be sacred and inviolable. Property acquired as a result of one's own labour (and the exploitation of other workers) became the most cru-

Rousseau's idolization and transfer to the Pantheon on 11 October 1794.

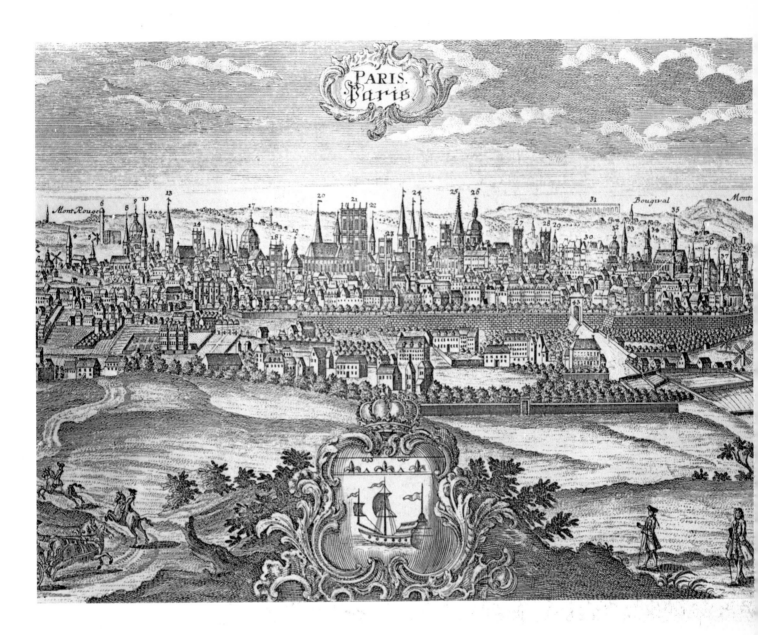

cial factor in determining the new social hierarchy, whereas the feudal property of the Crown, aristocracy and clergy was declared to be abominable, originating as it did (according to the ideology of the bourgeois revolutionaries) from unlawful conquest and force, that is, from theft. This moralizing division of ownership into two different forms allowed the revolutionary bourgeoisie to confiscate feudal property and to transfer it, to its own advantage, 'into the ownership of the nation'.

By tearing down class barriers and destroying feudal tradition, the bourgeoisie smoothed the way for the politically ambitious and ruthless, and the economically strong, and this movement found expression in the catch-phrase, 'Make way for

Paris in the mid-eighteenth century. Contemporary engraving.

efficiency!' The Revolution created ideal conditions for exploiting parcelled land-ownership and increasing industrial output through free competition. Moreover, the propertied bourgeoisie was able to make use of the nation's economic potential as it wished.

How can the sweeping successes and the triumphant advance of the Revolution be explained? One of the main reasons for its strength lay in the fact that France's industrial sector was already sufficiently developed and dynamic to supersede agrarian methods of production and the class-system which they supported, whilst the conflict of interests inherent in the emerging capitalist class-system was only present in embryonic form and had not yet come to a head. Thus it was possible for the Third Estate, which encompassed the propertied and the propertyless, to combine in the fight against feudalism and, despite all their social conflicts of interest, to act in unison at least until the overthrow of the monarchy. During the first four years of the Revolution, the bourgeoisie kept the lower classes in tow. Not until 1793 did their spokesmen emerge with separate demands. The sansculottes had, in fact, played a crucial part in all the battles fought against the domestic and foreign enemies of the Revolution, but had been swindled out of their share of the glory after the victory, and were not able to seize political power for themselves. Only the bourgeoisie knew how to lead and complete the Revolution in a way which would enable the whole society to develop further.

There was, in fact, a glaring contradiction between the motives of the idealistic spokesmen of the Revolution and its results. The revolutionaries hoped to realize mankind's age-old dream and to make politics moral and morality political, whereas the actual effect – and the most important success – of the Revolution was to free the propertied bourgeoisie from its feudalist–absolutist and mercantilist chains and to smoothe the way for a capitalist social and economic system.

The French revolutionaries' hopes for a harmonious and stable brotherhood between all peoples have not been realized to this very day. Nevertheless, the concepts set out in the Declarations of the Rights of Man and Citizens of 1789 and 1793 now form the basis of every humane society. Since the Second World War they have taken effect throughout the entire world as the liberation movements of the colonial peoples have adopted the revolutionary principle of the right to national self-determination.

A generation after the Revolution had triumphed, the philosopher Hegel paid tribute to that great attempt to transform the Enlightenment dream of a reasoned world into political reality with the following words:

No one had foreseen that, while the sun still stood in the sky and the planets still orbited it, man would turn himself on his head, that is, on his thoughts, and build reality accordingly . . . It was, therefore, a glorious sunrise. All thinking beings joined together in applauding that age. It was dominated by a sublime emotion, an enthusiasm of the spirit flowed through the world as if, for the first time ever, the divine had been reconciled with the world.

The Old Regime during the Reign of Louis XVI, 1774–1788

At the head of France's pre-revolutionary class hierarchy stood the king, an absolute ruler passed off by the Church as God's representative on earth. The absolutist form of government had been developing gradually since King Louis XI had triumphed over his feudal rivals and unified the country in the second half of the fifteenth century. Absolutism reached its zenith during the reign of the 'Sun King', Louis XIV (1661–1715), who identified himself personally with the state and was an unrivalled model for all the rulers of Europe. On the eve of the Revolution, sovereign power was in the hands of King Louis XVI, who had married the Austrian Princess Marie-Antoinette, ascended the throne in 1774 and now ruled over 25 million subjects. Despite being forced to take account of the extensive system of traditional, class-based privileges enjoyed by the clergy and the aristocracy, he was still the country's supreme law-giver.

Under the old regime France was a stratified coalition of privileged bodies, which was based primarily on legal inequality and which regarded birth and

1.1 The coronation of Louis XVI in Reims Cathedral on 11 June 1775. The king swears always to obey the Catholic Church and persecute heretics.

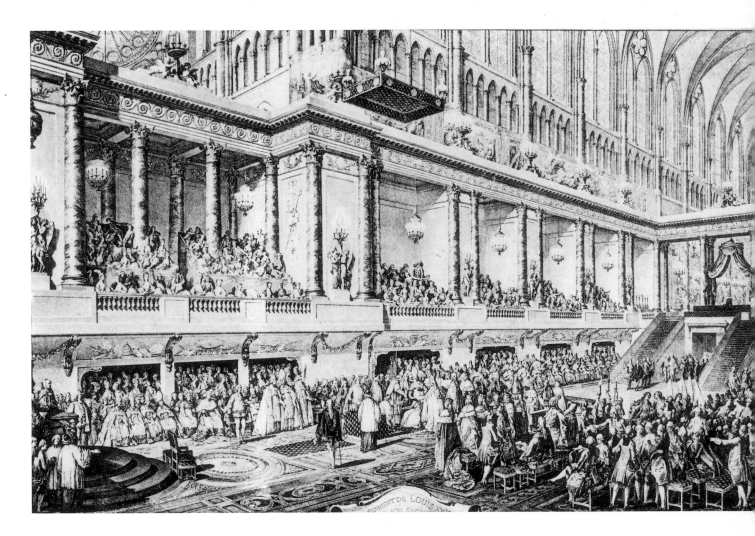

1.2 An idealized painting of the 'Forest of Versailles', where the court nobility would often stroll. In the eighteenth century these grounds served as a model for the countless royal residences throughout the absolutist states of Europe.

Overleaf: The Palace of Versailles was built at the end of the seventeenth century, during the reign of the Sun King, Louis XIV. The combination of baroque and classical set the style for the era of Absolutism. The light-flooded hall of mirrors, finished in 1686, lies at the centre of the palace, where the French kings lived.

1.3 King Louis XVI in his coronation robes. He ascended the French Throne in 1774 at the age of 20, after the death of his grandfather Louis XV, and had been married to the youngest daughter of Empress Maria Theresa, who lived in Vienna, since 1770.

descent as the major factors affecting the social order. The two politically privileged classes were the clergy, with around 120,000 members, and the aristocracy, which numbered around 350,000 (if family members are included). Over 98 per cent of the population belonged to the politically powerless Third Estate, which, in addition to the bourgeoisie, comprised the artisans and lower classes from the towns and the peasants and farm-hands from the country. France still had an agrarian structure, there being barely sixty towns with more than 10,000 inhabitants. More than 85 per cent of Frenchmen lived on the land.

The country's First Estate was the Catholic clergy, whose duties included not only spiritual welfare, but also the care of the poor, education and the maintenance of registers of births, deaths and marriages. The high-ranking clergy – 18 archbishops and 121 bishops – was drawn exclusively from the aristocracy. Even the majority of abbots and canons were aristocratic. The lower-ranking clergy, made up of around 20,000 monks, twice as many nuns and over 50,000 priests and chaplains, were of lower birth and shared the material poverty of the rural population. Whereas a bishop's annual income was at least 50,000 *livres*, a rural clergyman received only 700, his chaplain only 350 *livres*.

The prelates' economic power was based on the

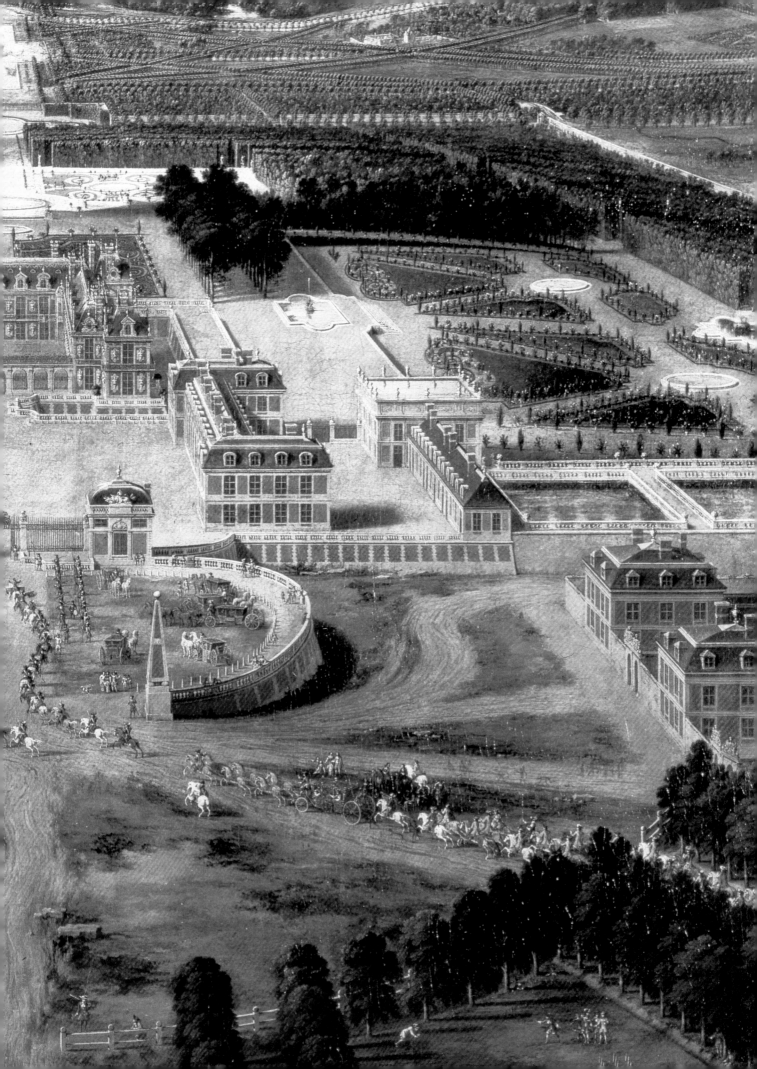

1.5 Queen Marie-Antoinette in her bedroom at the Palace of Versailles. A painter portrays her as a harpist amid a group containing members of the high nobility, who were entitled to enter the royal chambers.

levying of tithes and on the Church's ownership of approximately 10 per cent of the country's entire surface area. The tithe was that part of his crops and cattle yield which a peasant had to hand over. In the towns the Church owned numerous houses, from which it earned rent. The clergy, which had its own administration and courts, enjoyed significant legal and fiscal privileges, among them exemption from the payment of taxes. Every five years the high-ranking clergy met in order to discuss matters relating to religion and class. They had adopted a voluntary tax, the 'don gratuit', which was a clergyman's

only financial burden and was levied at a rate of less than 3 per cent of his average annual income.

Like the clergy, the aristocracy also encompassed wide class variations. Aristocrats were exempt from the payment of taxes and enjoyed economic, fiscal and honorary privileges, for example, a monopoly on higher-ranking officerships, ecclesiastical offices and administrative posts. It was forbidden for aristocrats to do manual work, and anyone who did so risked being ostracized by his class.

The Court nobility, which lived in the king's entourage in Versailles, numbered around 4,000

1.6 Queen Marie-Antoinette in her ceremonial court dress, around 1780. The lilies of the Bourbon standard are embroidered onto her purple robe in gold. Her intricate hair ornament consists of pearls, flowers and a bouquet of diamonds.

Overleaf:
1.7 The *Comédie Française* during an opera performance before an aristocratic audience in the court theatre at Versailles.

people. These courtiers used the greater part of their high incomes to maintain their social status, that is, to pay for their numerous servants, luxurious receptions, and costly theatre visits and hunt meetings. The *noblesse de robe*, which had been drawn from the affluent bourgeoisie since the sixteenth century, supervised the running of the administrative and legal apparati. At its head stood the members of the thirteen *parlements* of the monarchy, which served as High Courts and were additionally responsible for registering and recording royal legislation. The parliamentarians, who had bought their hereditary offices from the monarch, could not be removed from their posts and were steeped in the privileges of their class. On the lowest rungs of the aristocratic ladder stood the landed gentry, most of whom were financially dependent on the feudal taxes paid by their peasants. As these taxes had been fixed in the Middle Ages and the purchasing power of money had inevitably diminished, many lords of the manor had only meagre incomes. Some had the old archives searched for records of feudal dues payable by the peasants, but which had been long forgotten. Approximately 30 per cent of the land was owned

by the aristocracy.

The Third Estate likewise lacked uniformity. Those with capital, who had bought government stocks, lived from their interest. Many owned land which was worked by serfs. In fact, just under one fifth of the area of France was owned by the bourgeoisie. Many educated merchants, owners of manufacturing companies and mines, as well as members of the free professions, scholars, journalists and other thinkers of the Enlightenment, supported the Encyclopaedists and Physiocrats, and all voiced criticism of the defects of the regime. The master craftsmen and their journeymen rejected

1.8 In this idealized representation King Louis XVI is depicted as a benefactor of the people. In reality, he concerned himself little with the weal and woe of his subjects and spent his time either attending hunts and court festivities or in his locksmith's shop, where he made elaborate locks which he then showed off to visitors.

economic liberalism and the theory of competition, and their guilds, whose very existence was based on the supply-led economy, were intent on preserving their privileges. The situation of the wage-earner, whose working day could be as long as 16 hours, worsened as a result of continual price rises. The very lowest-ranking elements of the urban population were the day-labourers, errand boys, water and wood carriers, and domestic servants with no permanent position, all of whom spent up to four-fifths of their income on bread alone and lived in squalid accommodation.

The greater part of the Third Estate – over twenty

1.9 This is how a kitchen belonging to a serf or statute-labourer would have looked. They owned no land of their own and lived in abysmal poverty.

1.10 Anne Robert Jacques Turgot, Louis XVI's Finance Minister 1774–1776. He hailed from a wealthy, ennobled bourgeois family, and was a councillor in the Paris *parlement* and co-founder of the Physiocratic (liberal) school of economic thought. He tried in vain to reform the abuses of the old regime.

living as farm-hands and menial workers on estates owned by the aristocracy and rural bourgeoisie. In addition, there were a million serfs, inherited by the lords of the manor.

The bulging apparatus of state administration was incapable of carrying out its functions properly. The jurisdictions of those responsible for finance, the Church and the army often overlapped, invariably causing the rights and privileges of outside bodies to be infringed. Due to the fact that high-ranking office-holders could not be removed from their posts, laziness, corruption and venality were common among servants of the state. Since communication between the individual provinces was difficult, each region existed as a separate entity, their respective crop yields determining their cost of living. The variety of weights and measures in use, and the numerous tolls payable on bridges and roads hindered economic efficiency and contributed to the disorder and confusion. Internal customs duties increased production costs, with the result that French industry could often not keep pace with its English rivals. The legal system was in equal disarray, and magistrates in the provincial towns guarded their medieval privileges jealously. Northern France practised common law, whilst the South preferred Roman law.

When, in 1774, Louis XVI ascended his grandfather's throne at the age of twenty, he wanted to eliminate the increasingly widespread abuses which he found, and named one of the country's most respected Enlighteners, Turgot, as his Minister of Finance. Turgot was an administrative expert originating from the rich commercial bourgeoisie and was closely associated with the Physiocrats. He set himself the goal of removing all those obstacles which stood in the way of the free development of the economy. His appointment was greeted warmly by such as Voltaire and Condorcet, for they could now see a representative of their own school of thought in a position of power. Turgot lifted the restrictions on the traffic in grain in order to ensure that the population would have bread, replaced the peasant's statute labour with a general tax intended to increase income from the produce of the soil, reduced tolls, and abolished all feudal and guild privileges in order to encourage free trade and commerce. His programme also included administrative decentralization and increased powers for local and

million people – lived in the country, although few peasants were affluent or could live off the land. Most were tenant farmers and worked a small piece of land which did not even feed them. Although 35 per cent of France's surface area was owned by the peasantry, nine-tenths of all peasants were smallholders or tenant farmers forced to rely on common rights in order to survive. The lord of the manor administered the law on his land and collected the feudal dues. The enslaved tenant farmers had to do statute-labour, building roads or with the military forces. They groaned under the burden of numerous direct and indirect taxes. Particularly hated was the salt tax, which was extremely high in some parts of the country. As a result of the increase in prices, and both the king's and feudal taxation, the number of landless peasants grew. They eked out a miserable regional authorities.

These attempts at structural reform, aimed at freeing the state from the tutelage of self-interested bodies, encroached upon the traditional privileges of both the aristocracy and the craftsmen's guilds. The *parlements* refused to register the reforms. When Turgot would not provide the sums of money necessary to support the American colonies in their revolt against England, the king dismissed him. In doing so, the monarchy threw away its last chance to reform itself.

Turgot's successor was Necker, a banker from Geneva. He sought both to reduce the domestic deficit and to cover the cost of the war against England which had broken out in 1778, by loans, and was forced to put up with a further growth in the national debt. For a time he was popular, but he made enemies when he adopted several economy measures, abolished the pensions of parasitic courtiers, and reduced the number of tax-farmers, who advanced the state large sums of money each year, only to replace the taxes they had collected with ground rent and compound interest levied on the vassals.

In 1781, in an attempt to silence his critics, Necker produced a report which revealed the true state of the country's finances. Although the report understated the deficit in order to safeguard France's credit-worthiness, the privileged classes were furious that Necker had detailed the excessive extrava-

1.11 Jacques Necker, a protestant banker from Geneva, director general of King Louis XVI's finances from 1776 until 1781 and from 1788 until 1790.

1.12 Charles Alexandre de Calonne, Finance Minister to Louis XVI from 1783 until 1787. Like Necker, he was unable to restore financial soundness to the French budget.

1.13 The official opening of the Assembly of Notables on 22 February 1787 took place in the presence of King Louis XVI at the Palace of Versailles.

gance of the Court, and persuaded the king to drop him.

Necker's successors, who were neither willing to tamper with the exemption from taxation enjoyed by the aristocracy and the clergy, nor able to increase the taxes on the Third Estate, instead increased the national debt by raising even more loans. The trade agreement signed with England in 1786 led to a further worsening of the economic climate, as France was flooded with cheap English cloth, and numerous textile companies were ruined.

In 1786, recognizing that the Crown's authority was rapidly being undermined by the country's hopeless financial situation, Finance Minister Calonne suggested to the king a programme of fiscal and administrative reforms which was similar to Turgot's and also satisfied the demands of the commercial and industrial bourgeoisie. He wanted to limit the fiscal privileges enjoyed by the aristocracy,

but not to inflict too much damage on a class which he regarded as the mainstay of the Crown, since he feared the opposition of the *parlements*. Thus he happened upon the idea of having his reform programme approved by an assembly of notables.

February 1787 saw the assembly of 144 prelates, big landowners, and members of the various *parlements* and provincial diets, as well as other notables. They insisted uncompromisingly on retaining their old-established privileges, and defended them-

1.14 Caricature of the class-based privileged order. The peasant, whose stockings are torn and who wears clogs on his feet, carries the clergy and the aristocracy on his back. The receipts hanging from the pockets of the well-dressed members of the privileged classes show details of the clergy's prebends and pensions and the feudal dues and taxes which burden the peasants.

selves against every attempt to reform the French state and every suggestion that they should share their superiority with the upper middle classes. Calonne, who did not dare to impose his will on the privileged aristocratic classes, pleaded in vain for his reforms to be approved. But the notables would not ratify his plan, for they wanted to exploit the weakness and helplessness of the sovereign and to force a return to the practices which pre-dated absolutism. Since the aristocratic forces of reaction

believed that absolutism was ripe for capitulation, Calonne's consultation of the notables proved fruitless. In April 1787 Calonne was dismissed and fled to England in order to escape a charge of embezzling public funds.

The dissolution of the assembly of notables marked the beginning of the 'aristocratic revolt' which ushered in the Revolution. Calonne's successor was the Archbishop of Toulouse, Brienne, who to all intents and purposes put absolutism into cold storage, by establishing a finance committee to act as his most senior monitoring body. Lafayette, a marquis who belonged to the progressive wing of the assembly of notables and enjoyed a great deal of prestige because he had fought at Washington's side in the American War of Independence, asserted that only a body representing the whole population had the right to pass a finance bill.

This reference to the States-General, which had convened for the last time in 1614, was taken up by the Paris *parlement*, to whom Brienne had turned for registration of his programme of reform and his abolition of control over the trade in grain. The aristocratic parliamentarians, who were not prepared to surrender their privileges, believed that the convocation of the States-General would be a suitable means of subordinating the absolute authority of the Crown to their will once and for all. They presented themselves as the protectors of the organic laws of the kingdom and condemned the tyranny of the monarch in general and the king's secret arrest warrants in particular. The ultra-conservative Paris *parlement* even declared, on 3 May 1788, that 'the goal of any society should be the preservation of freedom, life and property'. This declaration resembled liberal concepts of Enlightenment and was designed to move the aristocratic and bourgeois opposition groups to join together against the weakened forces of absolutism. The aristocracy hoped to carry with it all those who were dissatisfied with the Government.

In response to this challenge Louis XVI ordered the creation of a *Cour pleniére*, a Court Assembly, over which the king himself would preside and which would have the sole right to ratify legislation, with the *parlements* losing this privilege. The reform, however, came too late. Throughout France the aristocratic and bourgeois opposition protested against Louis XVI's attempt to restore his absolute authority. On 7 June 1788 in Grenoble, the capital of the province of Dauphiné, the population, determined to prevent the dismissal of its *parlement*, clashed with troops on the streets. Opposition to the new 'instrument of despotism', as the *Cour pleniére* was generally known, also spread to the clergy. When Brienne convened a meeting of the high-ranking clergy and asked for a sum of 8 million *livres*, he received a rebuff. The meeting approved only 1.8 million, and *that* to be paid in instalments. Compared to the domestic deficit of almost 200 mil-

lion, it was a drop in the ocean.

In July 1788 a provincial assembly constituted of members of all three estates met in Vizille (Dauphiné). It demanded not only the abandonment of the *Cour plenière*, but also the convocation of the States-General, at which the Third Estate's representation would be as strong as that of the two privileged classes. These resolutions were indeed revolutionary. The social and political structure of the old regime was being rocked to its foundations.

Faced with a threatening alliance between the privileged classes and the bourgeoisie, as well as imminent financial collapse, the Government stated its readinesss to begin researching the method of nomination to the States-General, its electoral regulations, and the number of electors and deputies concerned. On 8 August 1788 the king's Council of State agreed to convene the States-General on 1 May 1789 and promised the representatives of the nation that they would be able to 'fully exercise all rights to which they are entitled'. At the same time, the *Cour plenière* was suspended. These moves were nothing short of wholesale capitulation.

A few days later, on 24 August, Brienne announced that the Government would have to suspend all payments. This could only mean national bankruptcy. The king dismissed the unsuccessful minister, recalled Necker and vested the *parlements* with their former rights. On 21 September 1788 the Paris *parlement* decided to reconstitute the States-General in its 1614 form, that is, divided into the three estates, with each having one vote. By these means, the aristocracy aimed to ensure ultimate victory, not merely over absolutism, but also over the Third Estate, since its representatives could always be outvoted by a coalition of the privileged classes, the clergy and the aristocracy.

Considering the advanced stage which the breakdown of the privileged order had reached, however, any such victory for the aristocracy was illusory. The anti-absolutist alliance between aristocratic and bourgeois opposition groups shattered. The Third Estate demanded that the number of its deputies in the States-General be doubled, so that its representation would equal that of the aristocracy and clergy together. In addition, it called for voting by head-count rather than by order, or estate. In December 1788 the Paris *parlement* agreed to the Third Estate's demand for doubled representation, but deferred a decision on the method of voting. Henceforth the bourgeoisie would lead the opposition.

The Beginning of the Bourgeois Revolution

In the first few months of 1789 price rises and shortages led to bread riots and local uprisings in several provinces. The previous year's harvest had been bad and the price of bread reached its highest level since 1709. Gangs of beggars and robbers roamed the countryside. In the lead up to, and during the elections to the States-General, the revolutionary atmosphere was unmistakable. The population's trust in the authorities was on the ebb, and the intellectual spokesmen of the politically powerless Third Estate called for the overthrow of the old regime. Their recommendations on a new social order were published in numerous pamphlets, broadsheets and treatises, and stimulated ever-increasing social and political agitation.

The most influential of the broadsheets to inflame public opinion on the eve of the Revolution began with the provocative words, 'What is the Third Estate? Everything. What has it hitherto been within the state's order of things? Nothing. What does it demand? The right to become something.' The author of these words

2.1 The cavalry attacks employees of the carpet-manufacturer Reveillon in the Paris suburb of St. Antoine on 28 April 1789. During their rebellion they threw furniture from the factory from the windows and set fire to it.

2.2 Abbot Emmanuel Joseph Sieyès, whose broadsheet *What is the Third Estate?* contained the programme of the bourgeois Revolution. He was a member of both the Constituent Assembly and the Convention, voted for the king's death, but kept in the background during Jacobin rule. He was envoy to the Prussian Court 1798/99. He was then elected to the Directory and planned Bonaparte's coup on 18 brumaire (9 November 1799).

2.3 Opening of the States-General in the '*Salle des Menus Plaisirs*' at the Palace of Versailles on 5 May 1789.

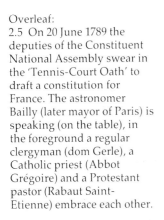

2.4 A procession in the States-General at Versailles on 5 May 1789. The procession is in three columns, with the aristocracy on the right, the clergy in the centre, and the Third Estate (with twice as many delegates) on the left.

Overleaf:
2.5 On 20 June 1789 the deputies of the Constituent National Assembly swear in the 'Tennis-Court Oath' to draft a constitution for France. The astronomer Bailly (later mayor of Paris) is speaking (on the table), in the foreground a regular clergyman (dom Gerle), a Catholic priest (Abbot Grégoire) and a Protestant pastor (Rabaut Saint-Etienne) embrace each other.

was the vicar-general of the diocese of Chartres, Abbot Emmanuel Sieyès, a free-thinker in priests' clothing, who was a member of the privileged clergy, but whose origins were bourgeois. In this broadsheet he outlined the programme of the power-seeking bourgeoisie, which, he maintained, was not prepared to attend the States-General simply for the purpose of debating matters of taxation or granting the old regime funds in order that it could continue its mismanagement. Concisely, and with great keenness of mind, he called for the Third Estate, which he identified with the bourgeoisie, to make itself the sole representative of the will of the nation. The Third Estate, he claimed, contained everything necessary for the shaping of a nation:

It is the strong and powerful man, whose one arm is still chained. If one were to eliminate the privileged classes, the nation would not be the poorer, but the richer. What, then, is the Third Estate? Everything, but a shackled and oppressed everything. What

would it be without the privileged classes? Everything, but a free and thriving everything. Nothing functions without it, yet without the others everything would function infinitely better.

As the general will, Rousseau's 'Volonté Generale', on which the new social order would have to be based, could only be developed by the majority, and as the Third Estate constituted the overwhelming majority of the population, its representatives would be 'the trustees of the national will'. It was not the temporary return of the States-General which was required, as the Government seemed to believe, but the constancy of national representation.

Sieyès also set out further demands, which made him one of the most important theorists of the Revolution. He borrowed Montesquieu's concept of the separation of powers, but rejected his notion of aristocratic supremacy, and whilst he accepted Rousseau's concept of the general will, he rejected that of

2.6 On 20 June 1789 the deputies of the newly-formed Constituent National Assembly, whose chamber has been locked on the instructions of King Louis XVI, go instead to the building in which the Versailles aristocracy used to play rackets (*Jeu de Paume*).

tuent Assembly and incorporated into the Constitution of 1791.

At the end of January 1789 Louis XVI issued regulations covering election to the States-General, which stipulated that the deputies representing the aristocracy, the clergy and the Third Estate would be elected separately from each other. All members of the aristocracy and all high- and low-ranking members of the clergy were entitled to vote. The Third Estate, however, was divided into two groups. Only French men over the age of 25 who had a permanent residence, and who paid direct taxes, were entitled to vote. This stipulation excluded 90 per cent of the adult population from participation in the democratic process, since only every tenth Frenchman had a sufficiently large taxable income. The election meetings, at which the intelligentsia, mainly lawyers, set the tone, first discussed the wording of petitions, which were then summarized for delivery by the deputies to the States-General. Only then were people chosen to sit in the electoral assemblies which would ultimately elect the deputies. The Third Estate's representation consisted exclusively of members of the bourgeoisie. Not a single peasant and not a single member of the urban lower clases was elected.

The elections to the States-General led to a huge increase in political awareness in all classes and social strata. The population's deeply-rooted respect for the traditional class-led authorities was replaced by faith in the strength of the new concept of the nation, which would obliterate all social conflicts of interest. It was widely believed that the new composition of the States-General would transform the kingdom into a harmonious unit, whose civil servants would henceforth take into account only the public interest.

An analysis of the approximately 60,000 petitions received, from all three estates, reveals that every single one called for a restriction of the king's powers. Demands for legal reform and a guarantee of press freedom were also common to all. However, whereas the Third Estate called for the abolition of tithes and all other feudal privileges, as well as the introduction of complete equality for the bourgeoisie, the aristocracy defended the preservation of its privileges and of voting by estate, and rejected legal equality and the admission of all Frenchmen to all offices of state. The aristocracy's spokesmen warned

direct democracy, which he replaced with representation such as that practised in the English system of government. He also rejected the imperative mandate, stressing that elected representatives should not be bound by the instructions of their electors. All these principles were adopted by the Consti-

2.7 At a sitting of the Constituent National Assembly on 23 June 1789 Mirabeau calls out to the master of ceremonies, Dreux-Brézé, 'We are here by the will of the people and we will not stir from our seats unless forced to do by bayonets.'

2.8 Honoré Gabriel de Riqueti, Count Mirabeau, who was elected to the States-General as a Third Estate deputy despite being an aristocrat, tried in vain to achieve an English-style constitutional monarchy in France.

that the abolition of the class structure would plunge France into democratic chaos and give way to the tyranny of undisciplined mobs. The lower-ranking clergy criticized the bishops' and prelates' accumulation of lucrative prebends. Many priests pledged that they would represent the interests both of their own class and of the poor in the States-General. It was not only at the clergy's meetings, but also at those of the Third Estate, that the existence of social tensions was apparent. Whereas the master craftsmen wanted to preserve their guild privileges, the industrialists and merchants spoke out in favour of their abolition. They also protested against the disastrous trade agreement with England, which would lead to the ruination of whole sectors of French industry. At village meetings the small-holders demanded the maintenance of parish property and general grazing rights, which guaranteed them a minimum subsistence, whilst the big landowners wanted to abolish common land and transfer it into private ownership. All peasants supported demands for the removal of all feudal dues.

As the elections were drawing to a close the dire need of the unemployed, who were excluded from the democratic process, increased dramatically. Food prices were exorbitant, and even those who were in work barely earned enough to buy bread. On 28 April 1789 rioting broke out in the Paris suburb of St. Antoine, and factories owned by a manufacturer of carpets and saltpetre, who was

2.10 On the night of 12–13 July crowds armed with guns, sabres, scythes and picks keep watch in Paris in order to prevent the town from coming under military occupation.

2.9 Camille Desmoulins, speaking in the gardens of the *Palais Royale* on 12 July 1789, appeals to the people of Paris to rebel.

2.11 Having plundered the weapon store of the armoury (*Hôtel des Invalides*), crowds march to the Bastille with cannons and guns on the morning of 14 July 1789.

accused of having joked about the dire need of the people at an election meeting, were plundered. Several hundred workers and unemployed people put up a spirited resistance to the soldiers deployed by the police chief to quash the unrest. More than twenty were killed and twice as many injured. Several of the leaders of this spontaneous revolt were sentenced to death and executed, others were sentenced to forced labour on the galleys.

The election results demonstrated that the revolutionary movement already contained members of the privileged classes. 291 clergymen, 270 aristocrats and 578 members of the Third Estate were elected. More than two in three of the clergy's representa-

tives were rural priests inclined towards support of the bourgeoisie's demands or liberal and progressive prelates. In addition, around a third of the aristocrats elected were prepared to work with the Third Estate on matters of joint concern, among them Lafayette, the Duke of La Rochefoucault, Count Clermont-Tonnerre and the Viscount of Noailles. The liberal priests included Abbot Gré-

2.12 Storming of the Bastille on 14 July 1789. The assailants position the cannons.

Overleaf:
2.13 The Bastille is demolished after its capture by the Paris crowds.

goire and Archbishop Talleyrand. Two members of the privileged classes who played an important part in the Revolution were elected as representatives of the Third Estate: Abbot Sieyès and Count Mira-beau. Roughly half of the Third Estate's deputies were lawyers (including Barnave, Le Chapelier and Robespierre) and no wonder, since the study of law prepared them for a political career. Due to their theoretical education and their practical legal work, lawyers were especially familiar with the outdated nature of the law as practised under the old system of government, and were predestined to become opponents of the privileged order. Moreover, the economic prospects were grim for many lawyers under absolutism and they hoped to be able to make careers for themselves under the new order. The

2.14 Marie-Joseph Motier,
Marquis Lafayette, former
comrade-in-arms of General
Washington in the American
War of Independence, as
commander of the National
Guard on the Paris Champs
de Mars.

political programme in his report, made no mention of the question of a constitution, and also said nothing as to whether voting was to be by estate or by head-count. His sole concern was the restoration of financial soundness. As before, the Government sought to preserve absolutism and simply wanted the States-General to eliminate the huge national debt. By adopting this attitude it passed up its last chance to form a coalition with the Third Estate and establish a bourgeois constitutional monarchy like that in England, where the bourgeoisie had transformed the aristocrat into a decorative figure-head during the 'Glorious Revolution' a century before, depriving him of his political privileges, but leaving him his social prerogatives.

The deputies representing the Third Estate, who regarded themselves as patriots and representatives of public opinion, acted boldly and were determined to destroy the old system of privileges once and for all. A group of deputies from Brittany formed the 'Breton Club', from which the Jacobin Club later emerged. In imitation of the British lower house, the deputies of the Third Estate adopted the term 'Deputies of the Commons' (*Députés des Communes*), rejected their enforced separation into classes, and called upon the deputies representing the clergy and the aristocracy to join forces with them. On 17 June, after a number of clergymen had gone over to the side of the Third Estate, this new alliance voted by a majority of 490 to 90 to transform itself into a national assembly, whose purpose would be to draw up a new constitution for France.

This decision, which transferred sovereignty from the king to the nation, was revolutionary, for it replaced the privileged order with a modern system of representation founded on legal equality. The National Assembly rushed to pacify the bourgeois public creditors with its first decree, in which it pledged to take responsibility for the debts of the bankrupt feudal regime.

On 19 June the clergy decided by a majority of twelve votes to join the National Assembly. The aristocracy, on the other hand, refused to yield and pressed the king to abolish the States-General. When the deputies of the newly constituted National Assembly found their meeting rooms locked on 20 June, they retired to an nearby hall, in which the Versailles aristocracy used to play rackets (*jeu de paume*). There they swore the 'Tennis-Court Oath'

bankers, merchants and industrialists were represented by around a hundred deputies, and more than fifty wealthy landowners, who had been elected by peasants, also represented the Third Estate. The remainder were scholars, journalists, doctors, officers and other members of the educated middle classes.

When the deputies were presented to the king on 2 May 1789, Louis made it known that he wished to preserve the traditional distinction between the classes and was not willing to permit discussion on the question of the country's plight. At the official opening session on 5 May, Necker did not include a

2.15 Patriots march
triumphantly wearing sashes
in the colours of the tricolor
and red liberty caps. They
carry a model of the stormed
Bastille.

2.16 Night-time sitting of the
Constituent National
Assembly in Versailles on
4–5 August 1789. The sitting
abolished feudal privileges.

DÉCLARATION
DES DROITS DE L'HOMME
ET DU CITOYEN,
Décretés par l'Assemblée Nationale dans les séances des 20, 21 23, 24 et 26 aoûst 1789, acceptés par le Roi
PRÉAMBULE
ARTICLE PREMIER
AUX REPRESENTANS DU PEUPLE FRANCOIS

2.17 The Declaration of the Rights of Man and Citizens adopted by the Constituent National Assembly on 26 August 1789 was later incorporated into the Constitution of 1791.

and pledged 'never to dissolve, but to meet in any place where the conditions would allow, until the constitution of the kingdom has been drawn up and rests on firm foundations'.

Three days later the king ordered the Assembly to reverse its decision. The Assembly, however, refused and proclaimed the immunity of its members. Mirabeau declared that the Assembly, elected as it was by the nation, would only yield in the face of bayonets. On hearing this, Louis XVI gave way, thereby surrendering his power, to all intents and purposes, to the representatives of the nation. He commanded the clergy and the aristocracy to join forces with the representatives of the Third Estate. On 9 July the deputies voted to adopt the name 'Constituent Assembly'. This marked the final laying to rest of the old order and the establishment of the first modern parliament on the European mainland.

Despite his concessions, however, Louis XVI hoped to break up the Assembly by means of armed force. Under the pretext of forestalling popular unrest, he ordered 20,000 men (including Swiss and German mercenaries) to mobilize in the area around Versailles. These troop movements did not go unnoticed. The masses were convinced that the aristocracy was hatching a plot to put a bloody end to the Revolution. Thousands gathered around the numerous wall posters put up in every square in Paris, which warned of the aristocracy's provocation.

When the king dismissed Necker on 11 July, even going as far as to banish him from France, and appointed an ultra-conservative cabinet under the chairmanship of the courtier Breteuil, the unrest reached a climax. The National Assembly protested and made a public appeal for 'National Guards' to be formed. The Paris electoral assembly, which had elected the deputies representing the Third Estate, decided to set up a revolutionary council and a civic guard. As military reinforcements began to advance on Paris, the church bells rang out. Numerous popular orators, including the journalist Camille Desmoulins, called upon the people of Paris to arm themselves in order to repel the troops. On 13 July mobs began to plunder gunsmiths' shops and weapon depots. The next day they occupied the armoury (*Hôtel des Invalides*) and took guns and rifles from the arsenal. Around a thousand demonstrators marched on the Bastille, a medieval stronghold which then served as a state prison and was a symbol of despotism. The walls of this citadel were 30 metres high and its water-filled moat measured 25 metres across.

The assault party, which was made up primarily of craftsmen, workers and other members of the lower classes, was reinforced by a detachment from the Civic Guard, which set up a battery of three cannons in front of the gates to the citadel. The Bastille's commander, de Launay, who had command of more than 30 Swiss and 80 *invalides*, tried to negotiate. The besiegers, however, succeeded in letting down the drawbridge and penetrating the citadel's courtyard. When those defending the Bastille opened fire, there was a short struggle which claimed several lives. De Launay surrendered and was lynched by the enraged mob, which then forced its way into the Bastille itself and freed the seven prisoners there. Shortly after its capture, the old stronghold was razed and the ground levelled.

The storming of the Bastille sealed the overthrow of the old regime and symbolized the victory of a people which was bursting its chains. Even on this first '*journée révolutionaire*', 14 July 1789, it was clear that the bourgeoisie needed the support of the common people if it was to win its struggle against the forces of yesteryear.

The Paris bourgeoisie took advantage of the victory and assumed the administration of the capital. The respected astronomer Bailly, who had taken the Tennis-Court Oath, was named as mayor, Lafayette as the commander of the National Guard. On 16 July the king agreed to reappoint Necker and set off for the National Assembly, where he promised to join it in restoring order and calm. On the next day he came to Paris, where Bailly presented him with a three-coloured cockade as a symbol of the 'everlasting alliance between the monarch and the people'. The tricolour bore the colours of the French capital, blue and red, and between them the white of the

Bourbon dynasty. By accepting the cockade, the king symbolically recognized the sovereignty of the nation and renounced the sacred nature of the divine right of kings.

The king's humiliation was too much for those ultra-reactionary aristocrats who regarded a coup as the only way out of the crisis. The king's youngest brother, the Earl of Artois (who would ascend the French throne thirty-five years later as Charles X), the Prince of Condé, the Duke of Polignac, and several other high-ranking aristocrats left France. Many more would follow.

The Paris Revolution had an enormous effect on the whole country. In every town new, bourgeois magistrates were elected and National Guards formed. Everywhere the destitute lower classes were convinced that the aristocracy was hoarding grain in order to drive the price of bread higher. Everywhere they demanded that indirect taxes be

2.18 Allegory on the fact that the Declaration of Human Rights did not apply to the French colonies: a black slave demands that the Declaration's pledge that 'men are born free and with equal rights and remain so' be met. On the left stand four demons: the aristocracy, selfishness, injustice and revolt.

abolished and corn-profiteers punished. Everywhere they feared that the aristocracy was enlisting the help of itinerant gangs of robbers in order to thwart the plans which they themselves hoped and believed would soon free all men. The magic word 'freedom', which was taken literally by the manual workers, fuelled hopes for liberation, not only from the chains of feudalism, but also from every form of injustice. Just as powerful as this hope, however, was the peasantry's fear of the nation's aristocratic enemies. In the second half of July and the first few days of August fantastic rumours spread like wildfire throughout France, engendering *la grande peur* in the common people. It was said everywhere that brigands in the employ of the lords of the manor were destroying crops and setting fire to farmsteads. The peasants armed themselves, marched on the palaces and the castles of the Teutonic order, and demanded the opening of the archives and the surrender of those documents on the basis of which they had to pay feudal dues. They lit fires on the village greens and in the woods and burned the old parchments. Should they be refused the documents, the peasants would set fire to the manor and string up its obstinate owner or administrator. They seized power in the villages and drove out the tax collectors and their agents.

Bourgeois landowners, who, like the aristocracy, possessed feudal rights, felt threatened by the peasants' uprisings. Bloody confrontations ensued between the municipal militia, intent on protecting the rights of the bourgeois landowners, and the peasants, who wanted to shake off all manifestations of subordination. Even during this first stage of revolution, it was possible to discern clear traces of class struggle.

Unnerved by the peasant unrest, the National Assembly took legislative action of far-reaching significance and in doing so dealt a fatal blow to the old, class-based order. The deputies recognized that the rural population's actions could no longer be reversed and had to be sanctioned in order not to jeopardize the unity of the revolutionary forces. Members of the Breton Club devised a method of eliminating feudal rights without having to fear for the inviolability of the bourgeoisie's right to own property. They maintained that ancestral rights relating to land-ownership represented a special form of ownership and were not inviolable because

2.19 Painted medallion depicting the torso of a black slave woman who is wearing a liberty cap and demanding that the promises made in the Declaration of Human Rights be kept. The inscription reads, 'I (want to be) free too 1789'.

they had been acquired by means of unlawful appropriation and acts of force. For this reason they should be made available for repurchase, enabling landowners to dispose of privileges which the statute-workers had, in any case, already snatched away from them.

At an evening sitting on 4 August 1789, the Viscount of Noailles (who possessed no land himself) suggested for the first time the abolition of statute labour, serfdom and all duties of service to the lord of the manor without compensation. Several progressive aristocrats lent their support and offered their privileges 'as a sacrifice on the altar of the new France'. The Assembly resolved to abolish all privileges and feudal encumbrances, but drew a distinction between personal duties and the rights pertaining to land-ownership. Whereas the former were, indeed, to be abolished, the Constituent Assembly

2.20 Headwear as a symbol of the Revolution: a young middle-class man sets a liberty cap on his head and throws his tricorn and wig to the ground.

2.21 The aristocrat and the clergyman are horrified when the citizen lying on the ground bursts his chains and seizes a weapon. In the background the Bastille is being demolished. Those who have just stormed the Bastille carry the heads of the commander of the stronghold, de Launay, and the merchant leader Flesselles on picks.

declared that tenant farmers would have to buy the right not to pay ground rent to the owner of the land. In this way the Assembly was able to abolish feudalism in theory, without abolishing it in practice. Many countryfolk who were too poor to pay damages to the original beneficiaries of such land-related rights were simply transformed from statute-labourers into wage-slaves. Although they acquired the right to freedom of movement, they were unable to acquire the land they worked. They often refused to pay the lord of the manor ground rent and remained a restive and dissatisfied element for the next four years. The greater part of the peasantry would have to wait for the Jacobin Convention's agricultural legislation of June 1793, which did away with the last vestiges of feudalism on the land.

In the course of the next few weeks the deputies drafted numerous parliamentary bills, and on 11 August 1789 the National Assembly announced that the feudal regime had been completely obliterated. Though this may have been an exaggeration, it is true to say that new decisions being taken would prove to be of great importance for the further development of the Revolution. All Frenchmen now enjoyed equal rights and duties, had equal access to all professions and public offices, and were subject to the same tax laws. All privileges and customary rights enjoyed by the various towns and provinces had been abolished and the sale of public offices outlawed. Justice was available to all free of charge. Since the fragmentation which had been a feature of the feudal era disappeared, the French state became a single territory, which could be structured and

organized in line with modern requirements.

As a constituent assembly, the National Assembly was principally responsible for the drafting of a written constitution. Using the Constitution of the State of Virginia, the American Declaration of Independence (both of 1776), and the American Constitution of 1787 as models, the Assembly decided that, like them, the new French constitution should also lead with an official 'Declaration of the Rights of Man and Citizens'.

From 20–26 August, every one of the seventeen articles contained in this 'catechism of principles of 1789' was thoroughly debated. The deputies submitted more than fifty different versions. Even Thomas Jefferson, one of the fathers of the American Declaration of Independence, who was the United

States Ambassador to the French court in 1789, was drawn into the process. The proposal that a Declaration of Duties should accompany the Declaration of Rights was rejected by a majority after several long debates.

The Declaration was drawn up in the spirit of the Enlightenment and was more polemic, more aggressive and more powerful than its American model. It expressed the political ideals and values of the victorious bourgeoisie, and its adoption can be regarded as an epoch-making event in the history of the world, a sentence of death for the old regime. The Declaration was based on a secular, rather than a religious, view of mankind and its watchword, 'liberation', appealed not only to the French, but to all the nations of the world. Maximilien Robes-

pierre, a lawyer from the northern town of Arras who, as a member of the Constituent Assembly, took part in the whole process of debate, underlined that the Declaration had 'created universal, irrevocable and imprescriptible principles of law in order that it should apply to all peoples'.

The Declaration of Human Rights strengthened those freedoms which existed as of natural right and independently from the state. It regarded the guarantee of the rights of the citizen as a function of the sovereignty of the will of the people, that is of the participation of the politically 'active' citizen, the *citoyen*, in public affairs. It was based on the conviction that the welfare of the community depended on the confidence of the public in the legal system and on the personal inviolability of each individual. Its first article stressed that, 'Men are born free and with equal rights, and remain so'. The second contained a catalogue of human rights: freedom, security, ownership and the right to resist oppression. The fact that ownership appeared as an inviolable natural right, testified to the bourgeois nature of the document.

Citizens had the right to contribute 'either personally or through their representatives' to the legislative process, for this was to be an expression

2.22 A banquet for the king's household troops in the opera hall at the Palace of Versailles on 1 October 1789, at which a tricolor was thrown to the ground and trodden on.

2.23 Parisian market women armed with stabbing weapons and a cannon march on Versailles on 5 October 1789. On the left is a noblewoman (wearing a trimmed hat), who does not join the procession.

of the general will. In the same way, each had access to all public offices and rank, regardless of his origins. No one could be accused of a crime or arrested except in such cases as the law stipulated. All citizens were equal in the eyes of the law. Every citizen was adjudged innocent until convicted of a crime and could only be punished in accordance with the law. No law could have retrospective force. All taxes had to be sanctioned by the nation, all civil servants accountable to society. Freedom of expression, whether in the written or spoken word, was permitted as long as it did not disturb the 'legally established order'. The final article stipulated that

property could only be expropriated in cases of 'legally proven need' and with 'just compensation', thus confirming the legality of the resale of feudal rights.

This individualistic declaration, which made no mention of a belief in the authority of some and the subservience of others, was characteristic of a liberal bourgeoisie which disassociated itself from the state and wanted to create an autonomous domain which no outside power would be able to violate. The Declaration of Human Rights did not contain a word about the social conditions which were of such vital importance to the lower classes.

The king refused to give his assent either to the decrees abolishing feudalism or to the Declaration of Human Rights. In order to meet him halfway, the Constituent Assembly voted by a majority of 575 to 325 on 11 September to grant him a 'suspensive veto', that is, the right to interfere in the law-making process, and to hold up 'with suspensive power and for the lifetime of two parliaments' any of the National Assembly's laws which did not suit him. Despite this, Louis XVI was still not prepared to give his assent to the August Decrees, for he had only outwardly reconciled himself to the upheaval and hoped to reverse the revolutionary shift in power.

2.24 On 6 October 1789 the demonstrators, joined by Lafayette's National Guard meet at Versailles. Soldiers fire their rifles in celebration as the king promises to transfer his residence to Paris.

Robespierre, who rejected every attempt by the king to interfere in the legislative process, called the suspensive veto 'a monster', which was 'incomprehensible in both moral and political terms'. On 16 September in his new newspaper, *The People's Friend* (*Ami du peuple*), the doctor and journalist Jean-Paul Marat warned that a powerful faction within the National Assembly intended to sabotage the nation's new political system. He had already appealed to the people to watch over the Revolution in a broadsheet on 1 July. A flood of newspapers, broadsheets and pamphlets reported on counter-revolutionary plots being hatched by the aristocracy and called upon the masses, hungry and desperate

2.25 Louis XVI and his family seated in a state coach drawn by eight horses. Under pressure from demonstrators, they have been forced to move their residence from Versailles to the Tuileries. The Parisian market women accompanying the procession joyfully wave sprigs of poplar.

as a result of shortages, to take political action.

When the king ordered new troop reinforcements at the beginning of October and the blue, white and red cockade was trampled underfoot by aristocrats at a banquet in the Palace of Versailles, the indignation of the people of Paris knew no bounds. On the morning of 5 October 1789 around 7,000 proletarian women and a Civil Guard unit of about three times that size (and containing a number of those who had stormed the Bastille), decided to march on Versailles. Lafayette and the Paris National Guard accompanied the procession. When the crowd reached Versailles, the king both refused to sign the Constituent Assembly's decrees and turned down a request for more regular supplies of bread. The next day bloody battles raged between the demonstrators, who invaded the Palace, and the king's household troops. Under pressure from the mob, Louis XVI gave way and declared himself willing to leave Versailles and move to his residence in the Tuileries, which lay in the heart of Paris. On hearing this, the National Assembly, whose meeting hall the masses had likewise invaded, resolved to follow the king and henceforth to meet in the capital.

For the second time within three months, the mass action of the people had nipped in the bud the counter-revolutionary plans of the Court and smoothed the way for the victory of the bourgeoisie.

The Work of the Constituent National Assembly

The bourgeoisie, which had deprived absolutism of its political power and dealt a fatal blow to the system of feudal privileges, intended to replace the old regime with a parliamentary state based on legal equality and personal freedom. According to the theories of the Enlightenment, this union of the citizens should not be regarded as an end in itself, as absolutism had been, but as an agent of reason, which would guarantee both social well-being and the fundamental individual and collective freedoms set out in the Declaration of Human Rights.

From the very outset such ideas were supported and propagated by the Jacobin movement, which had its origins in the Breton Club. Those members of the Constituent Assembly who joined the Jacobin Club in 1789 sought to establish a bourgeois parliamentary state based on the sovereignty of the people and the separation of powers. Although they preferred to achieve this goal by peaceful and reformist means, they did not, in principle, reject revolutionary force. In fact, they warmly greeted popular action such as the storming of the Bastille and the march

3.1 Following the closure of religious orders by the Constituent Assembly in February 1790, the monks and nuns move out of their cloisters.

on Versailles, which had forced the king's move to Paris. Even during the first phase of the Revolution the hard-line supporters of the old regime transformed the term 'Jacobinism' into a political byword for excess, fanaticism and bloodlust.

The most eminent representative of the early Jacobin movement was Antoine Barnave, who, in his *Introduction à la Révolution Française* (written early in 1792), offered a materialistic interpretation of the state's upheaval. He found an explanation for the events of the Revolution in the dynamism of social and economic development. Barnave belonged to the Constituent Assembly's left wing, which fundamentally approved of the Constitution of 1791, and which hoped to reach a compromise both with the Court and with the progressive wing of the aristocracy along the lines of England's settlement of the 'Glorious Revolution' of 1688.

After the National Assembly's move to the capital, the deputies who shared such aims held their meetings in the secularized Dominican Friary of Saint Jacques (founded in 1218) and therefore became known as Jacobins. According to the consti-

3.3 Ordinary people dance around a tree decorated with a liberty cap and sing the revolutionary song *La Carmagnole. Ça ira, réjouissons nous, le bon temps viendra* – things will be fine, let us rejoice, good times are on the way.

Overleaf:
3.4 The population of a provincial town in France plants a tree for freedom in the presence of the mayor and the National Guard. The National Guards wear sashes in the colours of the tricolor. Young girls and children with garlands in their hair sing to the strains of a wind band.
3.2 A meeting of the Jacobin Club in the library of the former Friary of St. Jacques in the rue St. Honoré. After June 1791 the Jacobin Club met in the church itself since there was more room. On the left of the picture (standing) is the President, at the lectern on the right is a speaker.

tution which they adopted in February 1790, their official name was the 'Association of Friends of the Constitution'. Membership of the club was not restricted to deputies, but was open to anyone who paid an admission fee of 12 *livres* and an annual subscription of 24 *livres*. This relatively high subscription effectively excluded workers from the membership. Even so, by the end of 1789 the Paris Jacobin Club had 400 members. Six months later the membership had reached 1200. From 1790 on, Jacobin Clubs sprang up throughout France and their number soon ran into several hundreds.

The Jacobins were only one of many revolutionary groups to emerge around this time, although probably the most important. The Cordelier Club, which met in Paris' Franciscan Friary, was a radical combat club, which, according to its constitution, had set itself the task of 'watching over the observance of human rights and denouncing any abuse of public power'. The Cordelier Club charged only a nominal subscription and even admitted women and poorer citizens. It also had several notable revolutionaries, such as Danton, Marat, Desmoulins and

Chaumette, as members. The club had links with the working-class political clubs (*sociétés populaires*) which had been springing up in the sections of Paris since 1791 and where the sansculottes came together. These clubs, which organized mass rallies attended by hundreds of people, adopted Rousseau's ideas on the inalienable sovereignty of the people. They rejected the principle of representation as a distortion of the general will, and demanded the introduction of direct democracy, according to which deputies would simply be delegated by the people and would be under the constant control of their electors.

During the life of the Constituent Assembly, the tone of the Paris Jacobin Club was set not only by Barnave, but also by other constitutional monarchists, including Lafayette and Mirabeau. Although both hoped for a strengthening of the King's executive authority and in their memoranda advised Louis XVI to reconcile himself with the Revolution, they were not capable of working together and regarded each other as rivals. Lafayette left the Jacobin Club in April 1790 and founded the 'Society of

Dans l'enthousiasme de cette Liberté que l'on croyoit
s'être donné, on imagina de planter des arbres pour
en perpetuer la memoire, ce qui ce fit dans chaque
section avec grand appareil, Les Gardes nationaux
accompagnoient le Maire, et une Musique brillante
rendoit cette fête interessante.

1789', a body of no political import. Mirabeau became a legal advisor to the Crown and sought to turn the monarchy into an institution for the protection of bourgeois interests, as it had been in England for a century. His intention to become a member of the Cabinet in order to steer the Revolution in his preferred direction was frustrated by the Constituent Assembly, which distrusted him. On 7 November 1789, the Assembly passed a decree stating that ministerial office was incompatible with the job of a deputy.

In a memorandum, Mirabeau advised the king to

free himself from the control of the people of Paris and to appeal to the French provinces for help in defeating the insurgent capital city. The advice was not heeded, nor were any of Mirabeau's other plans adopted. In May 1790 Louis XVI and Marie-Antoinette took the ambitious politician into their employ, but acted against his will when they forged an alliance with Emperor Leopold II of Austria, King Frederick-William II of Prussia and various other sovereigns, whose armed support they hoped to enlist for the purposes of crushing the Revolution. Mirabeau was convinced that this policy would lead to the downfall of the French monarchy. On 2 April 1791, the day of his death, he said, 'I am taking the shroud of the monarchy with me. The political parties can fight over its remains.'

The Constituent Assembly's first task was to solve the financial crisis which had been a direct cause of the outbreak of revolution. In order to reduce the national deficit Talleyrand, a progressive member of the aristocracy and Bishop of Autun, suggested that the Church's property should be taken into public ownership and that the state should take over responsibility for paying the salaries of the clergy. On 2 November 1789 the Constituent Assembly did indeed vote to nationalize the Church's property. Its value was estimated to be around 4,000 million *livres*. Six weeks later the Assembly accepted a proposal from the Finance Minister, Necker, that the

property of the Church and the Crown should be offered for sale for 400 millions, and that treasury bonds, so-called *assignats*, should be issued to this value. These *assignats* were confirmed as currency some months later and became an official form of paper money. In July 1790 the Assembly ordered the gradual sale of *all* the nation's property. Henceforth the *assignats*, originally intended to liquidate the national debt, would be used to eradicate the domestic deficit. In order to attract lots of buyers and enable poorer citizens to buy, the land was parcelled and could be paid for in instalments. In some villages the peasants bought land jointly, but day-labourers and landless peasants were only seldom able to afford a parcel. The sale of the nation's property – like the right to repurchase feudal rights – was of limited benefit to the poor countryfolk. Instead, it increased the dominance of the rural and urban bourgeoisie. The flood of paper money led to rocketing inflation and by the beginning of 1792 the *assignats* were only worth 35 per cent of their original value.

Thus the *assignats* had two effects. On the one hand they committed a section of the peasantry to the Revolution, since anyone who had acquired Church property was also willing to fight for it, for he would not wish to lose all his worldly possessions as a result of the Revolution being crushed. On the other hand, the inflation which they had

3.6 The press freedom introduced by the Revolution created a new profession: newspaper sellers. Hundreds of newspapers and journals sprang up, many of them only short-lived. A newspaper seller shouts out details of the issue of *assignats*. The '*Patriote français*' is handed out by Brissot, the leader of the Gironde, on the left of the picture. The newspapers posted up next to Brissot, the *Journal du Soir* and the *Chronique de Paris*, were apolitical.

3.7 At the federation festivities in Paris on 14 July 1790 Louis XVI and Marie-Antoinette swear an oath of allegiance to the nation and the law.

3.8 The federation festivities on the Paris Champs de Mars on 14 July 1790, the first anniversary of the storming of the Bastille. In the centre is the newly-erected 'altar of the fatherland', from which a tricolor flies. The enthusiastic crowd swears an oath of allegiance to 'nation, law, and king'.

Overleaf:
3.9 At the federation festivities on 14 July 1790 the Paris municipal authorities had wine and food distributed to the population on the Champs Élysées.

caused led to food shortages in the towns, because the peasants tended to keep back their produce for themselves. Speculators hoarded grain and raw materials, took advantage of the reduction in the value of money, and amassed vast fortunes. The workers, who were paid their wages in debased *assignats*, could not even afford to buy basic food-stuffs. Inflation brought with it the intensification of social tensions and led to bread riots and outrages in many places. It was also to be one of the root causes of the Terror.

As a consequence of the confiscation of Church property and the closure of the monasteries and religious orders, the Constituent Assembly was compelled to reassess the relationship between the Church and the state, pay the Church's costs, and transform the clergy into civil servants. In addition, the state took over responsibility for the care of the sick and the poor, which had been one of the Church's functions under the old regime. The 'Civil Constitution of the Clergy' of 12 July 1790 established the supremacy of the state in Church affairs. The number of bishops was reduced from 133 to 83, and their canonical institution by the Papal Court abolished. The clergy was to be elected throughout: bishops by the electors of the departments, priests by those in the districts. In place of the old lucrative prebendaries, a bishop now received an annual sal-

ary of between 12,000 and 30,000 *livres*, representing a fall in income, whilst a parish priest earned a minimum of 1,200 and his chaplain 700 *livres*, which in general represented an improvement.

Pope Pius VI, who had already officially slated the Declaration of Human Rights, condemned the Civil Constitution as heretical and as an attempt to destroy the Church. The antagonisms between the secularized French state and the Papal Court intensified when the enclave of Avignon in southern France, which had been papal since the fourteenth century, joined the new nation state. In November 1790 the Constituent Assembly required all incumbent priests to swear an oath of allegiance to the constitution of the kingdom. Only four French bishops, including Talleyrand, did so. Roughly half the priests refused to comply, feeling themselves to be more closely tied to the Papal Court in Rome than to the revolutionary nation-state.

On 10 March 1791 the Pope formally condemned the principles of the Revolution and the new collection of rules governing Church life, belief, and worship, and the schism became irreversible. Henceforth the political conflict would be accompanied by a religious one. The struggle between Church and state, and the open breach which existed between the state and Rome, opened up a whole new zone of activity for the counter-revolution, which had been

in decline until then. Many of the priests who had refused to swear the oath of allegiance joined forces with the enemies of the Revolution. Reactionaries, *émigrés*, and those members of the clergy who had remained true to Rome formed a united front and marched together under the banner of religion.

The popular movement was gathering strength and demanded an improvement in material living conditions. In view of this increased strength, the deputies considered it imperative that they should politically safeguard such power as they had already acquired. This purpose was served by a property qualification and the division of the population into 'active' and 'passive' citizens, both of which excluded the masses from having any say in the general will, that is, the democratic process. On 22 December 1789 the Constituent Assembly voted by a narrow majority of ten votes (453:443) to adopt an electoral law which divided citizens into four groups. It contained a property qualification, according to which those without property could neither vote nor be elected; they were to be politically powerless 'passive' citizens. Those who paid annual taxes amounting to at least three days' wages could elect other voters to the electoral colleges and were to be known as 'active' citizens. Only those who paid annual taxes amounting to at least ten days' wages could become members of an electoral college, and to be a deputy it was necessary either to be a landowner or to pay annual taxes amounting to

at least 54 *livres*. Out of 25 million French citizens, around a quarter, i.e. more than six million, were adult men (the age of majority for voting purposes was 25). Of these, more than two million were 'passive' citizens and over four million 'active' citizens, 50,000 were eligible for election to the electoral colleges, and only a few thousand were entitled to become deputies.

The democrats fought the property qualification tooth and nail, because it contradicted the basic principles of the equality of all citizens, and replaced nobility by birth with nobility by wealth. Robespierre called the placing of conditions on the right to vote or be elected a flagrant violation of human rights. Marat predicted in his newspaper that the population, which had already thrown off the yoke of the aristocracy, would also throw off the yoke of the wealthy.

The bill introduced by the deputy Le Chapelier and passed on 14 June 1791 likewise served the interests of the upper middle classes. It was enacted when signs of an organized labour movement began to appear in the work-shops of Paris. Joiners, masons, carpenters and printers took their grievances relating to low wages and poor working conditions to the National Assembly, citing their belief in human rights. They founded 'friendly societies' and described the employers as despots and enemies of the public good. The opposing side also inundated the National Assembly with a flood of

3.10 Soldiers of the National Guard on their way to the Palais Royal on the anniversary of the storming of the Bastille. They wear liberty caps to demonstrate their support for the Revolution and are surrounded by jubilant girls and children.

3.11 On 14 July 1790 a
ceremony takes place on the
spot where the demolished
Bastille had once stood. The
spot has been decorated for
the occasion, but sections of
the foundations walls of the
Bastille are still visible to the
left and right of the entrance.

protests and accusations, claiming that the workers'
'wage conspiracies' ran contrary to the public interest and should therefore be banned. In the *Peoples'
Friend* of 8 and 12 June, Marat came to the defence of
the workers, saying that they alone had been
responsible for the victory of the Revolution and
that they were now being sucked dry by these 'vam-
pires', these enemies of the people. 'It makes one
turn red with shame and groan with agony to see
such a productive class of poor people at the mercy
of a handful of villains, who gorge themselves on
the sweat of others and rob them of the meagre
fruits of their labour like monsters.'

The National Assembly took the part of the
employers almost without debate. Le Chapelier's
law was based on the principle of unlimited free-

3.12 At the federation festival on the site of the Bastille people dance and celebrate through the night in the glow of countless Japanese lanterns.

and that on trade unions remained in force until 1884.

A Constituent Assembly decree replacing the old provinces with eighty-three easily supervised departments of roughly the same size permitted the establishment of modern legal and administrative systems. The departments were divided into smaller units, districts and cantons, whose administrative and fiscal authorities were elected by 'active' citizens. The urban administrations were granted wide powers, including the right to assess and levy taxes, jurisdiction over the police, and the right to maintain public order. The special powers exercised by the provinces and regions under the old regime, and the control by the privileged classes of the legal system, were replaced by new regulations. Civil cases were tried by justices of the peace in the cantons, by county court judges in the districts, and by chief justices in the departments. A court of assize was established in each department to try criminal cases, and Paris acquired a court of appeal. Judges were elected and administered the law in the name of the nation. Any person accused of a crime had to be brought before a court within twenty-four hours of his arrest and judgement was pronounced in public. Proper legal representation was guaranteed.

As had been the case in earlier bourgeois revolutions in the Netherlands and England, the French Revolution also brought emancipation for the Jews. The Jews had been driven out of France in the fourteenth century, but at the beginning of the Revolution around 40,000 still lived on French soil. Paris, with its population of approximately 600,000, had a Jewish community of around 1,000 people. Roughly a quarter of French Jews lived in the south-western coastal towns of Bayonne and Bordeaux and came from mainly affluent families of Spanish-Jewish

dom for the employer and forbade the workers either to form combinations to safeguard their common economic interests, to establish trade unions, or to call strikes. The proletariat was thus exposed to unlimited exploitation. The concept of freedom was interpreted by the employers in a way which would serve the interests of their own class. They maintained that the wage-earner's freedom consisted entirely of his right to make a 'voluntary contract' with his employer, that is, to sell his labour on the open market. Those without property had no right to demand participation in the administration of the state or to have a say in matters of public concern, because only ownership could bind the individual to the interests of the state. Le Chapelier's law was blessed with a long life, for the ban on combinations and strikes was not lifted until 1864,

3.13 A coffee morning for patriotic women. The speaker reads from the *Moniteur* and the participants donate money for the nation.

descent, but the greater part of France's Jewish population lived in Alsace, which had not been annexed until the seventeenth century.

For three days in December 1789 the Constituent Assembly debated the emancipation of the Jews from the special legal restrictions placed upon them, as well as their complete integration into France's national and social life. The most eminent champion of Jewish emancipation was the liberal priest Abbot Grégoire, who also spoke out vehemently for the liberation of the Negro slaves in France's West Indian colonies. It was during this debate that the Earl of Clermont-Tonnerre, who belonged to the progressive wing of the aristocracy, expressed the famous and often quoted view that, 'As a nation the Jews should be denied everything, as individuals they should be granted everything. They may not form any political body or class within the state, but

should be individual citizens.' This principle, which abolished traditional autonomy under the leadership of the rabbis within the Jewish community, eventually formed the basis of the law which emancipated the Jews. In January 1790 Jews of Spanish descent were freed from all previous disabilities and disadvantages, and on 28 September 1791 the Ashkenazim living in Alsace were granted that same freedom. They had to swear an oath of allegiance, were granted the same status as the non-Jewish majority of the population, and could apply for all public offices. The decree which granted emancipation stated that 'any citizen who agrees to carry out his constitutional duty, also has the right to enjoy the advantages which the Constitution promises'.

The constitution drafted by the Assembly was primarily shaped by, and beneficial to, the landed

3.14 The postmaster Drouet, who had recognized the king and thwarted his attempt to flee at Varennes on 22 June 1791 by barricading a road and thus stopping the carriage containing the royal family. He is dressed as a valet.

and educated middle classes, as well as members of that faction within the progressive wing of the aristocracy with which they had links. The document was a compromise between moderate and radical tendencies and sought to link contradictory theories of the state. On the one hand, it was influenced by the teachings of Locke and Montesquieu, who had favoured a system whereby the state's power would be limited and controlled by mutually checking authorities; on the other, it contained elements of Rousseau's 'Social Contract'. In line with his theory of the general will, or *Volonté Générale*, Rousseau regarded any subordination of the individual to the will of another as unlawful. The Constitution retained the constitutional monarchy, whilst at the same time insisting on the democratic principle of the non-transferable sovereignty of the people. It proclaimed the formal legal equality of all citizens, but left the political, economic and social inequality of the population untouched.

The monarch's authority was no longer anchored in the realm of the religious and supernatural, as it had been in pre-bourgeois societies, for the king had been stripped of his divine right to rule. In the place of personal loyalty to a hereditary royal house, the monarchy drew its rational derivation and legitimacy from the constitution of the united nation. A monarchy which had undergone such an ideological transformation as this would hopefully be able to find support in patriotism. The majority of the Constituent Assembly's members hoped to persuade the king to forge an honourable alliance with the bourgeoisie, in order that the aims of the Revolution could be accomplished with a minimum of force and so that the masses did not need to become involved, thereby threatening bourgeois property. The Constitution therefore assigned to the monarchy the role of mediating between conflicting interests, whilst at the same time acting in accordance with the inalienable will of the people.

The king was deprived of his right to dispose freely of funds. Like the English monarch, he received a civil list, which was set at an annual rate of 25 million *livres*. For his protection, he was given a guard comprising a 1,200-man infantry and 600 cavalrymen, all to be paid from the civil list.

The Constitution, which would serve as a model for numerous liberal monarchist constitutions abroad in the nineteenth century, brought about many fundamental changes, but it also permitted the continued existence of many relics of the pre-revolutionary order. Though the Constituent

3.15 The royal family returns to Paris on 25 June 1791 under the watchful eye of the National Guard. On the left of the carriage sit Louis XVI, Marie-Antoinette, and the two children. On the right sit the king's sister Madame Elisabeth and a lady's maid. The deputies Barnave and Pétion, who are accompanying the carriage, are partly hidden.

3.16 The Constitution, drawn up by the Constituent Assembly, to be handed over to the king on 3 September 1791.

3.17 On the Champs de Mars on 17 July 1791 the National Guard carries out a massacre of republican petitioners at the orders of Lafayette.

Assembly had abolished the hereditary nobility and its privileges, it was inclined to retain certain elements of the old system of rule in order to keep the demands and independent actions of the property-less lower classes in check. The hereditary ruler, who fictitiously appeared to be the supreme representative of the nation, could only take political decisions with the agreement of the National Assembly, though he retained the right to name ministers and could not be called to account. At command level at least, the control of the army, which had been profoundly shaken by the revolutionary attack, remained largely in the hands of the king, who had only outwardly yielded to the Constitution's restriction of his old absolute powers. By means of the suspensive veto, the king was able to cripple the legislative process. Ministers and diplomats were responsible, not to the legislature, but to the Crown, and were chosen, not from the ranks of the Assembly, but from the old aristocracy, as they had been before the Revolution. The abolition of feudal rights had earned the formerly privileged lords of the manor a not inconsiderable bonus.

In its foreign policy the Constituent Assembly distanced itself officially from the aggressive traditions and tendencies of absolutism. On 22 May 1790 it voted never to wage a war of conquest and never to use French troops 'against the freedom of another people'. This resolution was incorporated into the Constitution of 1791. It was to prove ambiguous, for it left the door open for French armies to *liberate* neighbouring peoples from the yoke of their despots.

The Constitution of 1791 had nothing in the way of material benefits to offer the peasants and artisans who formed the major part of the French nation. Through the division of the population into 'active' and 'passive' citizens, and as a result of the ban on trade unions, the ordinary wage-earner and the propertyless citizen had been politically gagged and condemned to economic impotence. Even the middle classes were unable to take part in the direction or control of the state. In the main, the work of the Constituent Assembly served the interests of the propertied bourgeoisie, which owed its success to the revolutionary actions of the lower classes on 14

July and 6 October 1789, yet rejected the social demands made by these classes and saw the unruly popular movement as a danger to the security of property.

For a long time, however, this class conflict within the victorious Third Estate had been overshadowed by the intoxicating thought of national self-liberation. On the first anniversary of the storming of the Bastille, 14 July 1790, solemn public demonstrations of patriotism, so-called 'federation festivities', took place all over France. On the Parisian Champs de Mars, which had hitherto served as a parade ground, tens of thousands of people built a stadium, in which Talleyrand celebrated a mass and the National Guards paraded before the king. On this newly-erected 'altar of the fatherland' Lafayette, their commander, swore an oath of allegiance to 'nation, law and king' and all those present repeated it after him.

Louis XVI, who had stood centre stage during this 'festival of fraternity', was determined to set aside the work of the Constituent Assembly and to restore his absolute rule. For this he would need the help of foreign powers. Several times he hypocritically professed his loyalty to the Revolution, which, he said, had 'eradicated abuses dating back centuries'. Secret correspondence of his discovered later revealed that at the same time he was planning, with the help of royalist émigrés, to flee the country. He intended to escape to Belgium, which at that time was ruled by Austria. There he would establish contact with the army of Emperor Leopold II, his brother-in-law, and use military intervention to put an end to the Revolution.

The escape was arranged by the Swedish cavalry colonel Axel Fersen, the queen's favourite, who ordered a large carriage with room for ten passengers: the royal family and their servants. On the evening of 20 June 1791 Lafayette, who had connived at the escape, left a gateway in the *Jardins des Tuileries* unguarded. Whilst the king's brother, the Earl of Provence, later to become Louis XVIII, took a different escape route and reached Belgium, the royal couple did not follow plans designed to guarantee their safety. Louis failed to stick to the timetable which had been agreed with the military orga-

3.18 On 14 September 1791 King Louis XVI swears an oath of allegiance to the Constitution drafted by the Constituent National Assembly.

Je soutiendrai la Constitution   *Je détruirai la Constitution*

3.19 A caricature of the king's points up his insincerity and two-facedness: he promises the deputies of the Constituent Assembly that he will uphold the Constitution at the same time as he is telling the priests that he will destroy it.

nizer of the escape, Marshal Bouillé, in Metz.

Near Varennes, not far from the border, a post-master by the name of Drouet recognized the king from his picture on an *assignat*. Drouet arranged for a bridge to be barricaded in order to stop the carriage. The citizens of Varennes sounded the alarm bells and alerted neighbouring peasants. The next day the Constituent Assembly sent three deputies, including Barnave, to accompany the runaways back to Paris.

The escape had failed less as a result of the king's bad time-keeping than because the peasants and citizens in the provinces had taken up arms in order to prevent it, and the hussars stationed in Varennes had been fraternizing with them. The episode led to a new wave of emigration amongst the aristocracy and among priests who had refused to swear the oath of allegiance.

The attempted escape also gave the popular movement an enormous lift. The democratic wing of the Jacobin Club, led by the deputies Robespierre and Pétion, described Lafayette as an accomplice, because he had known of the plan and had not foiled it. The Cordelier Club went further. It declared Louis XVI to be an enemy of the nation and called for the immediate abolition of the monarchy and the establishment of a republic. The radical newspaper *Révolutions de Paris* demanded that the king be tried as a political criminal and traitor.

The liberal, upper middle-class majority in the Constituent Assembly wanted to end the Revolution as quickly as possible. It was hoped that this would prevent intensification of the upheaval and renewed intervention by the masses. Work on the monarchist Constitution was almost complete, but because the Constitution itself was under threat as a result of the king's removal from the Throne, the Assembly spread a fictitious rumour to the effect that the king and his family had not tried to flee, but had been kidnapped by agitators. The Constituent Assembly also ordered the recruitment of 100,000 volunteers, who were to be sent to France's northern border in order to repel a possible invasion by foreign troops. The royal family was placed under mild house arrest and Louis XVI suspended pending final clarification of his part in the matter of the escape. He would resume his post only when he had once again accepted, and sworn allegiance to, the Constitution.

The king's prestige had suffered irreparable damage and agitation, for the notion of a republic readily found favour in the working-class political clubs. On the second anniversary of the storming of the Bastille, 14 July 1791, the *Patriote français* called for the mandate to be withdrawn from the deputies in the Constituent Assembly and for the people to arm themselves for rebellion should this demand be refused. Whilst a bitter battle of words raged between the radical and moderate wings of the Jacobin Club, the Cordelier Club and members of the working-class political clubs drew up a joint petition calling for the Constituent Assembly to declare a republic. On 17 July this petition was submitted to the population of Paris on the 'altar of the fatherland'. Thousands of demonstrators streamed

3.20 King Frederick William II of Prussia, Emperor Leopold II, and the Elector of Saxony, Frederick Augustus III, discuss their joint 'Declaration of Pillnitz' of 27 August 1791. It is regarded in France as a threat and the beginning of an anti-revolutionary crusade.

to the Champs de Mars to add their signatures to it.

The Constituent Assembly, however, was not prepared for the popular movement to dictate how it should act. The mayor, Bailly, was instructed to break up the demonstration. Lafayette advanced with his National Guard and without warning ordered his troops to fire on the unarmed crowd. This 'massacre on the Champs de Mars' claimed fifty lives. Hundreds were wounded.

During subsequent moves to suppress the uprising, numerous leaders of the republican movement were arrested and several newspapers forced to take a stand. The leading members of the Cordelier Club, Marat and Danton, had to remain in hiding for some time, and the Club was temporarily closed. With elections to the Constituent Assembly imminent, the political and ideological antagonisms within the

Assembly intensified.

A split developed in the Jacobin Club when members drew a clear distinction between royalism and revolution. The loyalist majority, including Barnave and other members who had supported the property qualification, left the Club and founded a new, moderate, society in the Friary *des Feuillants*. At this point Robespierre, Pétion and Brissot took over the leadership of the Jacobin movement, and most of the Jacobin Clubs in the provinces sided with them.

After the massacre on the Champs de Mars, the Constituent Assembly revised the Constitution in order to strengthen conservative elements and avoid a new popular uprising. The property qualifi-

cation, which determined whether or not a citizen could be elected to a departmental electoral college, was increased and membership of the National Guard restricted to 'active' citizens. By May 1791 the Constituent Assembly had decided that none of its members should be permitted to become deputies in the new Legislative Assembly.

On 3 September 1791 work on the Constitution was complete. Eleven days later Louis XVI swore an oath of allegiance to it. To celebrate the occasion a general amnesty was declared and the arrested democrats freed. When the last sitting of the Constituent Assembly took place on the 30 September the affluent bourgeoisie regarded the Revolution as over.

3.21 On 14 September 1791 the liberal-monarchist Constitution is proclaimed on the Paris marketplace *des Innocents*.

Revolutionary Escalation, 1791–1792

The notion that the Revolution could be halted at that particular stage in its development was illusory, since the Constituent Assembly had been unable, in the sphere of either domestic or foreign policy, firmly to anchor the results of the upheaval, or to make them irreversible. The ruling bourgeoisie was harried from both sides: by the counter-revolutionaries, who were far from having to admit defeat, and by the urban and rural masses, who demanded tangible material improvements. The unity of the Third Estate had been shattered by the bloodbath on the Champs de Mars, the division of the nation into 'active' and 'passive' citizens, and the reinstatement of the treacherous king after his unsuccessful attempt to escape. As a result, it now proved necessary to extend the Revolution far beyond its original goals, so that those fruits of the victory which were ripe for plucking could be reaped by the bourgeoisie.

4.1 The black slaves in Haiti revolt against the white plantation-owners, Autumn 1791.

In the autumn of 1791 a new wave of unrest spread throughout France. In many areas the peasants refused to continue paying feudal dues, and a number of castles

belonging to aristocratic *émigrés* were set alight. In the towns, markets were plundered, cargoes of grain attacked, and shops stormed. Inflation meant that the inhabitants could not even afford to buy bread or other basic foodstuffs. For the first time ever, working-class political clubs in the sections of Paris called for governmental price control, for the supply of essential commodities to the population to be guaranteed, and for profiteers and speculators to be prevented from hoarding vital goods. Such demands were inconsistent with the sacred bourgeois principle of unchecked economic freedom.

The unrest also gripped France's colonies in the Caribbean. There had been insurrection here as early as 1790 since the promise of freedom contained in the Declaration of Human Rights had not been extended to the coloured slave population working on the sugar and coffee plantations in Haiti. In May 1791, after a great deal of shilly-shallying, the Constituent Assembly granted France's constitutional freedoms to the 'free coloureds', that is, the mulatto half-castes, but withdrew them again under pressure from the white plantation owners. In August 1791 the negro slaves, under the leadership of an extraordinarily capable and intelligent negro by the name of Toussaint Louverture, a former coachman, finally revolted. They seized land belonging to the plantation aristocracy

4.2 Following the abolition of slavery in February 1794, the black slave François-Dominique Toussaint-L'Ouverture, cautious and talented leader of the revolts in Haiti, entered the service of the Republic. As a general, he successfully fought off the English invasion of Haiti and in 1800 declared the colony's independence. Expeditionary troops sent by the First Consul, Bonaparte, forced a surrender. He was deported to France and died in a fortress prison.

4.3 As a member of the Constituent Assembly the cleric Henri Gregoire drafted the Civil Constitution of the Clergy and later became the constitutional bishop of Blois. He was a leading champion of emancipation and equality for the Jews and of the abolition of slavery in the Colonies.

and began to establish independent institutions of state.

The intensification of class conflict in France and in the French colonies took on particular significance when international tension increased. Since the king's unsuccessful attempt at escape, the Revolution had ceased to be a matter of concern within France alone, and the question of war began to dominate the political scene. Exiled French aristocrats, who had set up their headquarters in Coblenz, pressed for armed intervention by the powers of Europe. The European sovereigns in general, and those of the German constituent states in particular, feared that flying sparks from the Revolution might spread to their own countries and made preparations to extinguish the source of the fire. The Courts in Vienna and Berlin buried their old differences. At the end of August 1791 Emperor Leopold II of Austria and King Frederick-William II of Prussia, met at Castle Pillnitz in Saxony and declared their readiness 'to employ the most effective means' of placing Louis XVI 'in a position to strengthen the foundations of his monarchist regime'. Neverthe-

less they attached a condition to their military intervention, namely that other powers should also take part. This was an indirect call for England to offer financial support for the invasion by Prussia and Austria, but the English Government was not prepared to do this, because it regarded the French Revolution as a welcome political and economic weakening of its rival. The Pillnitz appeal for an anti-revolutionary crusade was, however, taken seriously in France and contributed to the nurturing of a war psychosis.

The 745-strong Legislative Assembly, which met for the first time in the *Manège* (former indoor riding arena) of the Tuileries on 1 October 1791, was a body of relative social uniformity. The deputies of the Constituent Assembly were not members of this new body, but bourgeois lawyers and owners were still the dominant force. There were few members of the aristocracy or clergy, and the lower classes were not represented at all. Those in favour of a constitutional monarchy had formed the left wing of the Constituent Assembly, but had now shifted to the right. Having achieved their political aims and

founded the Feuillants Club, they now rejected any further democratization. 264 of the delegates to the Assembly belonged to this faction, and one of their best-known spokesmen was Theodor Lameth. In the Feuillants Club as a whole, which had over 1,000 members, it was Barnave who set the tone. He had advanced to the position of advisor to the royal couple after their unsuccessful attempt to escape, although they mistrusted him just as much as they had mistrusted Mirabeau before him. In addition, several Feuillants were supporters of Lafayette, who in October 1791 relinquished his command of the Paris National Guard in order to stand for election as the new bourgeois mayor. Lafayette hoped to succeed Bailly, but was defeated by the Jacobin Pétion. Of the 80,000 'active' citizens in Paris only 10,000 took part in the election.

The centre ground in the Legislative Assembly was occupied by 345 independent deputies, all loyal to the Constitution, and these adopted various

4.4 The cartoon depicts a meeting of the Paris Jacobin Club in January 1792 at the height of the fierce debate on the subject of war and peace with the allied forces of Austria and Prussia. The four speakers on the platform, clearly Girondins, are calling for war, but are opposed by the President of the Club (on the right). One member bares his behind, and in the centre stands a group of figures wearing boots and the clothing normally associated with the aristocracy. The figures either sport horns or have the heads of birds. Members of the public are seated on the balustrade above.

stances. They were motivated largely by fear: they feared the growth of counter-revolutionary forces just as much as they feared further radicalization or intensification of the Revolution within society. On many issues these deputies voted with the left, sometimes out of conviction, but often under pressure from the Jacobin spectators in the stands, who took the greatest possible interest in the meetings of the Legislative Assembly.

On the left of the Assembly were 136 liberal deputies, mainly lawyers, journalists, and academics by profession. Above all, they represented the interests of the affluent *bourgeoisie d'affaires*, that is, of the merchants, entrepreneurs and industrialists, many of whom lived in the flourishing business towns and ports. Most of these deputies belonged to the Paris Jacobin Club. They were known as 'Brissotins' or 'Girondins', because their spokesmen were Brissot, a talented journalist and brilliant speaker, and the deputies Vergniaud, Gensonné and Guadet, all from Bordeaux in the department of Gironde. In addition, the Legislative Assembly contained a few staunch democrats, such as Lindet, Couthon and Carnot. They spoke out in favour of the introduction of universal suffrage and later took up posts on the Jacobins' 'Great Committee of Public Safety'.

The Jacobin Club was now growing in importance. After the departure of the Feuillants, it had undergone appreciable democratization and had now become a meeting place for master craftsmen, shop-keepers, traders, office workers, and other members of the petty bourgeoisie and their immediate social 'superiors'. Many of these people attended meetings every evening in order to listen to speeches by Robespierre, Brissot and the other revolutionaries. As was also the case at the well-attended meetings of the Cordelier Club and in the working-class political clubs, discussion here invariably centred around the international crisis and possible ways of relieving the desperate economic situation.

Reports of sabre-rattling by the loyalist *émigrés* in Coblenz, and the news that Austria and Prussia were arming themselves in preparation for military intervention, were welcomed by several of the political groupings in France, although for various, quite different reasons: the Court, the Feuillants grouped around Lafayette, and the Girondins were all keen to see the outbreak of war. Louis XVI and

4.5 As a result of inflation and the economic crisis many craftsmen and owners of small workshops were unable to find their rent and were thrown out onto the streets by their landlords.

Marie-Antoinette wanted war because they believed that the revolutionary troops would come off badly in any battle against the well-drilled armies of Prussia and Austria, and that a French defeat would make it possible for them to restore absolutism. On 8 September 1791, in a letter to her brother Emperor Leopold II in Vienna, the queen wrote, 'Armed might has destroyed everything, armed might can restore everything.' Three months later in a personal letter Louis XVI asked the Prussian king for military assistance.

Unlike the royal couple, Lafayette and his sup-

4.6 Pierre Victurnien Vergniaud, a lawyer from Bordeaux. Vergniaud was a member of the Legislative Assembly and the Convention and was a brilliant speaker for the Gironde. He was executed on 31 October 1793.

that the war would cause the peoples of neighbouring states, also oppressed by despotism, to rise up in revolt. For this reason they emphasized the Revolution's ability to liberate the world. On 29 November 1791 in the Legislative Assembly, the Girondin Isnard warned that the French were quite capable of 'changing the face of the earth and making all tyrants shake on their fragile thrones'. He also warned 'that if the cabinets of Europe embroil their kings in a war against the people, then we will embroil the people in a war against the kings.' Solemnly he proclaimed that 'France will utter a mighty cry and the peoples of the world will respond. The world will be bedecked with warriors, and the names of the enemies of freedom will be stricken from the list of mankind!' In the same vein, Brissot claimed a month later that 'the time has come for a new crusade; it will be a crusade for the freedom of the world.'

porters in the Feuillants Club, including many high-ranking officers, hoped for a French victory, believing that they would then be appointed to positions of great power and would be able to force their will not only on the Court, but also on the Legislative Assembly and the popular movement.

Brissot and his Girondist friends hoped that the war would unleash a storm of national passion, deflect attention from France's domestic social conflicts, and carry the Revolution beyond the borders of France. Largely for economic reasons, the Girondins were convinced that the war was in the interests of the nation: the bourgeois community, which hoped for huge orders to supply the army, was keen to restore the value of the *assignats* by means of a war economy.

The Girondins did not seek their allies from amongst the ranks of their nation's own lower classes, whom they mistrusted, but hoped instead

4.8 The Legislative Assembly meets in the riding arena of the Tuileries. On the left is the President's table and chair, behind that a plaque quoting the Declaration of Human Rights, and on the right a speaker at his lectern. The public watches from the stands, and guards armed with pikes keep order.

4.7 Jean-Marie Roland de la Platière. Roland was Minister of the Interior in Louis XVI's 'Gironde Government' from March until June 1792, and after the overthrow of the monarchy from 10 August 1792 until January 1793. He fled to Normandy after the overthrow of the Gironde and committed suicide when he heard news of his wife's execution.

Overleaf:
4.9 On 25 April 1792 at the home of Mayor Friedrich Dietrich of Strasburg (seated on a chair in the centre) Captain Rouget de L'Isle sings his newly-composed *War-song of the Army of the Rhine (Marseillaise)*.

4.10 Tens of thousands of copies of the sheet music of the *Marseille March* are printed and distributed among soldiers in the army and in the hinterland. The *Marseillaise* was translated into German six times during the Revolution.

Robespierre was one of the few politicians who had kept a cool head in the face of all this wartime propaganda. The willingness of his political opponents, the Court, and the Feuillants, to go to war made him suspicious, but he turned most violently of all on Brissot's idea of exporting the Revolution to neighbouring countries on the point of a bayonet. In his speeches to the Jacobin Club he pointed out that the army was badly organized, the soldiers inadequately armed and equipped for a lengthy bout of war, and the fortresses without ammunition. Before rushing into some wartime adventure elsewhere, it was necessary for France to end the Revolution within its own borders and to secure the achievements of that Revolution. In France itself equal rights could still be found only in the Constitution. They were by no means a reality, but were misinterpreted and trodden underfoot daily. In a speech on 2 January 1792, Robespierre maintained that,

to want to grant others freedom, before we have won it ourselves, is to ensure our own slavery along with that of the whole world. The most extraordinary idea ever to take origin in the head of a politician, is the notion that it is enough for an armed people to invade another people in order to move the invaded population to adopt the laws and constitution of the invading people. No one loves armed missionaries, and the first piece of advice offered by nature and caution is that the invaders should be repelled as enemies.

Robespierre recognized that the Girondins would be unable to win such a war if, as was the case, they were keen to prevent any advance in the process of democratization and to keep the fruits of the Revolution solely for the affluent bourgeoisie. He warned that the outbreak of war and the mounting of a crusade for freedom would bring with them unforeseen dangers for the Revolution unless the material needs of the masses were met and the domestic counter-revolution defeated. The Legislative Assembly ignored the warning.

The Prussian and Austrian rulers feared that the Girondins' calls for liberation could lead to revolutionary uprisings among their own subjects and came to the conclusion that a passage at arms was inevitable. On 7 February 1792 Emperor Leopold II and the King of Prussia, Frederick-William II, forged a military alliance and pledged that each country would send 20,000 men into the field should France attack. A few days later the Duke of Brunswick was appointed as commander-in-chief of the Prussian troops, and in Berlin work began on plans for the summer offensive.

The Paris Legislative Assembly, which cited the escaped aristocracy's noisy campaign against the Revolution as the main cause of the war, voted to confiscate the *émigrés'* property and to use the proceeds to finance the armed conflict. Towards the middle of March 1792 the king appointed a new, Girondin cabinet: the administrative genius Roland, whose clever and ambitious wife ran a well-known salon, became Minister of the Interior, General Dumouriez was appointed Foreign Minister, the banker Clavière took over responsibility for the state finances, and Marshal Servan became Minister for War. The dominant figure in the cabinet was Dumouriez, whose strategy was similar to that of Lafayettee: he planned a limited war and to enlist the help of the victorious homecoming army to secure a leading political position for himself.

In the meantime Emperor Leopold II, who had allowed himself to be drawn into the preparations for war only with extreme reluctance, died on 1 March. His son and successor, Franz II, who had an obsessive fear of the Jacobins, had not the slightest intention of making any concessions to French revolutionaries who called upon his subjects to revolt, not even for the purposes of preventing the war. He left unanswered an ultimatum in which the French Government called upon Austria to reduce the number of its troops and arms in Belgium, and on 3 April he assured the designated Prussian commander-in-chief, the Duke of Brunswick, that he would do everything within his power to rescue the French monarchy and save 'Europe from the spread of anarchy'.

On 20 April 1792, in an ecstatic frenzy of enthusiasm, the Legislative Assembly declared war on 'the King of Hungary and Bohemia', Franz II. Although the declaration avoided describing Franz II as the head of the 'Holy Roman Empire', Prussia rejected the possibility of a neutrality and declared a few weeks later that a state of war existed between it and France. The French declaration of war referred explicitly to the Constituent Assembly's decree of 20

4.11 Manon Roland (née Philipon), wife of the Minister of the Interior and twenty years his junior. Girondist deputies often met in Madame Roland's salon. She was a passionate opponent of the radical Jacobins and was executed on 8 November 1793.

4.12 General Theobald Dillon is murdered on 29 April 1792 in Lille. At the beginning of the war he had given the order to retreat and was accused of treason by his own troops.

May 1790, which had renounced wars of conquest. The National Assembly affirmed almost unanimously (only seven deputies voted against) that the French nation 'is taking up arms only in order to defend its freedom and independence; that the war which it is forced to undertake is not a war between nations, but the just defence of a free people against the unjust attack of a king; that France will never confuse its brothers with its real enemies.'

Contrary to the expectations of its authors, the war was to last almost a quarter of a century, with few interruptions, and would not end until 1815. It would considerably intensify revolutionary upheaval in France itself and transform the political and social scene throughout the continent of Europe. Its

first victim was Louis XVI's monarchy. At its very roots the revolutionary war stemmed from the political and ideological tensions which existed between a bourgeois and dynamic France and the class-based, feudal, absolutist nations of Europe. These tensions were so acute that they forced both sides to explode. In the end if would be the newer order which would demonstrate its superiority in this epoch-making struggle: the French nation dis-

4.13 The masses force their way into the Tuileries on 20 June 1792. They are protesting against both the dismissal of the Girondist ministers and the king's veto.

played a great measure of political maturity and revealed enormous vitality and revolutionary creative genius.

On 25 April 1792 a certain Captain Rouget de l'Isle, alive with patriotic fervour, composed a rousing 'war-song for the Rhine Army' whilst at the home of Mayor Dietrich of Strasburg. This stirring tribute to the Revolution was taken to southern France by a friend of Dietrich's and three months later, at the end of July, the Marseille volunteers sang it as they marched into Paris. The song achieved immortality as the Marseillaise and was adopted as the French national anthem in 1879.

The Girondins' hopes for an early and victorious surprise attack on Belgium, which would settle the war before the Prussians and Austrians could even mobilize their troops, came to nothing. Robespierre's warnings proved well-founded. Almost two thirds of the army officers had left the country, stocks of weapons were low, the discipline of the troops in tatters, and their morale at rock-bottom. Commanding Generals Rochambeau, Luckner and Lafayette were men of no substance. Generals Biron and Dillon ordered a retreat during the army's very

first skirmish on the Belgian border and the latter was slain by his own soldiers. Several army units made up of foreign mercenaries deserted to the Austrians *en bloc*.

The realization that the Revolution was fighting for its very existence as a result of this defeat gave a new impetus to the radicalization of the masses, and the persisting belief in a plot by the aristocracy gained ground. From then on the Paris sansculottes grew into a political force destined to play a crucial role during the next couple of years. They were the dominant force in the assemblies of the Paris sections and in the working-class political clubs, but they did not yet have a well-developed proletarian, political consciousness. Their name referred to their clothing: unlike the aristocracy, the sansculottes did not wear knee-length breeches (*culottes*), but preferred long trousers (*pantalons*). They were predominantly wage-slaves in the employ of numerous small businesses, or some other kind of ancillary workers: retailers and grocers, journeymen and unskilled labourers, apprentices and errand boys,

4.14 A crowd armed with picks, swords, scythes, and pitch forks carry placards saying 'Up with the sansculottes!' and 'Down with the veto!' into the royal chambers. One sansculotte has climbed onto a chair and is pointing at Louis and Marie-Antoinette. The king turns for help to the officers of the National Guard.

4.15 Volunteers leave for the front following the Constituent National Assembly's appeal on 11 July 1792, which claimed that the fatherland was in danger and that it was the duty of all citizens to defend their freedom.

4.16 Duke Charles William Ferdinand of Brunswick, the commander-in-chief of the allied Prussian and Austrian armies. On 25 July 1792 he issued a manifesto threatening Paris with destruction and on 19 August he invaded France. Following their defeat in the cannonade at Valmy he ordered his troops to withdraw.

4.17 Jerôme Pétion de Villeneuve, a member of the Constituent Assembly and mayor of Paris from November 1791 until November 1792. In the Convention he sided with the Gironde and after their fall from power fled to Normandy. Following the defeat of the federalist revolts he went underground and, when discovered in June 1794, committed suicide.

carters and day-labourers, wood-carriers and washer-women. Above all, they shared a hatred of and enmity towards the aristocracy and the rich, as well as a hope that the Revolution would help them to achieve a way of life fit for human beings. These 'passive' citizens bore the brunt of the Revolution and had already fought on the front line on 14 July and 6 October 1789. One of their most eminent spokesmen was Jacques Roux, the 'red priest', who in May 1792 began to demand the death sentence for any speculator or profiteer who feathered his nest at the expense of the poverty-stricken people.

In view of the army's many defeats at the front and the ever-louder protests of the masses, the

Legislative Assembly voted to banish those priests who had refused to swear the oath of allegiance and who were denounced as troublemakers by at least twenty citizens. It also voted to dissolve the king's aristocratic guard and establish a military camp for 20,000 men, the plan being that the latter would protect Paris and prevent a possible surprise raid by the generals. King Louis XVI used his veto against this decree, dismissed his Girondist cabinet, and re-appointed a Feuillant government.

The antagonisms which existed between the monarchy, the National Assembly and the popular movement, associated as it was with the radical wing of the Jacobin Club, soon came to a head. On

4.18 Louis XVI and his family retreat to the chamber of the Legislative Assembly, where it is decided to remove him from office. The battle between the rebels of 10 August and the Swiss Guard is visible in the background (right). The commander of the Swiss Guard has a rope tied around his ankles and is being dragged through the streets on his back.

20 July 1792, the anniversary of the Tennis-Court
Oath and the king's flight to Varennes, tens of thousands of demonstrators marched from the slums of
St. Antoine and St. Marceau to the Tuileries for the
purposes of protesting against the army's defeats,
the king's veto and the dismissal of the Girondist
Government. The crowds forced their way into the
palace and compelled the king to put on a liberty cap
with a blue, white and red cockade fastened to it,
and to drink the health of the nation. When Louis
refused to withdraw his veto and reinstate the dis-

4.19 Rebellious patriots
storm the Tuileries on 10
August 1792 using artillery
and cannon volleys.

missed ministers, the demonstration fizzled out, proving that nothing could be accomplished without the use of force.

Meanwhile, the allied armies of Prussia and Austria began to march. They were joined by a corps of *émigrés* under the command of the Prince of Condé, a cousin of Louis', which was stationed in the Rhineland, near the French border. Military intervention was imminent. On 11 July the National Assembly declared that the fatherland was in danger, called all National Guards to arms, and recruited new battalions of volunteers. 15,000 Parisians signed up for military service. The sansculottes' sectional branches, which by then were in permanent session, formed a central committee and demanded the dethronement of the king.

Robespierre, Danton and Marat, who presented themselves in the Jacobin Club as being in the forefront of the popular movement, repeated this demand and called for the establishment of a republic. In his newspaper *The People's Friend*, Marat violently attacked the Girondins, whom he called 'accomplices of despotism', picking in particular on Brissot, who in his eyes was a 'scoundrel and traitor'. Brissot gave tit for tat, describing Marat as a counter-revolutionary in disguise and rejecting both the king's dethronement and the introduction of universal suffrage.

Completely misjudging the balance of political power and the mood of the French people, Queen Marie-Antoinette pressed the emperor's Ambassador to Paris, Mercy d'Argenteau, to exert his influence on the royalist *émigrés* to issue a manifesto which would give the Jacobins a fright before the invasion of France. This manifesto, a tactically inappropriate and arrogant document drawn up by the *émigrés*, was issued by the Duke of Brunswick, commander-in-chief of the allied troops, on 25 July 1792. It would seal the fate of the French monarchy. The manifesto threatened to court-martial all officers and soldiers who resisted the invasion, called upon the French to subordinate themselves to their rightful sovereigns without delay, and made the members of the National Assembly and Paris' municipal council personally responsible for ensuring that not a hair on the heads of the royal family was harmed. Otherwise, they would be 'condemned by a court martial without any hope of mercy', Paris would have to expect 'revenge the likes of which had never been seen

before and which would never be forgotten', and the town would be exposed to 'a military execution and absolute ruination'.

The manifesto was made public in Paris on 1 August. It did not daunt the population, as the Court had expected, but had quite the opposite effect. On behalf of forty-seven of the forty-eight sections of Paris, the mayor, Pétion, demanded the immediate dethronement of the king. The excitement reached boiling point when the representatives of the radical wing of the Jacobin Club called upon the population to save the Revolution. On the night of 9 to 10 August 1792 the alarm bells rang out. Tens of thousands of sansculottes and patriots from all over France, who had come to the capital as volunteer 'confederates' over the previous few weeks in order to strengthen the popular movement, armed themselves and headed for the Tuileries. The sections of Paris sent representatives into the town hall to dissolve the old municipal council and establish a new 'Commune'. This new council, set up not through the normal legal channels, but by a decision of the people, later became the most important instrument of the Revolution and would play a decisive political role over the next two years. The new Commune dismissed the commanders and

4.20 One of the sansculottes who took part in the storming of the Tuileries on 10 August 1792. He is wearing the red liberty cap and long striped trousers (*pantalons*) in the national colours (red, white, and blue), not knee-breeches (*culottes*) such as those worn by the aristocracy. He is armed with both a sabre and a gun.

Overleaf:
4.21 The Swiss Guards defending the Tuileries are mowed down on the evening of 10 August.

officers of the National Guard and appointed reliable revolutionaries in their place.

The National Guards in the Tuileries, who were supposed to be protecting the king, left their positions. Some even went over to the rebels. The Swiss Guard, on the other hand, greeted the assailants with volleys of gunfire, and bitter struggles took place in the inner courtyard of the king's palace. When the sansculottes and their confederate reinforcements positioned cannons, the Swiss surrendered. Most were slain by the furius crowd, for it had suffered several hundred casualties, some fatal.

The king and his family retreated to the chamber of the National Assembly. The Assembly voted to suspend him temporarily from his post and to form itself into a National Convention which would be elected by equal and universal suffrage. Furthermore, the distinction between 'active' and 'passive' citizens was abolished in line with the demands of the sansculottes and radical Jacobins. The Girondins, who had attempted to back up the monarch despite his perjury and double dealing, and who had wanted the war, but had not known how to conduct it, were not able to prevent the process of political democratization.

The 'journée révolutionnaire' of 10 August 1792 was one of the most critical days of the Revolution. Its significance outstripped even that of 14 July 1789, when the Parisian people had rescued the Revolution for the first time. Whilst only the symbol of despotism had been destroyed in the storming of the Bastille, this time the Throne itself had been toppled and the institution of the monarchy removed. Though the storming of the Bastille and the king's repatriation to Paris on 6 October 1789 had borne no traces of a direct link between the Constituent National Assembly and the revolutionary people, this time those bourgeois intellectuals from the Jacobin Club who were sympathetic to the people had formed an alliance with the sansculottes. By doing so, they hoped to put an end to the continued treachery of the counter-revolution and to safeguard their democratic achievements to date.

The sansculottes used the assemblies of the various sections and of the Paris Commune to establish revolutionary institutions. But although it was the appearance of the sansculottes in the political arena which made victory possible, it was a victory for the bourgeoisie. Thanks to its economic and intellectual might, only the bourgeoisie knew how to politically direct the Revolution. Although the conflicts of interest which existed between the Jacobins and sansculottes were still discernible, their combined efforts to topple the monarchy consolidated the alliance between bourgeois and plebeian democrats. The alliance was to last over a year and secure the final victory of the Revolution over its enemies at home and abroad.

4.22 The 'Temple', formerly the meeting house of the Knights Templar, served as a state prison during the French Revolution. Louis XVI and his family were held prisoner here after 13 August 1792.

The Conflict of Interests between the Girondins and the Montagnards

The *'journée révolutionnaire'* of 10 August 1792 and the toppling of the monarchy radically transformed the political landscape. The constitution of 1791, which had guaranteed the existence of a constitutional monarchy and which had been drafted only with a great deal of effort and a great many compromises, was now a thing of the past. The loyalist Feuillants abandoned the Legislative Assembly and disbanded, and the popular movement became a major political force. The next six weeks were characterized by the rivalry between the 288-strong Paris Commune, which had contributed considerably to the victory and chiefly comprised members of the petty-bourgeoisie, and the Legislative Assembly, whose key posts were held by the Girondins. The National Assembly's decree of 11 August abolished the distinction between 'active' and 'passive' citizens; all French men over the age of 21 would be entitled to vote in the forthcoming elections to the National Convention without distinction of income or ownership.

The 'Provisional Executive Committee' appointed by the Legislative Assembly

5.1 Between 2–4 September 1792 many unsworn priests being held in the former monastic prison of the abbey (*l'Abbaye*) in the rue de Saint-Germain-des Prés were massacred as counter-revolutionaries. Here the crowd celebrates amid bodies which have been thrown out onto the street. One man carries the head of one of the victims on a pike.

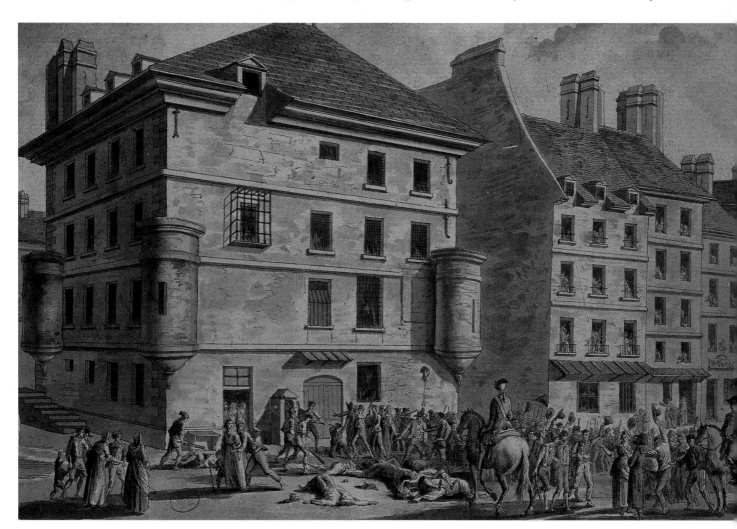

had a Girondist majority, since Roland, Clavière and Servan were reappointed to their old ministerial posts and Lebrun was named as Foreign Minister. Danton, a radical Jacobin, became Minister of Justice. The popular movement saw to it that a whole series of decrees were passed: property belonging to *émigrés* was released for sale and parcelled, so that even poor peasants could afford to buy, priests who refused to swear the oath of allegiance were threatened with deportation to Cayenne, Devil's Island, and royalist newspapers were banned. Pending trial, the Commune had the king and his family incarcerated in the tower of Temple, an old stronghold in Paris. In an attempt to recompense the people for their sacrifices, a quite extraordinary revolutionary court of law was set up, whose task was to bring to justice traitors and those who had been responsible for the bloodbath on 10

August. Lafayette tried in vain to persuade his army to march on Paris, then deserted to the Austrians, who naturally distrusted him and held him prisoner in the Moravian stronghold at Olmütz for five years. The Commune's newly-established surveillance committees carried out house searches in the hope of finding arms and had numerous suspicious citizens and unsworn priests arrested. At the end of August there were around 2,600 prisoners incarcerated in Paris.

Although the capital was in great agitation over the imminent invasion by enemy troops, the Girondins again wanted to emphasize the internationalist nature of the Revolution. On 26 August 1792 the Legislative Assembly voted to grant French citizenship to foreign personalities who had 'undermined the foundations of tyranny and cleared the way for freedom' so that they could be elected to the Natio-

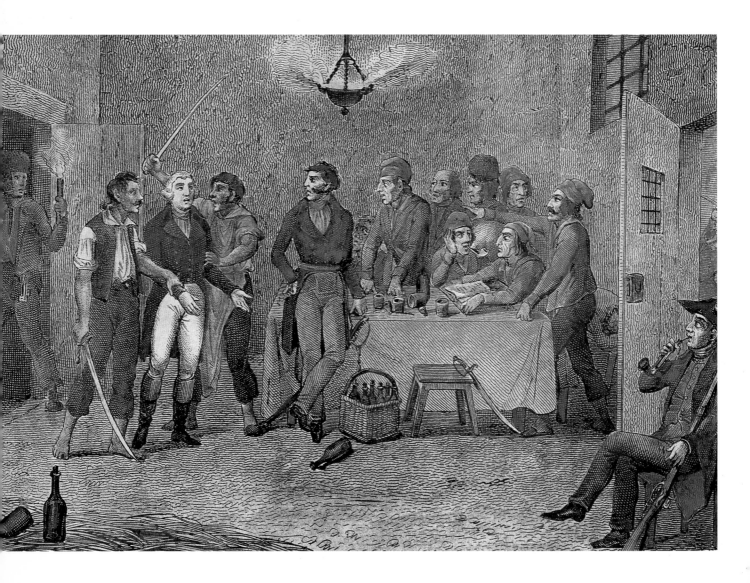

5.2 A detainee, clearly
identifiable by his clothes as
an aristocrat, is brought
before the 'Tribunal of
People's Justice' which went
into session in the abbey
prison during the September
Massacres of 1792.

5.3 The *Hôtel de la Force*
(formerly a palace belonging
to an aristocrat) in the rue du
Roi de Sicile served as a
prison during the
Revolution. In September
1792 prisoners being held
here are beaten and
beheaded with hatchets and
pick-axes.

Overleaf:
5.4 The cannonade between
the Prussian army under the
command of the Duke of
Brunswick and the
revolutionary forces led by
Generals Dumouriez and
Kellermann at Valmy on 20
September 1792. There was
no close combat, and on the
next day the invading army
began to retreat.

nal Convention. Eighteen pro-revolutionary politicians, generals, and writers from the United States, England, the German Empire, Italy, Poland, the Netherlands and Switzerland thus became French citizens. Among the Germans were the poets Klopstock and Schiller, the Brunswick pedagogue Campe, and the Prussian Baron Cloots of Cleve. The latter had been living in Paris since the beginning of the Revolution and was an active member of the Jacobin Club. Proud to call himself a citizen of the world, he had made a name for himself in 1790 as the 'orator of the human race' and adopted the classical name Anacharsis in honour of a Scythian sage of noble birth, who had travelled to Athens to take part in the blessing of Solon's constitution.

On 19 August the allied troops began their invasion of France. Although Prussia took to the

battlefield only as an ally of Austria's, it stationed an army of 42,000 men on the Rhine. The *émigrés* assured the Duke of Brunswick that the advance on the French capital and its subsequent conquest would be perfectly safe, a mere stroll. On 23 August the stronghold at Lonwy surrendered to the Prussians without a fight, and on 2 September word reached Paris that Verdun, the last stronghold before the capital, had been surrounded. The Commune announced that the enemy was outside the town and called upon the people to take up arms. Volunteer route battalions formed on the Champ de Mars, ready to go to the front. In a speech, Danton proclaimed that 'the peal of the alarm bells is calling for the enemy of the fatherland to be crushed. It will take courage, more courage, and yet more courage. Then France will be saved!'

UNITÉ·INDIVISIBILITÉ
DE·LA·RÉPUBLIQUE
LIBERTÉ·EGALITÉ
FRATERNITÉ·OU LA·MORT

5.5 This poster from the autumn of 1792 bears the slogans of the Revolution. A fighter sits half-naked in a classical pose and with a huge liberty cap suspended above his head, a tricolor blowing in the wind on either side of him. He is leaning on a placard which reads 'Death to the tyrants', and beneath him is a stone block with the inscription 'Unity, Indivisibility of the Republic, Freedom, Equality, Fraternity, or Death'.

Whilst thousands of Parisians began to construct fortifications outside the town in order to block the enemy's path, rumours spread that counter-revolutionary prisoners were about to stage a break-out from the jails. A panic-stricken mob made its way to the prisons to settle with its captured enemies. In several prisons the Commune's Surveillance Committee set up provisional 'Tribunals of People's Justice', which sentenced dozens of prisoners to death and also acquitted a few. The massacres lasted from 2 to 6 September. During this, the Revolution's first taste of the Terror, prison guards, Commune soldiers and National Guards murdered around 1,100 detainees. Of these, more than a half were common criminals, 300 unsworn priests, 150 aristocrats (including some women), and 50 Swiss Guards who had surrendered during the battle on 10 August. The Minister of Justice, Danton, who could possibly have put a stop to the butchery, did not step in and as a result was later accused by the Girondins of being partly responsible.

Thomas Jefferson, who had helped to draw up the American Declaration of Human Rights and who was President Washington's Secretary of State in 1792, made the following comments on the 'septembrissades':

In the course of the battle, which was necessary, many culpable people died without proper trials, and with them, some innocent people. I mourn for these more than anyone else, and I will mourn for them until the day I die. But I mourn for them in the same way as if they had fallen in battle. It was necessary to use the arm of the people – a machine which, although not as blind as bullets and bombs, is still somewhat blind . . .'

The first day of the September Massacres also marked the beginning of the elections to the National Convention. These were by means of indirect, equal, universal suffrage, and of the more than six and a half million people who were entitled to vote, only a million did so. More than a third of the 749 newly elected deputies had parliamentary experience: 191 had been members of the Constituent Assembly and 78 were formerly deputies in the Legislative Assembly. Almost 60 per cent of the 'Conventionnels' had studied law and were either lawyers, administrators or civil servants, 9 per cent were merchants or enterpreneurs, 7 per cent were clergymen, 6 per cent artists, writers or scientists, 6 per cent doctors, 6 per cent landowners, and 5 per cent officers. In addition, seven aristocrats (1 per

5.6 General Charles François Dumouriez, commander of the victorious revolutionary forces who fought at Valmy (20 September 1792) and Jemappes (6 November 1792). He lost the Battle of Neerwinden on 18 March 1793 and deserted to the Austrians three weeks later.

5.7 On 29 September 1792 the French army under the command of General Adam Philippe Custine attacked the town of Speyer. The picture shows an army division crossing the Rhine.

5.8 The 13,000-strong army under the command of Custine marches into the stronghold of Mainz, which surrendered without a fight on 22 October 1792.

cent) were elected to the Convention, one of whom was Philippe d'Orléans, the king's cousin, who joined the Jacobins and called himself 'Philippe Égalité' (Equality). There were also a few deputies of working-class origin, including a weaver, a cooper, a baker, a gunsmith, and a grave-digger. Of the eighteen foreign revolutionaries to whom the Legislative Assembly had granted French citizenship, two took up seats in the Convention: Anacharsis Cloots, and the writer and democrat Thomas Paine, who had made a name for himself in the American War of Independence and whose theoretical revolutionary treaties *The Rights of Man* (1791) had become a gospel for radical democrats throughout Europe.

When the Convention first met, just under 180 of its deputies were members of the liberal Girondist group, which tended to be rather upper middle class. A further 110 or so were members of the left-wing, Jacobin 'Mountain Party' (*Montagne*), which was closely allied with the people. These radical deputies were known as 'the Mountain' (or Montagnards) because they occupied the back benches in the riding arena of the Tuileries, where the sittings took place. The benches were raised off the ground and could only be reached by steps. The twenty-four deputies elected in Paris were all Montagnards. They included Robespierre, Danton, Marat, Desmoulins, Billaud-Varenne and Collot d'Herbois. The leading Girondist and Jacobin deputies all came from the same social stratum: the educated middle classes. Neither the Girondins nor the Montagnards were organized political parties with constitutions or programmes, but merely displayed two diverging bourgeois patterns of behaviour, both ideologically and in practice.

The centre of the Convention, which contained 450 deputies, was known as the 'Plain' (*Plaine*), or derisively as the 'Swamp' (*Marais*). Many of these deputies, who initially voted with the Gironde, had bought property confiscated and sold off by the nation and had made a pretty penny out of the Revolution. Some, like Barère and Cambon, joined forces with the Montagnards and were given leading roles within that group.

At its first sitting on 21 September 1792 the National Convention sanctioned the uprising of 10 August by unanimously voting to abolish the monarchy and establish a republic that was 'one

5.9 The Battle of Jemappes (Belgium) on 6 November 1792, which saw the revolutionary forces under the command of General Dumouriez score a victory over Austrian troops led by Duke Albert of Saxe-Teschen.

and indivisible'. The internationalist Abbot Grégoire paid tribute to the decision, describing it as an event of huge significance for the history of mankind. 'The abolition of the French monarchy' was, he said, 'the first step towards an alliance between all the peoples of the world.' Before this vision of universal fraternity could be realized, however, enemy troops would have to be driven off French soil. The tens of thousands of volunteers who had responded to the announcement that the fatherland was in peril by rushing to arm themselves, had also brought about a democratization of the French army and transformed its social composition. It had largely become an army of peasants and sansculottes, who identified patriotism with self-liberation. They knew that they were fighting in their own interest because they knew that a victory for the counter-revolutionary invaders would also mean the return of the aristocratic *émigrés* and the reintroduction of tithes and feudal dues.

After the Prussians had taken Verdun nothing appeared to stand between them and Paris. However, the commanders of two French army groups, Dumouriez and Kellermann, succeeded in positioning 50,000 men near Valmy. In an artillery duel the sansculottes' army held firm against the Prussian cannonade, and the Duke of Brunswick did not dare to give the order for his infantry to attack. Between bursts of cannon-fire the peasants and craftsmen fighting in the French army cheered their nation, much to the amazement of their opponents. This revolutionary army of 'tailors and glove makers' won a moral victory over the drilled mercenaries, who had been tailored to follow orders blindly, and on 21 September, the day on which the Convention first met, the invading army began to retreat towards the German border. The Battle of Valmy was the revolutionary army's first victory and marked an important turning point because, as Goethe wrote in his *Campaign in France* thirty years later, it ushered in 'a new epoch in the history of the world'. An army of 17,000 men under the command of

General Custine advanced into the Rhineland and occupied the towns of Speyer, Worms and Mainz. On 6 November General Dumouriez's troops scored a victory over the Austrians near Jemappes and soon occupied the whole of Belgium. The advance of the revolutionary army appeared to be unstoppable.

It was chiefly the struggle for power between the Girondins and the Montagnards which prevented this from being the case. Whilst the monarchy had still existed the joint struggle of the bourgeoisie and the working classes against feudalism had remained the centre of attention. The conflicts of interest between rich and poor, which had been concealed until then as of necessity, now became glaringly obvious. The September Massacres widened the gulf between the moderate and radical factions in the bourgeois camp, since the Girondins distanced themselves from the people's self-administered justice and regarded the goals of the Revolution as having been attained. When the sansculottes-dominated Paris Commune suggested several revolutionary measures to alleviate the effects of the desperate economic situation (controlled rates for the *assignats*, the confiscation of stockpiles of essential commodities, draconian punishments for speculators and profiteers, and the introduction of price ceilings), Brissot remarked that the 'hydra of anarchy' was raising its ugly head. These demands,

5.10 A French cartoon mocks the defeat of the Prussian and Austrian troops in the autumn of 1792. The Austrian commander is saying, 'How these wretched sansculottes fight!' The Prussian King Frederick William II (who was present when his troops were defeated at Valmy) is answering, 'Who would have believed it!' The two are sitting back to front on their horses, and are being drawn by a double-headed eagle with the words 'News of new conquests' in its beak.

Freiheit und Gleichheit

5.11 German peasant girls, priests and French revolutionaries dance around a tree planted in the name of freedom and adorned with a liberty cap. A child holds high a flag bearing the words 'Freedom and Equality'. The scene was painted by an unknown artist during French occupation of the southern Rhineland (October 1792 – March 1793).

he said, contradicted the right of the citizen to dispose of his property as he saw fit. At this, Robespierre took the part of the 'real patriots, who are trying to found the republic on the principles of equality and in the public interest', and described his Girondist opponents as 'false patriots, who are establishing the republic for themselves alone, and who would govern in the sole interest of the rich and the civil servants'. Marat adopted an even harsher tone. The *People's Friend* described the Girondins, who had condemned the excesses of the September Massacres, as schemers and traitors who intended to do away with the people's newly acquired freedom. It demanded that a dictatorship be established to thwart the Girondist conspiracy, and that the sittings of the National Convention be transferred to a huge hall, whose stands could hold 4,000 spectators. Here it would be 'constantly under the watchful eye of the people, who can then stone the Convention if it forgets its duties'.

The antagonism between the spokesmen of these two bourgeois factions became so intense that on 10 October 1792 Brissot and his supporters were expelled from the Paris Jacobin Club. By taking such action the Jacobins had drawn an indelible line between liberalism and revolutionary democracy. The passionate debate on the aims of the Revolution, and how they could be achieved, continued in the Convention. Whereas Brissot, Roland, and their friends wanted to reserve all political and economic privileges for the bourgeoisie and deny the working classes every opportunity to direct the state, the Jacobins, who represented the interests of the lower middle classes, interpreted the equality clause set out in the Declaration of Human rights as an appeal for the democratization of public life. It was, then, their diametrically opposed attitudes towards the masses which determined the diverging political

paths followed by the Jacobins and Girondins. In fact, the Girondins' policies contained certain contradictions: they instructed the victorious Generals Dumouriez and Custine to call upon the people of the neighbouring countries to rise up against their tyrants, but rejected all political and social demands made by the French lower classes because they feared that such demands would represent a danger to bourgeois ownership.

Whereas to the Girondins 'freedom' meant first and foremost the absolute right to dispose of one's property as one wished, for the Jacobins it was rooted not in the concept of ownership, but in the nature of man. They regarded freedom as a function and feature of equality and therefore not only postulated liberation from the feudal yoke, but also turned on the political privileges inherent in plutocracy. Robespierre and Marat contrasted the right of ownership with the right of the destitute masses to

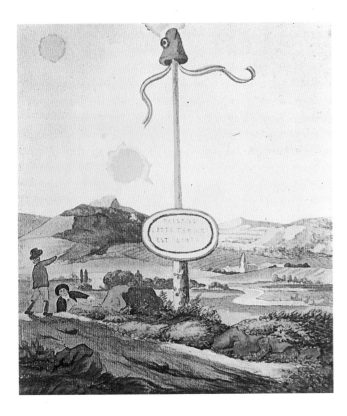

5.13 A water-colour painted by Goethe in the autumn of 1792, during the French occupation of the Rhineland. From its position on the river bank the 'freedom tree', which has been decorated with a liberty cap and a tricolor, acts as a kind of border post and announces to those passing that the country all around is free.

5.12 An advance party of the French Mosel army marches into the duchy of Zweibrücken on 10 February 1793. On the following day the troop planted a 'freedom tree' adorned with a liberty cap on the square in front of the duke's residence and promised to bring his subjects freedom and equality. The duke himself had fled to Mannheim.

live and physically exist, the egoistic interests of the individual with those of the community as a whole. The Jacobins, who regarded their main task as being the defence of the land and of representative parliamentary democracy, used the militancy of the sansculottes as the motor of the Revolution. They realized that an alliance with the propertyless lower classes was imperative if they were to defeat their enemies at home and abroad. Their policy was therefore to unite all petty bourgeois and working-class forces, to eradicate class antagonisms, and to try to narrow the gulf between the propertied and propertyless. Out of a sense of responsibility to the nation, and because of the demands of the war, the Jacobins were prepared to allow certain curtailments both of the right of ownership and of personal freedom, if the social interests of the masses required this. Despite their willingness to co-operate, however, the Jacobins did not regard the sansculottes as equal partners, but rather as vital reinforcements in the struggle against the Royalists and Girondins. According to Jacobin doctrine, the running of the state had always to remain in the hands of those democratic representatives of the educated middle classes who were sympathetic to the people.

Through its occupation of Savoy, Belgium and the southern Rhineland, France's defensive war had taken on the character of an expedition of conquest. Although an assembly of the citizens of Chambéry, the capital of Savoy, had decided to seek union with France only three weeks after the occupation, the French experienced serious problems in the Rhineland. The sansculottes army had marched into the Rhineland chanting 'Peace with the cottages, war on the palaces', and General Custine had issued an 'Appeal for the oppressed people of the German nation' to rise up against their royal despots. Nevertheless, the Mainz Jacobin Club, founded on 23 October 1792, was able to mobilize only a minority of the population.

On 19 November the Girondin Government launched a propaganda campaign by issuing a decree which announced that the Convention would 'offer fraternal assistance to all peoples who wish to win back their freedom'. The suggestion that France should extend its territory to its 'natural borders', i.e. should annex Belgium and the Rhineland, gained popularity. On 15 December the Con-

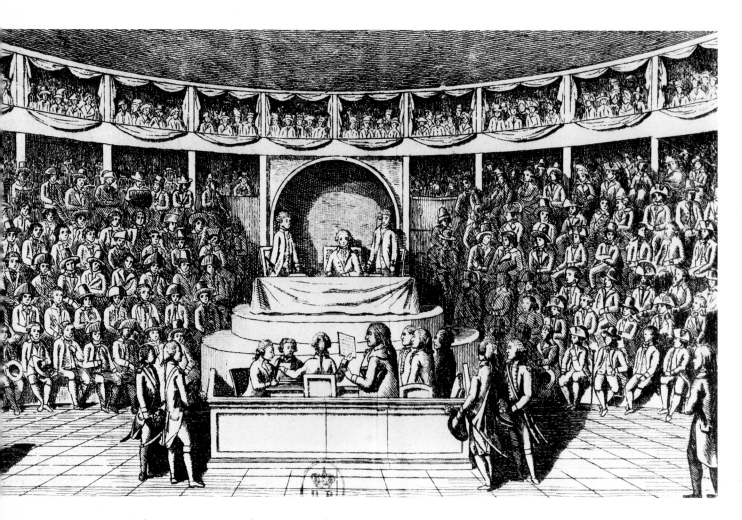

vention voted to set up revolutionary administrations in the occupied territories. Preparations were begun for elections which would enable the Rhenish people to decide for themselves whether they preferred to establish an independent republic or to be annexed by France.

At the same time, the National Convention in Paris began the trial of Louis XVI. During a search of the royal apartments in the Tuileries, a secret drawer had been found in an iron cupboard, which contained the royal couple's correspondence with counter-revolutionary *émigrés* and foreign monarchs. The letters proved that the king had conspired against the Revolution even after his unsuccessful attempt to escape and his formal swearing of an oath of allegiance to the Constitution. The Girondins feared, quite rightly, that the king's trial and conviction would bring about an intensification within society of the Revolution. The Montagnards, on the other hand, considered it absolutely essential for the king to be brought to trial, because this would force the Convention either to find the per-

5.14 On 11 December 1792 the king's trial opens before the Convention. The deputy Bertrand Barère (in the centre) presides over the sitting and is questioning the king, whom he addresses as 'Louis Capet' and who is visible in profile. The deputy Valazé (with his back to the onlookers) shows the king documents bearing his signature and upon which his crimes against the nation are based.

5.15 The king's second hearing on 26 December 1792. The deputy chairing the sitting is Defermon (on the right with a document in his hand). The king is standing in the background. On the left, at the table, are his three defence counsel Malesherbes, Tronchet, and De Sèze, who is summing up.

jured king guilty or to condemn his overthrow on 10 August. Saint Just declared that the king had become a rebel and public enemy, since he had violated the laws of the people. But in any case, he maintained, every king was a usurper, for the sovereignty of the people was alienable. 'One cannot become a king without burdening oneself with guilt . . . This man must rule or die.' Robespierre's argument followed similar lines: 'It is better that Louis dies', he said, 'than that a hundred thousand honest citizens should lose their lives. Louis must die, because the fatherland must live.'

On 11 December 1792 the Convention, which had resolved itself into a tribunal, began to hear the case against the king. Louis was stripped of all his titles and addressed as 'Louis Capet'. The charge detailed all his actions from 1789 on and branded him a conspirator and traitor. The king's public defender, De Sèze, disputed the Convention's right to try him. He maintained in his summing-up that the king enjoyed immunity under the Constitution and could therefore not be called to account. These argu-

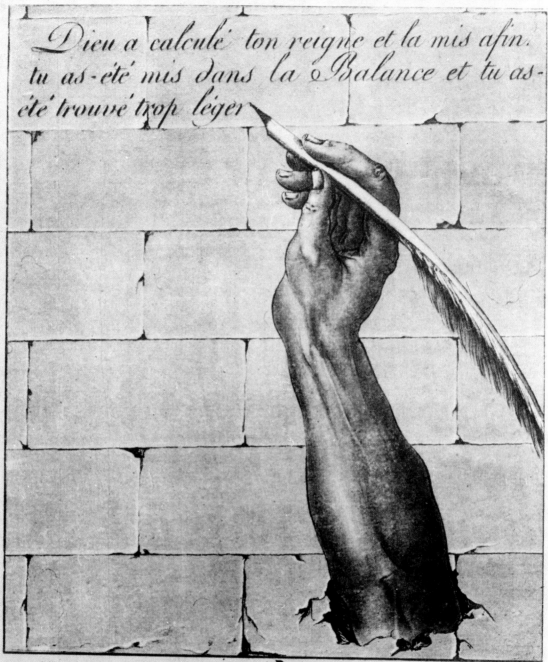

Dieu a calculé ton reigne et la mis afin. tu as-été mis dans la Balance et tu as-été trouvé trop léger

Cent fois coupable et cent fois pardonné, **LOUIS LE** au peuple pour ne pas se rendre cette justice, qu'il doit avoir seule pourroit depuis quatre ans, lui avoir conservé Sa cruel; et que n'est-il possible de l'abandonner à ce tour- la loi la plus sacrée, le salut de vingt-quatre millions France attachée au jugement de la génération actuelle dans l'etat actuel l'Europe, comment considerer se monstre point de ralliment des _____ contre contre-revolution Alors la meme politique tot ou tard deviendroit la cause de la Sub-

Elle attend le Coupable

DERNIER a trop éprouvé la bienveillance et la générosité épuise tous les sentimens d'humanité qu'un reste de pitié consience est sans doute pour lui le bourreau le plus ment interieur, mille fois pire que la mort; mais d'hommes exige qu'il soit jugé, et la gloire de la et des générations futures veut qu'il soit puni de la France et dans l'agitation dangereuse de sous un autre rapport que sous celui d'un revolutionnaires et comme un noyeau de permet-elle en sa faveur une grace qui, version de la république.

Extrait de la reponse

du C Duvachez au reflechon de l'quisieur Necker

ments were rejected, and the Convention decided to submit four questions to the deputies.

The vote as to whether Louis Capet 'was guilty of conspiring against freedom and attacking national security' was carried *nem con*, with 14 abstentions.

The question as to whether the judgement should be submitted to the people for approval was rejected by 426 votes to 278.

In the relevant ballot, 387 deputies voted for the immediate execution of the death sentence; 334 voted for imprisonment or raised objections to the execution.

The Girondins' proposal that the guillotining should be deferred was rejected by 380 votes to 310.

On 21 January 1793, on what is now the Place de la Concorde in Paris, Louis XVI was beheaded. It was a grave defeat for the Girondins, the majority of whom had voted against the execution and attempted to prevent it. The execution demonstrated, however, that the Jacobins, supported by the sansculottes, were beginning to win the upper hand. The counter-revolutionary press in Germany described the guillotining in gruesome detail. Few contemporary observers were able to see through the apparent radicalization of the Revolution. Those, like the Mainz Jacobin Georg Forster, who regarded Louis' decapitation as a 'security measure' and believed that he had had to be convicted 'not in accordance with the law books, but in accordance with natural justice', were not merely ostracized by the Conservatives, but were also loathed by the Liberals. When Friedrich Schiller, an honorary citizen of France, learned of the king's execution, he called the French 'vile henchmen'. Even Klopstock, who had thanked Roland, the French Minister of the Interior, for his honorary citizenship only two

5.16 This handbill announcing the death sentence imposed upon King Louis XVI reads, 'Louis, traitor, read your sentence.' The hand breaking through the wall writes on the wall the words which the prophet Daniel (ch. 5, vv. 26 and 27) spoke to the Babylonian despot Belshazzar: 'God hath numbered thy kingdom and finished it. Thou art weighed in the balances and art found wanting.' Beneath the guillotine are the words 'Waiting for the guilty'.

5.17 Louis XVI on 18 January 1793, three days before his execution.

Overleaf:
5.18 Louis XVI, accompanied by his confessor Abbot Edgeworth, glances back before climbing the steps to the guillotine.

5.19 A cartoon mocking 'the coalition of the kings or crowned villains against the French Republic' after England and Spain had entered the war early in 1793. The animals are singing a 'dramatic pot-pourri'. No. 1: the fox, Pitt with an open purse on the table; No. 2: the turkey, George III of England (in a cage because his powers are limited); No. 3: the ostrich, Emperor Franz II; No. 4: the bitch, Catherine II (the Great) of Russia, at whose breast the emigrant brothers of the late king are suckling (the Tsarina provided them with money); No. 5: the toad, William V of Orange, stadhalter of the Netherlands; No. 6: the owl, King Frederick William II of Prussia; No. 7: the bat, William V's wife; No. 8: the pig, the Duke of Brunswick; No. 9: the horned billy-goat, King Charles IV of Spain (whose wife was the mistress of the Prime Minister Godoy); No. 10: the dachshund, King Ferdinand of Naples and Sicily; No. 11: the hare, Queen Maria I of Portugal; No. 12: Victor-Amadeus III, King of Piedmont and Sardinia; No. 13: the ass wearing the tiara on its head, Pope Pius VI.

months before, was morally indignant and cursed the king's 'lunatic judges' in several poems and odes.

Louis' execution resulted in the extension of the war. When the English Government expelled the French Ambassador to London, the Convention made a simultaneous declaration of war on both England and the Netherlands at the recommendation of Brissot. A few weeks later, on 7 March 1793, France broke off diplomatic relations with Spain. When war was declared on the Spanish Court, the deputy Barère proclaimed that 'an enemy more for France is a triumph for freedom!' With the exception of Switzerland, Scandinavia, the majority of the Italian states, Russia, and Turkey, the French republic found itself at war with the whole of Europe in the spring of 1793.

France's military encirclement and the maritime blockade imposed by England aggravated the economic crisis. Many peasants were only prepared to sell grain against hard cash, causing the *assignats* to fall to half their nominal value. As a result of inflation and shortages, the Paris sansculottes, who received their wages in paper money, could not afford to buy essential supplies. At the end of 1793 hunger riots broke out in Paris, and the desperate mobs began to plunder bakeries and grocery shops. Premises belonging to more than a thousand small retailers were attacked. As spokesmen for the starving, Jacques Roux, a priest in the section of Gravillier, and Jacques Hébert, the editor of the sansculottes' newspaper *Le Père Duchèsne*, demanded the punishment of speculators and profiteers who hoarded food and thereby pushed up prices. They also insisted that the poor and the families of volunteer soldiers fighting at the front should be supported out of public funds. A deputation of sansculottes, who appeared before the Convention on behalf of the sections of Paris, stated in their petition that 'it is not enough to have declared that we are French republicans. The people must also be happy, they must have bread, for where there is no longer bread, there is no law, no freedom, and no republic.' In the National Convention Jacobins and Girondins blamed each other for having engineered the unrest. Neither Marat nor Robespierre showed a great deal of sympathy for the people's plight, proving that despite their radicalism they still retained their bourgeois values. Robespierre suggested that

5.20 A sansculotte on watch. The slogan on the tricolor reads 'Freedom or Death!' The folk-singer Chenard, who took part in the festival of freedom in Savoy on 14 October 1792, was the model.

5.21 William Pitt the Younger, English Prime Minister from 1783. He belonged to the Tory Party and had been financing the anti-French coalition ever since England had entered the war in February 1793. In the war of the second coalition (1798–1801) Pitt once again organized and financed the powers fighting the French.

5.22 A meeting at the working-class political club in one of the Paris sections. It was through these clubs that the sansculottes made their social and political demands in the years 1792–94.

5.23 Inhabitants of the Paris slums appease their hunger in the street, where the cook of an eating house provides hot meals.

the revolts were a 'plot against France's patriots' and appealed to the sansculottes not to rise up 'for the purposes of collecting sugar, but to strike down the enemy instead'. On 18 March the Convention enacted a law, supported by both the Montagnards and the Girondins, which outlawed demands for 'equality of ownership'. Such demands had already been made by a few working-class political clubs and would henceforth carry the death penalty.

Social problems and the desperate economic crisis caused the fighting spirit of volunteers at the front to slacken off, with many soldiers returning to their native villages. When the Convention ordered the recruitment of 300,000 volunteers for the spring offensive, only half this number registered for military service. In the Vendée, a region of western France where the Church's 'Inner Mission' had put down strong roots and where unsworn priests had gained influence over the rural population, the peasants revolted against the levy. Their bitter opposition testified to the fact that it was not only the revolutionary notion of self-emancipation which could lead to serious violence when the masses were moved by it, but also the desire to retain a traditional social order. The peasants of the Vendée were steeped in pre-revolutionary notions of allegiance

and obedience to the local aristocracy. The Jacobin watchword 'patriotism' meant little to them. They were outraged by the execution of God's appointed monarch and were not about to go into battle against some unknown enemy on the orders of the atheistic 'regicides' who had seized power in Paris.

Although the counter-revolutionary rebels were badly organized at first, they nevertheless managed to procure weapons and equipment by means of surprise raids and sudden attacks on the National Guards who had been despatched against them. On 19 March 1793 the National Convention unanimously voted for a decree which introduced the death penalty for any rebel captured with a weapon in his hand, as well as the confiscation of his property. All the same, the rebels continued to score significant successes for several months, and the uprising began to threaten the Revolution. The armed peasants of the Vendée, who placed themselves under the command of experienced aristocratic and royalist officers, attempted to join forces and build a 'Catholic and monarchist army'. In May 1793, after the National Guards had suffered several defeats at the hands of the Vendée rebels, the Convention started to withdraw regular troops from the front and also mobilized volunteers. It was October

5.24 An *assignat* to the value of 50 *sous* (two and a half *livres*).

5.25 *Nouveaux-riches* speculators and soldiers of fortune, for whom the devaluation of paper money is a source of enrichment, on their way to a banquet.

before the Government's troops were able to gain the upper hand. The struggle lasted until the end of the year.

In mid-February 1793 the Girondist General Dumouriez began an offensive against the Netherlands from his base in Belgium. After two weeks, however, Austrian troops under the command of the Duke of Coburg succeeded in seizing the initiative. Early in March the French army began to beat a hasty and disorganized retreat. In the light of this renewed military threat, Danton appealed in the National Convention for Girondins and Jacobins to set aside their differences and act in the spirit of revolutionary unity. The Convention decided to despatch 'delegates *en mission*' with unlimited powers to all eighty-three departments. Their task would be to 'speed up the process of mobilization and revive the spirit of the Revolution'. Danton also proposed the establishment of a revolutionary tribunal to forestall terroristic outrages such as the massacres which had taken place in the prisons of Paris in September 1792: 'Let us be terrible, so that the people do not need to be!' The Revolutionary

5.26 Several skirmishers from the revolutionary forces position a cannon. They fought, not in close formation, but in scattered skirmish lines.

5.29 A meeting of the Paris 'Society of Revolutionary Republican Women' led by Pauline Léon and Claire Lacombe, which existed from May to October 1793.

5.28 A soldier of the Revolutionary Army in battle dress. He is armed with a gun and a sabre.

5.27 In the summer of 1793 women also take part in the struggle to defend house and home.

Tribunal established on 10 March comprised a chairman, five judges, a public prosecutor, two substitutes and twelve jurors, whose judgement was to be public and final. In addition, watch committees were formed, which would track down aristocrats and other enemies of the Revolution and compile lists of suspicious persons. The Convention also ordered the death penalty for anyone who called for the damaging of 'property in the realm of trade and commerce', or who plotted to restore the monarchy.

General Dumouriez had himself become guilty of this last crime. After his troops had suffered a crushing defeat near Neerwinden in March 1793, he began to negotiate with the commander of the Austrian forces, the Duke of Coburg, and promised to quit Belgium completely. Dumouriez planned to march back to Paris at the head of his army, break up the Convention, and restore the monarchy in favour of the executed king's infant son. On hearing

of this treason, the Convention sent the Minister of War, Beurnonville, and four other officials to Belgium to call Dumouriez to account. As the deputation entered Dumouriez's headquarters, he had the five arrested and handed them over to the Austrians. His coup failed, however, because he had reckoned without his army: his soldiers and most of his officers refused to betray the Republic. On 5 April Davout, the commander of a battalion of volunteers and a man who would rise to the rank of marshal under Napoleon, ordered his soldiers to fire on Dumouriez. At this, the treacherous Dumouriez deserted to the Austrians, accompanied by his adjutant, the son of Duke Philippe of Orleans (Égalité). Marat, whose *People's Friend* had prophesied Dumouriez's treachery months before, proved to be as correct in this case as he had been in forecasting the treachery of Louis XVI and Lafayette. Whilst Dumouriez's career ended with this episode, his adjutant still had a brilliant future in front of him,

5.30 Having invaded the town, royalist counter-revolutionaries in the Vendée tear up the tree planted in the name of freedom, chop it up, and burn the guillotine. In the background a procession led by clergymen and carrying a flag bearing a cross make their way to the church.

for after the July Revolution of 1830 he was crowned the 'Citizen King' Louis Philippe.

In the same week as Dumouriez went over to the enemy, General Custine, who in the autumn of 1792 had conquered the southern Rhineland, suffered a major defeat. At the beginning of April the Prussian troops succeeded in surrounding the stronghold at Mainz. Its eventual surrender was simply a matter of time – it was to follow just under four months later, on 23 July 1793.

The loss of Belgium and the Rhineland signalled the failure of the Girondins' war objective (to push forward to the 'natural borders' of France and carry the blessings of the Revolution to the neighbouring peoples). This led to a weakening of the Girondist movement in the Convention and the consolidation of the alliance between the Jacobins and sansculottes. A deputation from the sections of Paris demanded that all those demonstrably implicated in Dumouriez's treachery should be committed for trial. Number one on their list was Brissot, whose friendship and work with Dumouriez was public knowledge. In a speech to the Convention Robespierre adopted the sansculottes' demands as his own. Marat appealed to the oppressed to take drastic measures and demanded that they organize 'the despotism of freedom' and crush the 'despotism of kings'.

The Montagnards recognized that extraordinary measures were essential if the Revolution was to be saved. The deputies on the 'plain' voted with the Montagnards when they took the step of declaring a state of emergency. The Convention voted to confiscate property belonging to *émigrés* and to set up 'Revolutionary Committees'. The committees would have the power to issue identity cards and to arrest suspicious citizens and foreigners. Another decree concerned the sending of three deputies to each of the eleven armies of the Republic. These deputies would 'closely observe the behaviour of the members of the Executive Council, army suppliers, and industrialists, as well as the attitudes of the generals, officers and soldiers'. In addition, a fixed rate was agreed for the *assignats* in the hope of checking inflation and pacifying the starving sansculottes.

The Convention's most notable decision, however, was to establish a central institution, for in the next few months this institution, the Committee of

5.31 Rebellious peasants in the Vendée hide among the broom bushes. They are fighting revolutionary forces.

Public Safety, was to become of paramount importance. The Committee was endowed with executive powers and was set the tasks of supervising and encouraging better administration of the state, and co-ordinating the defence of the Revolution both at home and abroad. The meetings of the Committee, which was divided into four sections (External Affairs, Domestic Affairs, War and Navy) were secret. The Council of Ministers was placed in its charge and all government departments had to implement its decisions without delay. The members of the Committee were to be changed on a monthly basis as necessary.

The composition of the first Committee of Public Safety, which had nine members, demonstrated just how much the Girondins had fallen behind. The Montagnards sent five deputies to the Committee, the 'plain' sent three, and the Girondins only one. Danton headed the Committee and the other Jacobin committee members were Dalacroix, Barère, Cambon and Lindet. The balance of power within the Council of Ministers was also shifting. The former Minister of the Interior, Roland, had resigned and was replaced by Garat, who was busy distancing himself from the Girondins, whilst Lieutenant Bouchotte, a supporter of the sans-culottes, took over the Ministry for War.

On 13 April the Convention voted, at Danton's request, to end its interference in the affairs of other countries and to leave the liberation of neighbouring peoples from the yoke of feudalism to home-grown revolutionaries. This signalled the failure of the notions of a 'crusade for freedom' and the establishment of a 'Worldwide Citizen's Republic', which Brissot and a few others (including the 'orator of the human race', Anacharsis Cloots) had demanded. The war once again became what it had originally been: a struggle to defend the achievements of the Revolution.

The Girondins attempted to win back the ground which they had lost and directed their major attack against Marat, whom they regarded as the personification of anarchy. The deputy Guadet demanded that the 'People's Friend' should be committed for trial before the Revolutionary Tribunal, firstly because he had described the Girondins as traitors and criminals in a Jacobin Club circular, and secondly because he had demanded the recall of all those deputies who had voted against the execution of the king. Since many of the Montagnards had been sent to the provinces or to the army camps as 'delegates *en mission*', the Girondins managed to win a majority in the Convention for the bringing of charges against Marat. In order to avoid arrest, the

5.32 Camille Desmoulins, a journalist who had appealed to the masses to storm the Bastille. He was a deputy in the Convention and published the weekly newspaper *Le Vieux Cordelier*, which in December 1793 accused Robespierre of being a tyrant and demanded an end to the Terror.

5.33 Maximilien Robespierre, a deputy in the Constituent Assembly and the Convention, member of the Committee of Public Safety, head of the Jacobin Government from July 1793 until July 1794.

'People's Friend' was forced to go into hiding until the hearing began. He presented himself to the Tribunal as an 'apostle and martyr of freedom'. As the charge against him was shaky, the jurors were unanimous in acquitting him. Jubilant sansculottes adorned him with wreaths and carried him back to his seat in the Convention on their shoulders. Catching sight of his Girondist accusers he said, 'Now I have them. They will have their triumphal procession, but to the guillotine.' Even this forecast would come true, although only after Marat's death. Their revocation of the privilege of parliamentary immunity (in order to silence Marat and remove him from the Convention) would eventually prove disastrous for the Girondins. Its violation would soon return to haunt them.

The Girondins were not prepared to leave the field to their opponents without a fight. In a letter to the citizens of Paris the Girondin Pétion warned that the Jacobins and sansculottes represented a threat to ownership and freedom. In response, Robespierre set out the Jacobins' basic position on the question of ownership in a speech to the Convention on 24 April 1793. Since, in his view, the state was obliged to guarantee the right of all its inhabitants to material goods, he considered certain curtailments of the rights of ownership and personal freedom to be justified, if such action was necessary to secure public well-being. He suggested that ownership should be linked to society and secondary to the needs of society: the economically strong should not reap undue benefit. He accused the Girondins of violating the 'most sacred natural human right', since to link freedom with ownership benefited above all 'the rich and the insatiable, speculators and tyrants'. In an effort both to achieve harmony between the classes and to bind the sansculottes to the Jacobins with the prospect of a social democracy, he suggested that the Declaration of Human Rights be reworded. His draft not only proposed a legal tax-free subsistence level for the poor and the introduction of a system of progressive taxation, but also obliged the nation as a whole to 'take responsibility for supporting all members of

5.34 Georges Danton, founding member of the Cordelier Club, Minister of Justice after 10 August 1792, deputy in the Convention, member of the Committee of Public Safety from April to July 1793, leader of the *Indulgents* in the Jacobin Club from November 1793 until March 1794.

society, either by providing them with work, or by guaranteeing those who are unfit for work a means of survival'. Furthermore, it limited the right of ownership by linking it with a duty to respect the rights of others and not to erode their security, freedom or livelihoods.

Although Robespierre did not impugn the bourgeois right of ownership, his draft went too far for the Convention. It was not adopted, nor was it incorporated into the Declaration of Human Rights contained in the Jacobin Constitution of June 1793, which was installed after the overthrow of the Girondins.

The Conventions' setting of a fixed rate for the *assignats* did not pacify the sansculottes, since farmers would not take the devalued paper money in return for grain, leaving the poor urban population to spend up to 80 per cent of its income on bread alone. The Paris Commune issued an ultimatum demanding that price ceilings be prescribed by law. On 4 May the Convention gave way and set a 'maximum' for corn and flour. In order to supply

the market, the districts were to seize stocks from the farmers, confiscating them, and paying compensation if necessary. For the first time, the basic principle of economic freedom had been undermined for the benefit of the poor. On 20 May the Convention decreed a further economic measure demanded by the sansculottes: it forced a compulsory loan of a billion *livres* upon the wealthy, in order to finance the armaments necessary for the war. The deputies could not, however, agree on the establishment of a 'revolutionary army', as demanded by several of the sections of Paris, which would call counter-revolutionaries and profiteers to account and requisition supplies of grain.

The Girondins, whose support was strongest in trading towns such as Marseille and Lyon, went on

5.35 The radical democrat Thomas Paine, who lived in America from 1774 until 1787 and, as a journalist, played an important role in the War of Independence, was granted honorary French citizenship by the Legislative Assembly and became a member of the Convention. His book *The Rights of Man* (1791) became a gospel for republicans all over Europe. He objected to the execution of Louis XVI and was imprisoned from December 1793 until after the fall of the Jacobins.

5.36 Jean Paul Marat. He was originally a doctor, but did not practise after the outbreak of revolution. In his newspaper *L'Ami du peuple* (the *People's Friend*) he called for enemies of the Revolution to be fought relentlessly and correctly prophesied the king's treason, and that of Generals Lafayette and Dumouriez, and of the Gironde. As a deputy in the convention he resolutely spoke out on behalf of the sansculottes.

5.37 Louis Antoine de Saint-Just, deputy in the Convention, member of the Committee of Public Safety, friend of Robespierre, represented the Convention as a commissioner in Alsace and on the northern front.

the attack in the provinces. In league with members of the aristocracy, they drove the 'delegates *en mission*', who had come to mobilize recruits, out of Marseille and formed a General Committee to take over the administration of the town, close the Jacobin Club and arrest its members. In Lyon the wealthy merchants were not prepared to make any sacrifices for democracy. On 29 May 1793 Girondins and royalists together overthrew the Jacobin municipal authorities and imprisoned the president of the Jacobin Club, a man by the name of Chalier. He was guillotined in Lyon during the bloody civil war, which lasted almost five months. The town councils of Bordeaux and Nantes were also taken over by Girondins.

5.38 Marat is acquitted by
the Revolutionary Tribunal
on 24 April 1793. The crowd
decorates him with a
citizen's crown.

In mid-May the conflict between the Girondins and the Montagnards entered a crucial phase in Paris. The Girondins' submitted a motion to the National Convention calling for the Commune, controlled as it was by the sansculottes, to be dissolved. It was, they claimed, an 'anarchist authority' intent on taking over government. The motion was defeated, but the Convention did, however, sanction the formation of a twelve-man commission of inquiry to suggest ways of maintaining public order. On 21 May the committee, whose members were all Girondins, had several radicals arrested, including Hébert, deputy to the procurator of the Commune, Chaumette. In his widely read sansculotte newspaper, *Le Père Duchèsne*, Hébert had described the Girondins as 'accomplices of Capet and Dumouriez' and stated that they were hindering the Revolutionary Tribunal set up on 10 March.

The arrests triggered off the final showdown. A deputation from the sections appeared in the Convention to demand the release of Hébert and his comrades and the dissolution of the Commission of Twelve. The recently established 'Society of Revolutionary Republican Women', led by the actress Claire Lacombe, demonstrated in support of the detainees. Robespierre and Marat declared their solidarity with the Commune and the demonstrators. They also succeeded in getting a motion passed in the Convention which would release the detainees and dissolve the Commission of Twelve.

When the Girondins objected, an insurrectionary committee of the Commune was mobilized. Henriot, a friend of Marat and Hébert, who had taken part in both the overthrow of the monarchy and the September Massacres, was named as commander of the National Guard. On 31 May the alarm bells rang out and the warning cannons roared. Thousands of sansculottes marched to the Tuileries, forced their way into the chamber of the Convention and demanded the expulsion and arrest of the leading Girondins. They also demanded that the price of bread be lowered, that arms factories be set up to arm them, that all officers of noble birth be dismissed, and that the state should support poor soldiers' families and care for the elderly and the infirm. The Convention rejected these demands and merely dissolved the Commission of Twelve.

This partial success did not satisfy the revolutionaries. On 1 June the National Guard remained under arms; the Commune was preparing for the decisive battle. Early on 2 June Marat climbed the tower of the town hall to ring the bells himself. 80,000 demonstrators responded to his call, marched to the Tuileries, and again demanded the surrender of the Girondin leaders. After hours of wrangling, the Convention gave way to force. Twenty-nine Girondist deputies, including Brissot, Vergniaud, Guadet, Isnard, Pétion and Gensonné, as well as the Ministers Clavière and Lebrun, were placed under house arrest. Roland, whose name was likewise on the proscription list, escaped arrest by fleeing, but his wife, in whose salon the leading Girondins had often held political debates, was detained.

This was the 'journée révolutionnaire' of 2 June 1793, the day on which the Girondins fell from power. Within a period of less than ten months the Paris sansculottes had twice saved the Revolution and pushed it forward. Now they demanded the right to take part in the decision-making process. It was a turning point in the Revolution and assumed even greater dimensions than the storming of the Tuileries and the overthrow of the monarch on 10 August 1792, for the sansculottes were attempting to achieve goals which went far beyond the horizons of the landed bourgeoisie.

Jacobin Rule, 1793–1794

The Jacobins came to power as a direct result of the *'journée révolutionnaire'* of 2 June 1793, the day on which the intervention of the Paris masses forced a change of political direction for the third time. The Revolution was now reaching its zenith: the Jacobin Government was composed of uncompromising patriots who were intent on defending both the nation and the Revolution, and who were determined to mobilize all possible reserves and resources in order to achieve victory over France's enemies at home and abroad.

The Jacobins immediately began to fulfil the material promises which they had made during their long years of agitation. As the champions of the small-scale property owner, they sought to strengthen their alliance with the peasantry by linking the economic interests of that particular group with the political interests

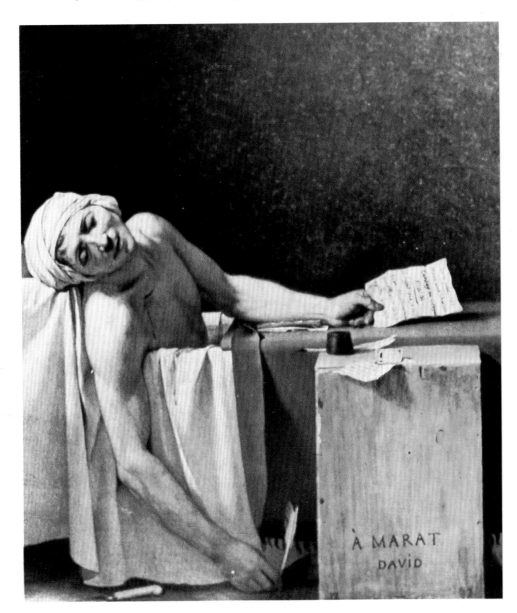

6.1 Jacques-Louis David's painting 'The Dead Marat' was commissioned by the Convention and hung in its chamber. The martyr of the Revolution lies dying in the bath, in which he sought relief from the pain caused by his skin disease. In his right hand he still holds a quill, his political weapon, which is contrasted with the murder weapon lying on the ground. In the left hand he holds the petition which his murderess used to gain access to his home.

of the Revolution. The peasantry should not merely supply the Jacobin Republic with willing taxpayers and recruits, but should also be fired with civic pride. On 3 June 1793, at its very first sitting after the overthrow of the Gironde, the Convention agreed terms for the sale of property which had once belonged to *émigrés*: the peasants were to receive small parcels of land virtually free of charge, since payment was to be in devalued *assignats* and could be spread over a period of ten years. Another decree ruled that the peasants could divide up the common land in their villages in proportion to the number of people in their families. A few weeks later the Jacobin Convention abolished all remaining feudal rights without compensation, thereby finally honouring the pledge made at the celebrated sitting of the Constituent Assembly on 4 August 1789. Thanks to the Jacobins, three million peasant families, who had tried in vain to persuade the Constituent Assembly, the Legislative Assembly, and the Girondin Convention to abolish feudal dues, were now liberated from the onerous yoke of landlordism.

The new agrarian legislation cleared the way for a

6.2 Charlotte Corday is led away after having murdered Marat.

6.3 Charlotte Corday is led to the scaffold after having been sentenced by the Revolutionary Tribunal (17 July 1793).

democratic, republican constitution. Drawn up within a matter of days by the deputy Hérault de Sechelles, the new Constitution was adopted by the Convention on 24 June 1793. Hérault de Sechelles had been elected to the Committee of Public Safety, along with Saint-Just and Couthon, on 30 May.

The Declaration of Human Rights which preceded the Constitution went further than that of 1789. It contained the rights to work and to a basic education, and obliged the state to provide poor relief. It proclaimed not only the right to resist oppression, but also the citizen's duty to rise up against a government which was hostile to the peo-

ple. The lifetime of a parliament was to be only one year, and all male citizens over the age of 25 were to take part in direct elections to the legislative body, without having to meet a property qualification. The legislature was to remain the supreme decision-making body, but was to be subordinate to the executive, and the exercise of national sovereignty was to be extended by means of a new system of public referenda.

The Constitution confirmed the principle of unlimited economic freedom; the Convention was not willing to meet the sansculottes' demands for equality in the social sphere. It also assumed the existence

6.4 On 16 July, his corpse having been embalmed, the murdered Marat lies in state on the deathbed of the Franciscan Friary in which the Cordelier Club met.

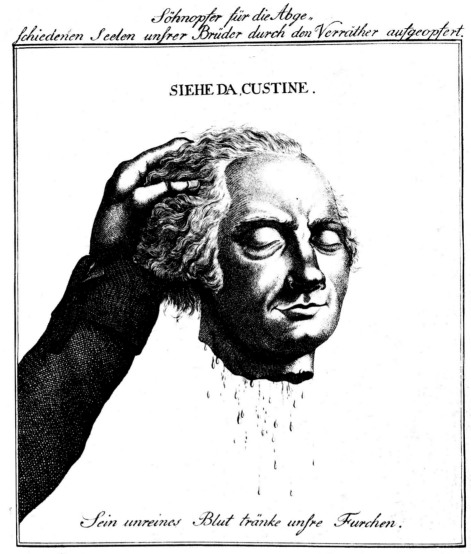

Söhnopfer für die Abge-
schiedenen Seelen unsrer Brüder durch den Verräther aufgeopfert.

SIEHE DA CUSTINE .

Sein unreines Blut tränke unsre Furchen.

SO MÜSSEN ALLE VERRAETHER DES VATERLANDES UMKOMMEN

den 28 Aug: 1793 im 2 ten Jahr der unzertheilbahren Republick, des Morgens um 10 Uhr und 30 Minuten.

6.5 The executioner holds up the head of General Adam Philippe Custine, who was guillotined on 28 August 1793 for having surrendered the Rhineland (conquered by his troops in the autumn of 1792) and suffered various setbacks in Belgium. The sentence beneath the dripping blood reads, 'their impure blood should water our fields', a translation of the last line of the chorus of the Marseillaise, 'Son sang impure abreuva nos sillons'.

of class distinctions and adopted the principle of an economy based on the division of labour and private-sector enterprise. Article 17 of the Declaration of Human Rights stated tersely, 'The citizen cannot be debarred from any type of work, living, or trade.' Such wording could easily be interpreted as a *carte blanche* for speculators and profiteers.

The Jacobin Constitution, which despite its shortcomings would serve as a prototype for political democracies in other European countries for the next two generations, defined the limits of the concessions which the bourgeoisie was willing to make to the working classes. The sansculottes were natur-

ally disappointed, since they had hoped that the Jacobins, who had after all come to power with their help, would offer them the prospect of equality of opportunity in the economic field and would proclaim a social democracy. On the day after the ratification of the Constitution Jacques Roux, speaking on behalf of the destitute population and several of the sections of Paris, went before the Convention and bellowed his 'Manifesto of the *enragés*' at the deputies:

Have you outlawed speculation? No! Have you imposed the death sentence for those who hoard food? No! Have you defined what constitutes freedom of trade? No! Have you forbidden trading with hard cash? No! Well then, we say to you that you have not done everything within your power for the good of the people. Freedom is no more than an illusion as long as one class can starve another and go unpunished. Equality is no more than an illusion as long as the rich man, by virtue of his privileged status, can decide the fate of his fellow man. The Republic is no more than an illusion as long as the counter-revolution is daily working to push up food prices to such an extent that three quarters of the population can only pay them with tears in its eyes. . . .

More than 1,850,000 Frenchmen (around 30 per cent of those entitled to vote) took part in the pleb-

iscite to ratify the Constitution, and this under civil war conditions. Of those, over nine-tenths gave their unreserved approval, and the result of the plebiscite was officially made public on 10 August 1793, the anniversary of the overthrow of the monarchy. The Convention, however, voted to suspend the Constitution until after a peace treaty had been concluded. Consequently, it never came into force, for the onset of the counter-revolution soon made emergency concentration of all governmental powers imperative. This was only possible by means of dictatorial coercive measures, and the Jacobins' subsequent actions therefore bore no relation to the suspended Constitution.

After the overthrow of the Gironde, rebellions against the Convention broke out in many parts of the country. Several Girondist deputies who had

6.6 A Jacobin broadsheet denouncing the 'White Terror' in Lyon in the summer of 1793. The counter-revolutionary, the symbol of the anti-Jacobin 'Society of the Sun' on his chest, tramples the Constitution underfoot. His accomplices beat an unarmed worker.

6.7 Antoine Quentin Fouquier-Tinville, public prosecutor for the Paris Revolutionary Tribunal during Jacobin rule. His merciless severity was notorious. Even after the fall of Robespierre he attempted to retain his post, but was arrested and tried by the Thermidorians. He defended himself, unsuccessfully, with the argument that he had only been following orders, but was guillotined in May 1795.

managed to escape from house arrest called a meeting in Caen (Normandy) on 13 June and issued a statement attacking Jacobin rule. Although for a time these 'federalist' uprisings, which were directed in particular against the Jacobins' attempts at centralization, were taking place in sixty departments – two-thirds of the country – they lacked a capable leadership and unified programme. The Girondists, who had provoked the revolts, developed from anti-Jacobins into counter-revolutionaries and worked hand in glove with royalists, aristocrats and unsworn priests in an attempt to smash the 'tyranny of the capital city'. Apart from Marseille, Bordeaux and Lyon, where the population had begun to perpetrate acts of violence against the Jacobins back in May, Toulouse, Toulon, Grenoble, Limoges and Caen also became centres of insurrection.

The federalist revolts were led by royalist generals and for several weeks they plunged the Revolution into its most serious domestic crisis yet. They failed, however, because the political measures being introduced by the Jacobin Convention at that time kept the masses from joining forces with the rebels. The peasants were pleased to have been emancipated once and for all and were therefore willing to fight under the patriotic banner for the 'one and indivisible republic' and for the farmland which they had so recently acquired. In addition, the proclamation of the Jacobin Constitution had won the support of many urban small-scale property owners. The Convention knew that it could divide the agitators from their popular base by promising federalist deserters exemption from punishment and by outlawing the escaped Girondins. These and other emergency measures quickly took effect. In Normandy the rebellion crumbled in mid-July 1793. Marseille was retaken at the end of August, Bordeaux in mid-September, and after a bitter and bloody battle Lyon fell to the Jacobins on 9 October.

Toulon, where the English had landed in August in order to lend support to the counter-revolutionary rebellion and to establish a bridgehead, was recaptured in mid-December.

The federalist rebellion led indirectly to the murder of Marat. His murderess, Charlotte Corday, who came from Normandy, had got to know several escaped Girondins in Caen. These men portrayed the radical people's friend as a bloodthirsty monster and enemy of the fatherland. Charlotte Corday travelled to Paris specifically in order to kill Marat and stabbed the unsuspecting revolutionary in his home on 13 July 1793 as he prepared a special edition of his newspaper to celebrate the fourth anniversary of the storming of the Bastille.

In an atmosphere of constant fear of France's enemies at home and abroad, this successful act of individual terrorism demonstrated the deadly peril which stalked the Revolution. It had been Marat who had most forcefully embodied the alliance

6.8 The public prosecutor sums up during the Revolutionary Tribunal's trial of several aristocrats.

6.9 A local revolutionary committee in session during Jacobin rule. These committees were responsible for watching and interrogating citizens, as well as receiving their requests and accusations.

Overleaf:
6.10 A Paris prison cell during the 'Great Terror' in the summer of 1794. A jailer, holding a list in his hands, calls out the names of 'suspects' to be taken before the Revolutionary Tribunal for trial.

between the radical, bourgeois democrats and the popular movement, and the Jacobins regarded his murder as proof of a large-scale conspiracy against the Revolution. As the 'Cassandra of the Revolution', Marat had accurately predicted the treachery of the king, the royalists, the generals and the Gironde. His own death as a martyr was to have far-reaching consequences. Although Corday testified at her trial that she had committed the murder 'in order to save hundreds of thousands', her actions actually tore down the gates of resistance to the measures proposed by the *enragés*, stirred up an immense lust for revenge, and gave new impetus to the revolutionary movement. Whilst the murderess

was led to the guillotine, the sansculottes organized a grand funeral ceremony for their hero. Hébert, the editor of *Le Père Duchesne*, and the *enragés* Roux and Leclerc took over where Marat had left off. Since 1790 Marat had been recommending the establishment of a dictatorship and the physical annihilation of all political opponents, and though the Jacobins had rejected this recommendation during Marat's lifetime, his murder contributed to its realization within a few short months.

In July 1793 the Republic was under threat from within and without: in the Vendée the republican troops suffered several setbacks; the leader of Lyon's Jacobin patriots, Chalier, who had been

imprisoned during the town's Girondist and royalist takeover at the end of May, was executed; the stronghold at Mainz, which had been under siege from a Prussian army for four months, capitulated; on the northern border Austrian troops under the command of General Coburg resumed their advance, captured strongholds in Condé and Valenciennes, and surrounded Cambrai. In view of these ill tidings from the various theatres of war, the Jacobins considered it essential that they establish a strictly organized government with extensive powers. Defending the achievements of the Revolution was France's primary consideration.

After Danton's expulsion, the Committee of Public Safety, which had hitherto been equal in rank with the other committees in the Convention, was reconvened as a revolutionary government. Under the leadership of Robespierre, who joined the Committee on 27 July 1793, the revolutionaries succeeded in overcoming the perilous crisis with which they were faced and in getting a grip on France's troubles at home and abroad. As the foremost representative of a national and at the same time democratic ideology, Robespierre, who commanded a great deal of respect in the Convention and enjoyed the confidence of the sansculottes, was the very embodiment of austere Jacobinism. He was highly suspicious of anyone who sought to capitalize on the Revolution at a personal level and demanded that all private interests be subordinated to the more general interests of the nation. This resolute and selfless man, who regarded the classical notion of virtue as man's most ambitious goal, was known to his friends as 'the Incorruptible'.

The other members of the 'Great Committee of Public Safety' were Couthon and Saint-Just, who together with Robespierre formed a 'triumvirate', Jeanbon Saint-André and Prieur de la Marne, who were generally *en mission* in various departments and rarely took part in the sittings, Lindet, who was

6.11 The Revolutionary
Tribunal tries Marie-
Antoinette ('Widow Capet')
on 14 and 15 October 1793.

6.12 Marie-Antoinette on the
way to her execution, drawn
by Jacques-Louis David on
16 October 1793 from a
window in the home of the
deputy Julien.

responsible for supplying the troops and the civi-
lian population, and Hérault de Séchelles and Barère, who were responsible for the diplomatic corps
and foreign policy. On 14 August Prieur de Côté
d'Or and Carnot were elected to the Committee,
followed on 6 September by Billaud-Varenne and
Collot d'Herbois. Eight of the committee members
had originally studied law, Jeanbon Saint-André
was a Protestant minister, Collot d'Herbois – who
had close links with the sansculottes – was an actor,
whilst Carnot and Prieur de Côté d'Or were weapon
engineers and military experts. Carnot, who possessed outstanding know-how and skills in the
fields of weapon technology, administration and

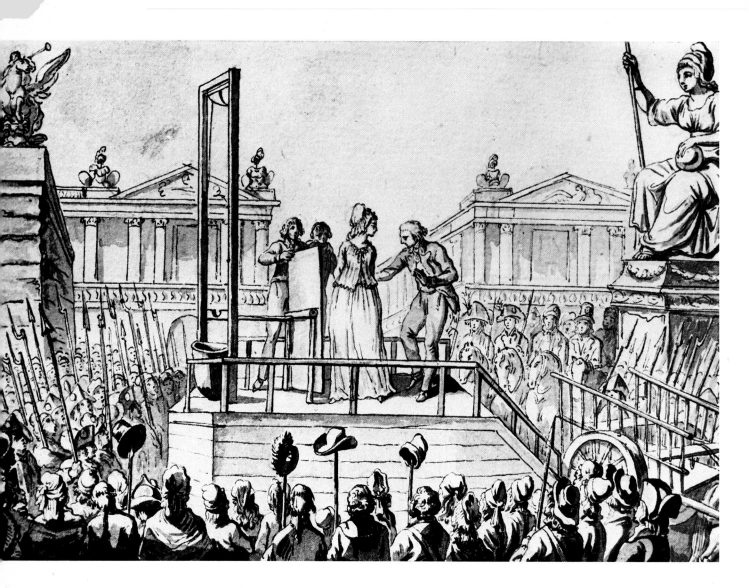

strategy, was rightly acclaimed as the 'organizer of the Revolution's victory'. Billaud concerned himself mainly with domestic problems and the administration of the departments. During their tour of duty on the Committee (which lasted just under a year) these twelve Jacobins, all very different in character, reached almost ten thousand decisions relating to political, economic, social, and cultural life, completely abolished the last vestiges of the privileged order, and adopted resolutions which fundamentally changed the social face of France.

On 10 August 1793, the anniversary of the overthrow of the monarchy, a rally took place on the Champs de Mars in Paris, to which many departments sent deputations. Once the result of the plebiscite on the Constitution had been announced, Robespierre gave a speech in which he called for the

6.13 Marie-Antoinette on the scaffold. The drawing depicts an anecdote according to which she unintentionally trod on the executioner's foot and apologized to him before the executioner's assistants placed her head on the guillotine.

Revolution to be saved. This would require the large-scale arming of the people, a matter close to the hearts of the sansculottes. On 23 August the Convention voted in favour of a proposal submitted by the Committee of Public Safety that a *levée en masse*, or conscription, be introduced. Conscription enabled the Government to mobilize all able-bodied single men and childless widowers between the ages of 18 and 25 for military service. They assembled in the major provincial towns and from there they were assigned to combat battalions. For as long as the enemy remained on French soil the Government would be able to call up all Frenchmen to meet the army's requirements and convert public buildings into barracks or munitions factories. The Republic was beleaguered from all sides and soon became one huge military camp. The first round of

6.14 The sentence passed on Brissot and 20 other Girondins is read out in the Revolutionary Tribunal on 31 October 1793. The condemned men rise indignantly from their seats, and the deputy Valazé plunges a dagger into his chest.

conscription produced an army of half a million men.

General conscription did not merely change the structure of the army, it also made state direction of the economy imperative. The Revolutionary Government recognized that it would have to subordinate the entire economy to the requirements of the war if it was to arm, equip and maintain the population. Furthermore, the state would have to set up its own productive and supportive systems and become the country's major employer. The demands of defending the nation made uncompromising coercive measures an absolute necessity.

The threat to the Revolution represented by the civil war and France's encirclement was not, however, the only matter which forced the Committee of Public Safety to transform the democracy as defined in the Constitution into a revolutionary dictatorship. The people of Paris, matured by the battles of the Revolution and driven to despair by hunger, also pressed the Jacobin Government firmly to suppress the counter-revolution and demanded that the Terror be placed on the agenda. The food shortages and the famine worsened at the end of August when the *assignats* fell to less than 30 per cent of their nominal value. As 5 September dawned, the Revolution had reached another – its last – *journée révolutionnaire*. The storming of the Convention was organized by workers who received their wages in devalued paper money and had no other source of income. Thousands of demonstrators from the slums, shouting for bread and wishing death on

6.15 The Girondins are loaded into two rack waggons with large wheels for transportation to their place of execution.

6.16 The courtyard of the Saint-Lazare prison, which housed 700 prisoners. This prison, in which numerous aristocrats were held, was known as a 'dandy's prison' (*prison des muscadins*) since the conditions were somewhat better than elsewhere: the prisoners were allowed to hire comfortable beds and keep servants. The picture shows several prisoners playing ball. No September Massacre took place at the Saint-Lazare prison, rue du Fauburg Saint-Denis.

profiteers and speculators, marched to the Tuileries and occupied the chamber of the Convention. On behalf of the Paris Commune the mayor, Pache, condemned the selfishness of the propertied classes. The procurator of the Commune, Chaumette, once again demanded the establishment of an 'internal revolutionary army' which would track down enemies of the Revolution, arrest suspicious individuals, requisition grain from the villages and transport it to Paris.

The Convention finally agreed to activate such a unit. It was to comprise 6,000 infantrymen and 1,200 mounted cannoneers, and its main task would be to secure for the capital the essential commodities which were so urgently required. The deputies wavered, however, when it came to placing restrictions on the sacred principle of economic freedom for the benefit of the sansculottes or meeting their demands for an extension of price ceilings. The Convention accepted Danton's suggestion that any citizen who took part in the assemblies of the Paris sections should be paid an allowance of two *livres* (40 *sous*) to cover loss of earnings, that the assemblies should cease to be in permanent session, and that the sittings should be limited to two a week. At the same time moves were made to eliminate the

6.17 A scene in Strasburg Minster, which was transformed into a 'Temple of Reason' during the dechristianization campaign led by the Jacobins Hébert and Chaumette in November 1793. In the foreground is the stone torso and arm of a toppled statue, probably of Saint Peter (there is still a key in the figure's hand). A Jacobin with a cap in his hand is preaching. In the background, on the altar, is an actress, who is meant to personify 'reason'.

leadership of the sansculottes movement: the *enragés* Roux and Varlet, who had been busy advocating people's power as the next phase of the Revolution and had shown up the inadequacy of the Montagnard democracy, were imprisoned, and Leclerc, who shared their views, was forced to discontinue publication of his newspaper. Shortly afterwards the 'Society of Revolutionary Republican Women', led by the suffragettes Pauline Léon and Claire Lacombe, was outlawed. Since the middle of September governmental power had further concentrated in the hands of the Committee of Public Safety: henceforth it would also appoint the members of the Committee of General Security, a body which carried out various policing functions, issued arrest warrants, carried out house searches, paid informers and agents, and supervised the local watch committees.

Such political measures were not, however, likely to alleviate the dire need of the masses. If this was to be achieved, then their economic demands would have to be met. The amount of pressure which the sections were forced to exert on the Convention pointed up the differences which existed between the Jacobins and the sansculottes. These two allies, who together had overthrown the Gironde, had completely different motives and aims. The sansculottes were not members of a homogeneous proletarian class, but represented a movement comprising the various plebeian elements of an economic system which had only recently outgrown the workshop-based productive conditions of the late eighteenth century. Some of these elements were facing economic extinction, whilst others were destined to join the ranks of the small-scale property owner or to become integrated into the future labour movement. The sansculottes, who were organized within the sections, did not wish to see the existing economic system replaced, but sought to maintain traditional practices and to preserve a standard of living which they believed to be under threat from the establishment of municipal authorities and from capitalist entrepreneurs and speculators. To some extent their thinking was still influenced by the attitudes of the old guilds. They eventually fell foul of the Jacobins by making egalitarian demands which went beyond the remit of the bourgeois Revolution. Among other things, they demanded restrictions on ownership, maintaining

that no one should be allowed to own more than one workshop or one shop, or to lease more land than he could work himself. This utopian social dream was based on the egalitarian notion of a harmonious society in which the needs of all members would be met by means of a planned economy. Private property would be retained, but its adverse effects on the economically weak would be obviated by state control.

The Jacobins, as bourgeois revolutionaries, held on tightly to the concept of competition and were reluctant to limit the right of an owner to dispose of his property as he saw fit, even for the duration of

6.18 The Church of *St. Jean en Grève* is pulled down during the dechristianization campaign.

the crisis. They were neither willing nor able to abolish the social distinctions which resulted from the inequality of ownership, but endeavoured in their economic policy to bridge the gulf between the material interests of the wealthy owners and the social aspirations of the propertyless classes, although without having to abolish capitalist forms of trade and production. The Jacobins, who were

6.19 Mass execution of
royalists and other counter-
revolutionaries in Lyon in
December 1793. The
shootings were ordered by
the Jacobin commissioners
Collot d'Herbois and Fouché.

torn between egalitarianism and elitism, democracy
and dictatorship, opposed the introduction of any
economic planning or state control simply for the
purposes of realizing the sansculottes' dream of
equality. They did not allow themselves to be
shaken from their role as leaders, but assigned to
the lower classes the task of securing victory for
the bourgeois Revolution on the battlefield and subordinating themselves to intellectual democrats.

Despite the threat facing the Republic, the Convention did not concern itself solely with political
and military matters, but extended its reforms into
the field of culture. It became clear that bourgeois
and working-class revolutionaries had very differ-

ent views on the issue of education. On the basis of
a project carried out by the Girondist Enlightener
Condorcet, the Convention had voted in December
1792 to introduce four years of free compulsory
education. Attendance at further education estab-
lishments was still barred to the children of the
poor. According to Condorcet, children from the
propertyless classes needed an education which
would prepare them early on for hard work, the offspring of the middle classes should be trained for
the lucrative professions, and the progeny of the
economically independent upper classes should be
prepared for a life of luxury. Just as it shaped the
economy, the market was also to determine the

6.20 The English fleet which landed in Toulon in the middle of August 1793 is driven out of France on 19 December. In the foreground (with the telescope) is the young artillery captain Napoleon Bonaparte, who headed the operation.

nature of education.

This concept of education contradicted Robespierre's dream of emancipation, since he believed that any moral political system would treat the interests of the whole as a priority. He submitted to the Convention a proposal worked out by the Jacobin deputy Michel Lepeletier, who had been murdered by royalists. According to this proposal, a system of compulsory social education would help to build the egalitarian structures of a future society and reduce inequality of opportunity. Equality within the education system would introduce the Jacobin notion of Virtue into the schools and break down class barriers. However, the contrast between rich and poor was only to disappear in the field of education: actual differences in ownership were to remain untouched.

The educative model conceived by Robespierre's friend Saint-Just provided for compulsory social education for all boys. Girls were to be educated in the parental home. The schools were to be financed through the sale of national and counter-revolutionary property. Saint-Just, who regarded the ultimate goal of the Revolution to be an egalitarian state of farmers, civil servants and warriors, wanted to promote a sense of community by organizing school classes in a quasi-military manner and by forming groups of sixty schoolchildren into

6.21 Lazare Carnot. Because of his outstanding military talents the Convention elected him to the Committee of Public Safety, where he acted, to all intents and purposes, as Minister of War. He organized the arming of the population, employed modern methods of mass warfare, and drew up, with great efficiency, operation plans for all fourteen of the revolutionary armies which defended France.

companies. The abolition of class distinctions in the field of education would, he believed, strengthen the virtue and brotherly love inherent in human nature.

The revolutionary leadership of the sansculotte movement regarded a large-scale programme of national education as absolutely vital to the defence of the Revolution. The section 'Panthéon français' appealed to the Convention to regulate adult education by law in order to accelerate the process of change in society, anchor the republican ideology, and enable the masses to take over all political offices.

In *Le Père Duchesne*, Hébert demanded that the state make available the funds necessary to ensure that every citizen, regardless of social status and income, received an equal education. The Convention, however, rejected not only the sansculottes' educational demands, but also Robespierre's suggestion that Lepeletier's concept of education should be adopted. The deputies were not keen on the idea of an egalitarian social order, but preferred to consolidate the social supremacy of the bourgeoisie.

The Convention knew that it could not win its battle against the counter-revolution at home and abroad without the active support of the masses and was therefore forced to resort to drastic coercive measures. On 17 September 1793 it gave way to pressure from the sansculottes: the 'Law of Suspects' initiated the Terror. The term 'suspect' was defined in extremely broad terms in order that it should apply to all counter-revolutionaries: it covered all those who, through their behaviour or their views, showed themselves to be 'enemies of freedom', all suspended civil servants, all those related to *émigrés*, and all those who were unable to show that they had 'carried out their civic duties' or 'how they supported themselves'. Local revolutionary committees were to keep tabs on local citizens, investigate their political views, and compile lists of suspects. The door had been opened wide for informers.

The Terror was, then, the expression and result of social antagonisms, that is to say, of the military crisis, the difficult economic situation and pressure from the starving and embittered Paris masses. The only options open to the Jacobins were either to be destroyed along with all the achievements of the Revolution, or to use terror to defend both the nation and the Revolution against rebellion and treachery, and thereby carry the day. The Terror empowered the governmental committees to use coercive measures to restore the authority of the state and to ensure that the welfare of the Republic was always the first priority. It also helped to awaken a sense of national solidarity and made governmental control of the economy possible, this being imperative if the war effort was to rescue the nation. The Terror inside France in no way detracted from the enthusiasm displayed by the sansculottes and peasants fighting for their own vital interests at the front.

With the judiciary now playing a greater role it became necessary to enlarge the Revolutionary Tribunal. From September on, it comprised four departments and had a total of nineteen judges and sixty jurors. Fouquier-Tinville had served as the public prosecutor since March. In the first half of the year the tribunal had tried 260 defendants and condemned 66 to death. In the last three months of 1793, however, it tried 395 defendants and sent 177 to the guillotine. The number of detainees held in the prisons of Paris trebled. By the end of 1793 they numbered more than 4,500.

On 29 September the Convention finally passed the 'Law of General Maximum', which had long been demanded by the sansculottes. The law extended the system of price ceilings, which had set a legal maximum price for bread and corn on 4 May, to all essential commodities and services. It also set a maximum wage. 1790 was taken as a base year, with the prices of basic foodstuffs, consumables and raw materials used in the manufacturing industries being calculated at base rate plus a third. Wages and salaries were also calculated using 1790 as the base and were fixed at base rate plus 50 per cent. All merchants were obliged to draw up inventories of their stock, and farmers to give notice of their supplies.

Although the maximums did nothing to relieve shortages, and although some continued to live 'like fat cattle' and others 'like beasts of burden', they did restrain the black market somewhat and enable the labouring classes to purchase enough to meet their daily needs at reasonable prices. The Government requisitioned large stocks of goods at the price set by the maximum for the army at the front. Inflation fell, and by the end of 1793 the *assignats* were once again worth 50 per cent of their nominal value.

The effects of the military reorganization were soon felt. Carnot, with his wealth of organizational talent and military skill, succeeded in transforming the bedraggled bevy which the first round of general conscription had thrown up into well-ordered and well-equipped armies. Workers, craftsmen and peasants, whose own interests were inextricably linked with the victory of the Revolution, overcame the military and technical superiority of the mercenary armies sent out against France. They employed modern skirmish tactics whereby soldiers no longer fought in close and rigid formation, but attacked the enemy in scattered lines. This enabled the soldiers to move more quickly and strike on every part of the battlefield.

On 8 September 1793 near Hondschoote, not far from the Belgian border, General Houchard's troops defeated the English army under the command of the Duke of York. Houchard neglected, however, to pursue the enemy, and his troops were themselves defeated in another battle shortly afterwards. The Convention, which had been extremely suspicious of army chiefs ever since Dumouriez's desertion, had already brought General Custine before the Revolutionary Tribunal and had him executed for

6.22 Bertrand Barère de Vieuzac, one of the best speakers in the Convention, was a member of the Committee of Public Safety. He composed communiqués to proclaim military victories and spoke out, along with Collot d'Herbois and Billaud-Varenne, for the Terror to be stepped up. In 1795 he was condemned to deportation to Devil's Island, but managed to escape. Given an amnesty by Bonaparte.

his military setbacks in the Rhineland. Now Houchard also fell under suspicion of treason. He was ordered back to Paris, sentenced to death, and guillotined.

The Committee of Public Safety filled the commands of the three main armies fighting on the northern border with young commanders who owed their careers to the Revolution and were prepared to employ Carnot's offensive tactics: Jourdan, Pichegru, and Hoche. Carnot, the 'organizer of the Revolution's victory', appeared in person on the Belgian front, and together he and Jourdan commanded the troops which defeated the Austrians at Wattignies on 16 October. Their success secured the northern front until the spring of 1794.

France's new-found success in defending itself enabled the Committee of Public Safety to consolidate its position of power. On 10 October 1793, at the request of Saint-Just, the Convention declared the French Government to be 'revolutionary until the peace'. In doing so, it legalized the Jacobin dictatorship and the draconian measures which accompanied it. The democratic principle of suffrage, which had characterized the Jacobin Constitution of June 1793, had been abandoned.

Now it was time for the Montagnards to settle with the counter-revolutionaries and their own enemies. On 16 October, after a trial lasting two days, Marie-Antoinette, the former queen – addressed by the judge as 'Widow Capet' – was executed for conspiring with the enemies of France. She was followed to the guillotine at the end of October by twenty-one leading Girondins, including Brissot, Vergniaud and Gensonné. They were accused by Fouquier-Tinville of having taken part in the federalist plot against the people, the Convention and the Republic. When seventy-five deputies protested against the death sentence imposed on these men, they were expelled from the Convention and imprisoned. The Girondins Pétion, Condorcet and Clavière committed suicide, and other members of the Gironde were executed in Bordeaux. Madame Roland mounted the scaffold at the beginning of November, and when her husband, who had escaped and was in hiding in the provinces, received news of her death, he also took his own life. The former mayor of Paris, Bailly, was tried for his part in the massacre on the Champs de Mars (1791). He mounted the scaffold along with Barnave, once a leading member of the Constituent Assembly, who had been found guilty of having had close links with the royal couple. Other prominent victims included Countess Dubarry, Louis XV's last mistress, and the Duke of Orleans (Philippe Égalité), who had been in prison since 6 April 1793 and was accused of having been involved in his son's desertion to the Austrians.

In the provinces the intensity of the Terror depended on the scale of each particular area's involvement in the counter-revolution and the attitudes of the commisioners sent by the Convention. On 9 October 1793 the insurgent town of Lyon surrendered, and the Convention ordered its destruction. Whilst Couthon, who was initially sent there, only followed these instructions symbolically, Collot d'Herbois and Fouché, who arrived in Lyon at the beginning of November, instigated a reign of terror. Because the guillotine worked too slowly, around 1,700 citizens sentenced by the local revolutionary tribunal were shot down by cannons *en masse*. After the collapse of the rebellion in the Vendée more than 600 condemned people were mowed down by case-shot in the town of Angers. In December 1793 and January 1794 Carrier, the deputy sent by the Convention to Nantes, had over 2,000 prisoners who were awaiting trial drowned in the Loire without trial or sentence. Most were rebels from the Vendée. More than 300 death sentences were carried out in Toulon after its recapture, and in Marseille, Bordeaux, Rennes and Arras the executions also ran into hundreds. Exact calculations have revealed that 16,594 people from all over France were condemned to death and guillotined on political grounds between the establishment of the Revolutionary Tribunal in March 1793 and the fall of the Jacobin Government in August 1794. In addition, another 20,000 or so died in mass executions by shooting or drowning, as a result of suicide, or through privation or illness in the prisons.

From October to December 1793 the public prosecutor in Alsace was Eulogius Schneider, a German Jacobin who had fled to the land of freedom. For six weeks he and the local revolutionary tribunal travelled around the small towns and villages in the area with a portable guillotine for the purposes of calling to account enemies of the Revolution. Of the 611 defendants brought to trial 29 were executed. Saint-Just and the deputy Lebas, who journeyed to

6.23 The 'Ultra-revolutionary' Jacques-René Hébert and his comrades in a rack waggon pulled by two horses on their way to the guillotine on 24 March 1794. On the right (in the background) is the entrance to the Jacobin Club with its inscription 'Equality, Freedom, or Death', in front of it a tree planted in the name of freedom.

6.24 The Festival of the Supreme Being on 20 prairial of the Year II (8 June 1794). The parade began at the Tuileries (left) and ended on the Champs de Mars, where a model of a mountain had been erected.

the German-speaking region of Alsace as 'delegates *en mission*' in order to boost the population's preparedness to defend the nation, considered all foreigners without exception, including tried and tested revolutionaries like Schneider, to be spies and agents in the pay of hostile powers. They had Schneider arrested and transported back to Paris so that he could stand trial before the Revolutionary Tribunal. 'This punishment', wrote Lebas in a letter to Robespierre, 'was born of the necessity to teach other foreigners a lesson. We should not trust these internationalist charlatans, but should rely on our-

selves alone.' This was Robespierre's view exactly. In a speech to the convention on 18 November 1794 he stressed that France was fighting a war in defence of its existence as a nation and would therefore forgo the pleasure of exporting the Revolution.

In the autumn of 1793 foreigners living in France came under increasing suspicion from the Jacobins. So too did the constitutional clergy, for many of the priests who had pledged allegiance to the Constitution tended towards support of the Gironde. Since the arrival on the political scene of the sansculottes, both the anti-clerical drift and the world-revolutionary cult had gathered speed. Some of the sections of Paris branded the Catholic Church a bastion of superstition and fanaticism.

At the suggestion of the deputy Romme, the Convention voted on 5 October 1793 to abolish the Christian calendar and introduce a republican calendar. The founding of the Republic on 22 September 1792 was taken retrospectively as the beginning of the new era, since this date marked the real

6.25 Camille Desmoulins embraces Georges Danton before their execution on 5 April 1794. The executioner's assistant grips Danton by the shoulder in order to lead him to the scaffold.

6.26 Citizens condemned by the Revolutionary Tribunal are transported to their place of execution in an open rack waggon. In the background (on the left) the outline of a guillotine is visible.

turning point in the history of mankind. The deputy Fabre d'Eglantine, a poetic genius, gave names to the twelve months, each of 30 days. Each name characterized a natural phenomenon: vendémiaire, brumaire, frimaire, nivôse, pluviôse, ventôse, germinal, floréal, prairial, messidor, thermidor, and fructidor. Weeks were replaced by periods of ten days (decades) so that the Christian Sunday would disappear, and the five (or six) remaining days of the year, the 'sansculottides', were to be celebrated as revolutionary festivals.

During the next few weeks the campaign to dechristianize France spread like wildfire. On 7 November the constitutional bishop of Paris, Gobel, appeared before the Convention, announced his resignation from the priesthood, and placed a liberty cap on his head. At the suggestion of the procurator of the Commune, Chaumette, the Cathedral of Nôtre Dame became a 'Temple of Reason', with an actress playing the part of the Goddess of Freedom at a dedication ceremony on 10 November. The Commune ordered the closure of all churches in Paris and their conversion into poor-houses or schools. In Reims, Strasburg and other places, anti-

clerical members of the 'internal revolutionary army' destroyed Gothic sculptures and pictures of the saints. Church bells were melted down and used to cast cannons.

Although as a deist Robespierre did not have much time for the Catholic faith, he regarded the excesses of the dechristianization campaign as a political mistake. He and his friends were not keen to lose the support of the peasantry and small-scale property owners, who generally took their religion seriously. He halted dechristianization and warned 'Ultra-revolutionaries' of Hébert's stamp, who had even been overturning altars, that they were doing the work of the counter-revolution. At the beginning of December, at Robespierre's suggestion, the Convention withdrew its anti-religious measures

6.27 Victims of the Terror are loaded onto carts after their execution and taken to burial grounds.

6.28 The Battle of Fleurus (in Belgium) on 26 June 1794, in which the northern army under the command of General Jean Baptiste Jourdan defeated Austrian troops led by Josias of Saxe-Coburg.

and restored the principle of religious freedom.

Recent victories on the battlefield allowed the Convention to provide the Republic with a dictatorial constitution; the 'Revolutionary Government Act' was enacted on 4 December (14 frimaire). The law brought about further centralization of the administration, curtailed the powers exercised by the Commune, placed all elected authorities under the control of the Committee of Public Safety, and suspended all elections for the duration of the war. This concentration of power failed, however, to prevent the emergence of factions with different social and political interests. The unity of the Montagnards was shattered, and the Jacobin Club split. The right wing, grouped around Danton and Desmoulins, wanted to enjoy the fruits of the Revolution straight away. Danton himself demanded that a compromise be reached with the foreign powers and that there should be an end to the Terror. He hoped that this latter demand would deprive the sansculottes of the position of strength which they

now occupied, since he regarded this as a threat. On behalf of the sansculottes, the left wing, gathered around Hébert and Chaumette, demanded an intensification of the Terror and governmental control of the economy, these measures being necessary if the battle against the enemies of the Revolution, war profiteers and the *nouveaux riches* was to be won.

The disclosure that a number of deputies had been implicated in a huge scandal involving foreign swindlers, soldiers of fortune, speculators and enemy agents, all living in France, greatly disturbed Robespierre and Saint-Just. They were convinced of the existence of a 'foreign plot' to destroy the Republic. In mid-December in the journal *Le Vieux Cordelier*, Desmoulins not only directed a frontal attack against Hébert and his comrades, but also described the dictatorship of the Committee of Public Safety, which the Committee consolidated by means of the Terror, as despotism. He demanded the appointment of a 'Central Committee of Clemency' and the release of all alleged suspects, of whom, he estimated, there were 200,000.

In a speech to the Convention on 25 December 1793, Robespierre cited the war as justification of the Terror and stressed that the Government was motivated not by despotism and mania, but by the public interest. 'It has', he said, 'to sail between two reefs, between weakness and recklessness, between moderation and extremism. Moderation bears the same relation to reticence as impotence does to chasteness, and extremism bears the same similarity to vitality as dropsy does to good health.'

Three weeks later, when Danton's friend Fabre d'Eglantine was arrested for his part in the scandal, Hébert and his comrades were jubilant. *Le Père Duchesne* spoke out not only against the *Indulgents* grouped around Danton, but also against the Committee of Public Safety's 'policy of balance'. Furthermore, it called upon the sansculottes to take control of the administration. The Jacobin method of government, which relied upon the harmonization of conflicting interests, at least until the final victory had been won, and on encouraging passive obedience from the sansculottes, threatened to run aground. The radical left-wing Cordelier Club, whose leading lights were supporters of Hébert, veiled a plaque quoting the Declaration of Human Rights which had been erected there, and several working-class political clubs demanded Danton's expulsion from the Convention.

Robespierre appealed to both factions to subordinate their own private interests to those of the public good. In a speech on the 'principles of political morality' on 5 February 1794 he explained the theoretical basis of his domestic policies. A policy of virtue was essential if the Government was to 'do the will of the people and seal the fate of mankind'. This meant nothing other than a love of the law and of the fatherland. The people would have to be guided by reason; the Terror, which must of course only be directed against the enemies of the people, was quick and strict justice, a product of virtue. 'Without virtue', he said, 'the Terror is a calamity, without the Terror virtue is powerless ... To punish the oppressors of mankind is an act of charity; to forgive them is an act of barbarity.'

However, the appeal had no effect, and the dissatisfied and destitute masses continued to press for their material needs to be met. The Convention, which finally redeemed the Constituent Assembly's pledge to abolish slavery in the Colonies, decided on a programme of extensive social reform. On 8 and 13 ventôse (26 February and 3 March 1794), at the suggestion of Saint-Just, two decrees were passed which allowed for the confiscation of all property belonging to suspected enemies of the state, and for this property to be used to pay damages to poor patriots. The programme represented a major revolution in the realm of property ownership.

This attempt to win the sansculottes over to the side of the Committee of Public Safety did not, however, pass beyond its initial phase, since it required a great deal of time-consuming work to establish the extent of the property involved in such a change of ownership. At the time of the Jacobins' fall from power the local committees were still processing around 40,000 applications. The decrees of ventôse were never implemented.

Robespierre's centre grouping was unable to bridge the gulf between the *Indulgents* and the 'Ultras'. It also failed to solve the problem of food shortages and guarantee supplies. The sansculottes' dissatisfaction and disappointment increased to such an extent that Ronsin, the commander of the 'Revolutionary Army', announced in the Cordelier Club that a rebellion against the Revolutionary Government was imperative. The Committee of

6.29 The Place de Grève, in front of the Paris town hall, on the afternoon of 9 thermidor of the Year II (27 July 1794). Armed sansculottes from several sections assemble for the purposes of freeing Robespierre and his companions, who were arrested in the Convention.

Public Safety, which had never identified with the social aims and political methodology of sansculotte-style direct democracy, now saw no alternative but to silence the 'Ultras' by force. Having been arrested in September 1793, the leader of the *enragés*, the priest Jacques Roux, had been sentenced to death in February 1794, but had committed suicide before the execution. On 13 March Hébert, Ronsin, and a number of others (including the 'orator of the human race' Anacharsis Cloots and several foreign spies) were arrested and brought before the Revolutionary Tribunal. Fouquier-Tinville accused them of having aided 'a foreign plot' and humiliated the Convention. They were executed on 24 March.

A few days later Robespierre and Saint-Just took steps to liquidate the *Indulgents*. Once again they

6.30 In the early hours of 10 thermidor of the Year II (28 July 1794) the gendarmes sent by the Convention force their way into the 'Hall of Equality' in the Paris town hall in order to rearrest Robespierre and his companions. A gendarme by the name of Merda shoots at the seated Robespierre with his pistol and shatters his jaw-bone. In the foreground is the wounded Georges Couthon, who has fallen to the ground and is trying to fight off an assailant.

used guilt by association to depict their political opponents as miserable blackguards and traitors: Danton, Desmoulins, and Hérault de Sechelles, a member of the Committee of Public Safety, were accused along with corrupt deputies, speculators and enemy agents of having hatched a conspiracy to destroy the Republic. Danton refused to take this lying down and shouted, 'I am no conspirator! My name is linked with every institution of the Revolution: conscription, Revolutionary Army, revolutionary committees, Revolutionary Tribunal, Committee of Public Safety.' When accused of corruption, he said, 'A man such as me has no price.' It appeared that he might be able to convince the jurors with his arguments, and fearing this the Convention decreed that defendants who had

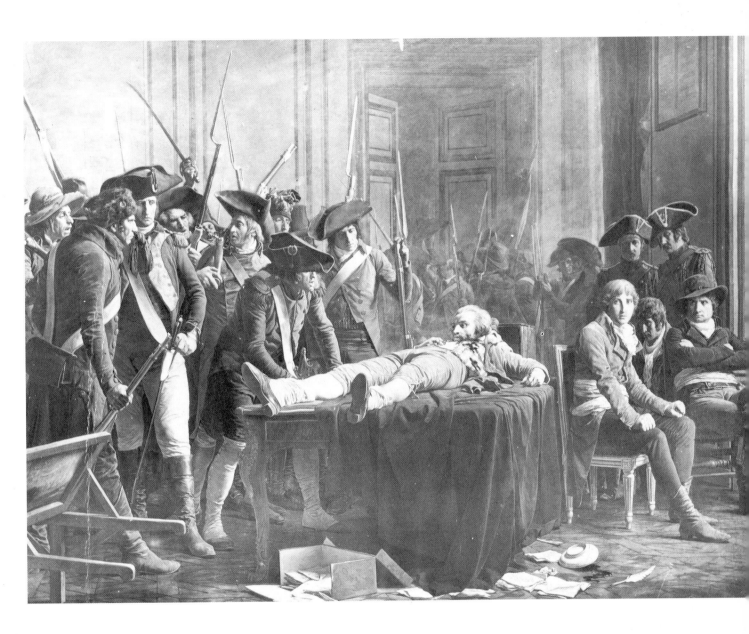

6.31 The morning of 28 July 1794. The seriously wounded Robespierre, whose head is resting on a wooden ammunition box, lies on a table in a meeting room used by the Committee of General Security.

'resisted or insulted the national justice' could be denied the right to speak. On 5 April 1794 all of the defendants, with the exception of the planted informer Lacroix, were condemned to death and beheaded.

A week later a third trial took place, which eliminated the remaining potential opposition. The procurator of the Commune, Chaumette, mounted the scaffold, and so too did the former Bishop of Paris, Gobel, and the widows of Hébert and Desmoulins. The Revolutionary Army was disbanded, and supporters of Robespierre took control of the Paris Commune. Pache was replaced as mayor by Fleuriot-Lescot.

The weakening of the democratic popular movement led, in the words of Saint-Just, to a 'journey' for the Revolution. The execution of the sans-culottes' leaders narrowed the political support-base of the Committee of Public Safety, paralysed political life in the sections of Paris, and widened the gulf between the Jacobins and the lower classes. The new local authority suppressed several strikes and administered Le Chapelier's law, which outlawed workers' combinations, with the utmost rigour. Once the left-wing opposition had been eliminated, the Government eased its control of the economy, asked for the co-operation of France's wholesale traders, and allowed the price ceilings fixed by the Law of General Maximum to be exceeded. As a consequence of all this the sansculottes, robbed of their leaders, were barely able to afford any commodity other than bread, the black market thrived, and the *assignats* fell again to 30 per cent of their nominal value. The measures also brought about a reconciliation between those who had benefited from the Revolution and the Jacobins, at least until the final victory was won on the battlefield. The Committee of Public Safety replaced the six ministries of state with twelve executive committees and extended centralization by recalling its 'delegates *en mission*'. It was now able to concentrate most of its attention on organizing, equipping and supplying the huge armies, which by the middle of 1794 had grown substantially and now contained a million men.

The doctrine pursued by Robespierre and Saint-Just was designed to establish a society without poverty, to nurture a sense of national solidarity more powerful than the interests of any particular class, and to commit the autonomous individual to the public good. In order to reinforce this vision metaphysically and to strengthen civic pride, Robespierre considered a pseudo-religious cult of the nation to be essential. On 20 prairial (8 June 1794) on the Parisian Champs de Mars a 'Festival of the Supreme Being' was held, in which the Convention and deputations from all over France participated. The festival was arranged by the painter David, and Robespierre, as high priest of the substitute religion, delivered a solemn speech.

The festival had been intended to heal France's ailing national unity and to gather the 'virtuous' together under the Jacobin banner. But according to Robespierre's view on political morality, virtue and terror were dialectic, causative terms, two sides of

6.32 The afternoon of 28 July 1794. 22 revolutionaries, including Maximilien Robespierre and his brother Augustin, Louis Antoine Saint-Just, and Georges Couthon, are driven to their execution on three rack waggons. The executioner is holding up the head of the first to be executed, and another is climbing the steps to the guillotine. Robespierre is the last to be beheaded. On the ground in front of the guillotine lies the deputy Philippe François Lebas, who had committed suicide when the gendarmes forced their way into the town hall. Several citizens celebrate the executions.

the same coin, and immediately after the festival's deification of virtue the Committee of Public Safety resorted to the 'Great Terror' in order (in the words of Collot d'Herbois) to 'exterminate the unteachable fellow-travellers of the tyrants'.

The law adopted on 10 June 1794 (Law of 22 prairial) encouraged denunciations and abolished the preliminary interrogation of defendants, their right to a defence, and the examination of witnesses. It defined the term 'enemy of the people' extremely broadly and introduced a vague 'moral proof of guilt'. If a defendant was found guilty the Revolutionary Tribunal had no option but to impose the death sentence. Following this tightening of the law, heads fell (in the words of the public prosecutor, Fouquier-Tinville) 'like roof-tiles'. In the final seven weeks of Jacobin rule 1,376 executions took place in Paris. During the entire period from March 1793 until the Law of 22 prairial there had only been 1,251.

On 26 June 1794 near Fleurus in Belgium the northern armies, under the command of Generals Jourdan, Kléber and Marceau, scored a decisive victory over the Austrians. The upper middle classes had for a time been repressed and restricted in their lust for profits, and after this military triumph they began to regard governmental control of the economy and attacks on the right of ownership as dispensable and superfluous. They also regarded the repression inflicted by the Terror, in fact by the Jacobin dictatorship in general, in the same light. They wanted a return to a liberal regime which would guarantee complete freedom of trade and production. Even the popular movement began to turn against the Jacobins. The dissatisfied and disappointed sansculottes, who had fought in all the battles of the Revolution yet had achieved neither social betterment, direct democracy nor an egalitarian redistribution of wealth, lapsed into apathy and

indifference. Their revolutionary fire was burnt out. With that the Jacobins lost the vital backing which had enabled them to defeat both their aristocratic and their bourgeois foes. The intensification of the Terror and the isolation of the 'triumvirate' (Robespierre, Saint-Just and Couthon) went hand in hand. The maximum wage announced on 23 July (5 thermidor), which meant a substantial loss of earnings for the workers, fuelled the bitterness felt by the lower classes and contributed to their alienation from the Jacobins.

In July 1794, with the Austrians in the process of completely quitting Belgium, French troops advanced as far as the German border. The question now arose as to whether the Government should move beyond defending the nation and embark on a war of conquest. Such action would contravene the Convention's resolution of 13 April 1793 not to interfere in the affairs of other countries. Robespierre could find no solution to the dilemma. For four weeks he attended neither the Committee of Public Safety nor the Convention, thereby providing his personal and political enemies with the opportuniity to hatch a plot to topple him. In the Jacobin Club he indicated ominously that those enemies of the people 'whose hands were covered in the blood of innocent victims' had to be destroyed. Those deputies, such as Fouché, Barras, Fréron, Carrier and Tallien, who had been responsible for terrorist outrages in the provinces and who had now been recalled to Paris, felt threatened and feared being hauled up before the Revolutionary Tribunal and executed. They established contact with the deputies belonging to the 'plain', who had always regarded the dictatorship of the Committee of Public Safety as a stop-gap measure. When the majority of the members of the Committee of Public Safety were initiated into the plot against the 'triumvirate' (Robespierre, Saint-Just and Couthon) the fate of the Jacobin dictatorship was sealed.

On 26 July 1794 (8 thermidor) Robespierre delivered a speech to the Convention in which he pleaded for the Terror to be sustained and promised to wipe out the enemies of freedom, although he mentioned no names. Predicting Bonaparte's usurpation of the state's power, he warned,

If for one moment you slacken the reins of the Revolution, then you will see how military tyranny will seize them and . . . scatter the dishonoured representatives of the people. We will perish for failing to speak in support of freedom at one particular moment in the history of mankind. The people will curse our memory, when it should in fact be dear to the entire human race!

The next day, 27 July 1794 (9 thermidor II), his guilty foes refused to let him speak. Amid widespread commotion, the assembly voted to place Robespierre, Saint-Just and Couthon on trial. Robespierre's younger brother Augustin and the deputy Lebas asked to share their fate. In desperation the 'Incorruptible', who had wanted neither the war nor to export the Revolution, but under whose rule France had nevertheless successfully warded off all its enemies, cried, 'The Republic is lost, the bandits are triumphing!'.

The Paris Commune was alarmed and managed to free Robespierre and his friends and take them to the town hall. The commander of the National Guard, Hanriot, tried in vain to mobilize the sans-culottes against the Convention, but the majority of the sections were not prepared to risk their lives for Robespierre and his associates. The Convention succeeded in mustering some troops, storming the town hall, and taking the five proscribed deputies prisoner.

On 28 July Robespierre, Saint-Just and Couthon, along with nineteen of their supporters, were beheaded without trial. The next day they were followed to the scaffold by another seventy-one adherents. By the beginning of August a total of 107 of Robespierre's supporters had faced the guillotine, including Mayor Fleuriot-Lescot, the commander of the National Guard Hanriot, and the members of the Revolutionary Tribunal and the Commune. The revolutionary Terror was over, but a new Terror, the White Terror, was just beginning.

The humanitarian dream of a just and classless 'empire of reason and virtue' died with the executed Jacobin leaders. The pendulum of the Revolution had swung as far as it could; now it began to swing back.

Thermidor and the Directory, 1794–1799

The overthrow of Robespierre marked the pinnacle of the Revolution. When the Jacobins fell from power the upper middle classes found that they were able to return to government and once again pursue their earlier strategic, political, and economic goals. The bourgeoisie's victory over the *citoyen* signified that this capitalist class of profiteers had finally arrived, though they owed their rise to the fact that the Jacobin dictatorship had successfully fended off every attack launched by the counter-revolution.

The Thermidorian Convention modified the composition of the Committee of Public Safety and removed it from its dominant position of power, purged the Revolutionary Tribunal of sansculottes, and disbanded the Paris Commune. The planned economy, which had solved the crisis of 1793, was abandoned, for it stood in the way of a liberal economic system. The abolition of price ceilings at the end of 1794 led to rocketing inflation. The *assignat* fell from 30 per cent of its nominal value in July 1794 to 20 per cent at the year end, 8 per cent in April 1795, and 3 per cent in

7.1 The Paris Jacobin Club in the rue Saint-Honoré is closed down on 11 November 1794 on the instructions of the Thermidorian Convention.

7.2 The French army under
the command of General
Pichegru enters Amsterdam
on 19 January 1795. The town
surrendered without a fight.

July 1795. Liberalization of the economy had aggravated class conflict; whilst poverty increased and
mortality rates rose rapidly in the slums of Paris,
army suppliers, currency smugglers, and those who
had bought up the nation's property in bulk lived
lives of ostentatious luxury. They threw sumptuous
parties and ridiculed the spartan puritanism which
had characterized the rule of the ascetic and virtuous Robespierre. The offspring of the *nouveaux
riches* and war profiteers, the so-called 'golden
youth' (*jeunesse dorée*), and gangs of dandies (*muscadins*) preyed upon Jacobins and sansculottes. In the
provinces too the White Terror reigned supreme. In
Lyon, Marseille, Toulon, and other towns numerous
members of the local revolutionary committees

were murdered. The Thermidorians allowed those Girondins who in June 1793 had protested against the expulsion of Brissot and his friends, and had been locked up as a result, to take their old seats in the Convention. The Paris Jacobin Club was closed down in November 1794, and the terrorist Carrier sentenced to death and executed for his part in the mass drownings in the Loire. A few months later Fouquier-Tinville, public prosecutor to the Revolutionary Tribunal, also stood trial. He and fourteen of the Tribunal's jurors were guillotined. Billaud-Varenne and Collot d'Herbois, both members of Robespierre's Committee of Public Safety who had had close ties with the sansculottes, were banished to Devil's Island. Their colleague Barère, who was likewise due to be deported, managed to escape.

The Thermidorians used France's concentration of military power, a product of the Jacobin system of conscription, to further the interests of their own class. They reaped the fruits of the Jacobin victories and readopted the idea, once expounded by the Gironde, of liberating other peoples. When France attacked the Netherlands in January 1795 the Convention rescinded the Jacobin decision of April 1793 not to meddle in the affairs of other countries. Once the Netherlands had been conquered by troops under the command of General Pichegru in May 1795 the country was renamed the 'Batavian Republic'.

The similarity between Girondist and Thermidorian slogans, the return to government of the upper middle classes, and France's new conquests did not, however, in any sense mean that France's military and political situation was the same as it had been in 1792. Girondist mottos such as 'Peace to the cottages, war on the palaces' had been conditioned by the fact that at the beginning of the war the absolutist powers abroad had fully intended to destroy France's bourgeois order. None of them had been willing to enter into an agreement with the

7.3 General Jean Charles Pichegru, conqueror of the Netherlands, 1794/95. He later went over to the side of the royalists, was deported to Guiana, fled to London, and took part in a royalist plot against Napoleon in 1804. He was arrested and found strangled in his cell.

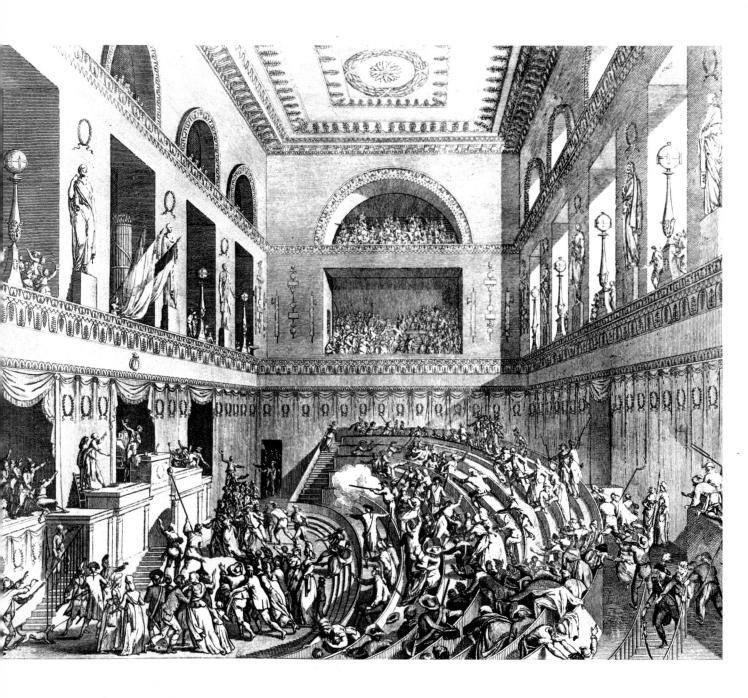

French. At that time the revolutionaries had regarded the powerless and oppressed peoples of Europe as potential allies. The Thermidorians, however, had no intention of urging other peoples to revolt. The peace concluded with Prussia in Basle in 1795 testified to the fact that France's rulers had discarded their old political goal of establishing a bourgeois order in central Europe and were ready to make deals with the absolutist monarchs. The peace treaty drew a demarcation line along the River Main, thereby protecting northern Germany from the war. In the South, France continued to battle

7.4 The uprising on 1 prairial of the Year III (20 May 1795). The sansculottes force their way into the chamber of the Convention. One rebel carries the head of the murdered deputy Jean Feraud on a pike and holds it out towards the President of the Convention, Boissy d'Anglas.

7.5 Republican troops led by General Hoche are victorious over the royalist *émigrés* landed on the peninsula of Quiberon (Brittany) by English ships on 3 thermidor of the Year III (21 July 1795). After the capture of Fort Penthièvre (on the left of the picture), over which a tricolor is already flying, the royalists surrender. 748 captured *émigrés* and rebellious peasants were executed after the victory.

against the Austrians until the signing of the Treaty of Campo-Formio at the end of 1797.

The fear of a resurgence of Jacobin forces or a sansculotte-led uprising at home was the root cause of the Thermidorian Convention's keenness to reach compromises abroad. Within a few weeks of the signing of the Treaty of Basle, the Paris sansculottes rebelled twice – on 1 April and 20 May – against the rule of speculators and war profiteers. These were desperate and hopeless attempts at calling to account profiteers who were growing rich at the expense of the starving and propertyless masses.

The rebels' programme referred to Article 35 of the Jacobin Declaration of Human Rights of 1793, which stated that it was the most sacred right and most urgent duty of the people to revolt if the Government should violate their rights. The sansculottes demanded the dismissal of the Government, the proclamation of the Jacobin Constitution of 1793, the election of a new legislative assembly, and effective measures to combat famine and inflation.

The working classes were, however, unable to force a democratic change of direction on the bourgeoisie, since they lacked a political organization of their own, a recognized leadership, and well thought-out tactics.

The insurrections were cruelly suppressed and thirty-six of the rebels condemned to death. Among these were six members of the Convention who had taken the part of the insurgents. These 'last Montagnards' stabbed themselves before their execution. The Thermidorian Convention, which had released from prison all opponents of the Jacobins, now had 3,000 revolutionaries disarmed, arrested and deprived of their civil rights.

In the light of this retrogressive development, the Royalists considered that the time had come to restore the Bourbon monarchy, but when *émigré* troops supported by the English navy landed on the peninsula of Quiberon (southern Brittany) in July 1795 the

attackers were soon repelled. This success and the signing of a peace treaty with Spain around the same time strengthened the Thermidorian regime, and on 22 August 1795 a new constitution was proclaimed.

The 'Constitution of the Year III' returned the upper middle classes with all due form to the positions of political power which they had been forced to vacate temporarily during Jacobin rule. The right of resistance, which had been anchored firmly in the Declarations of Human Rights of 1789 and 1793, disappeared. A two-part property qualification excluded the working-class masses from having any say in politics. Anyone who paid direct

7.6 The royalist uprising of 13 vendémiaire of the Year IV (5 October 1795). Troops under the command of General Bonaparte respond with volleys of cannon fire and are carrying out a bloodbath on the steps of the Church of Saint Roche.

7.7 General Lazare Hoche. The son of a stableman, he rose to the rank of general during the Revolution, commanded the Mosel army in 1793, and despite being innocent, spent several months in prison after having been denounced by General Pichegru. In 1795 he defeated the corps of *émigrés* which landed at Quiberon and fought the rebels in the Vendée. In 1797 he promoted the establishment of a republic on the German left bank of the Rhine, which would be set up with the help of Jacobins from the Rhineland. He died in Wetzlar at the age of 29.

taxes was known as an 'active citizen', but only those who could prove an income equal to 200 days' wages could become electors. Most of these were big landowners. It was these electors, of whom there were 30,000 throughout France, who elected France's deputies. The watered-down Declaration of Human Rights was coupled to a catalogue of duties. The Constitution declared the separation of powers to be the very basis of good government and divided the existing 750-strong Legislative Assembly into two chambers: the 'Council of Five Hundred' and the 'Council of Ancients'. One third of the members of each of these bodies were to be newly elected every year. The 'Council of Ancients'

appointed a five-man Directory, which in turn appointed ministers. Each year one member of the Directory was to stand down and a new one to be appointed in his stead. By establishing a second chamber and granting the Legislative Assembly the right to order house searches, ban working-class associations, and suspend the freedom of the press, the Thermidorians hoped to put a stop to any attempts to resurrect the Jacobin Government.

In order to prevent the royalists from winning a majority in the new assembly, the Thermidorian Convention stipulated that two-thirds of the new representatives should come from among their own ranks. The royalists, who had hoped to use the new

constitution to restore the monarchy, armed themselves for rebellion and managed to mobilize some 20,000 men. To counter this threat the Convention set up a defence committee under Barras and activated three battalions of the 'Patriots of '89', which consisted in part of Jacobins. When the royalists advanced on the Tuileries on 5 October 1795 (13 vendémiaire of the Year III) the commander of the republican forces, a 26-year-old artillery captain appointed by Barras, by the name of Napoleon Bonaparte, opened fire on the royalists with case-shot, and the rebellion collapsed.

7.8 During the rule of the Directory the extravagantly and fashionably dressed beneficiaries of the Revolution would meet at the 'Galerie de Bois'. In the centre is a spruced-up dandy (*muscadin*) wearing a high necktie, tightly-fitting frock coat with long tails, and soft pointed boots.

Following this victory the Convention called a halt to the White Terror in the provinces and declared a political amnesty which restored freedom to most of the imprisoned revolutionaries. The amnesty did not, however, apply to those who had been banished, unsworn priests, or *émigrés* who had fought against the Revolution, and Billaud-Varenne and Collot d'Herbois were consequently unable to return from Devil's Island. The first five members of the Directory were all 'regicides', men who had voted in the Convention in 1793 for the execution of King Louis XVI: Barras, La Revellière-Lépeaux, Letourneur, Ruebell, and the 'organizer of the Revolution's victory', Carnot, who had also served on Robespierre's 'Great Committee of Public Safety'.

Among those released from prison under the amnesty was the social revolutionary journalist François-Noël Babeuf, who had been incarcerated at the beginning of 1795 for 'incitement to riot'. Babeuf had adopted the name Gracchus, because he, like the two revolutionaries of the ancient world, hoped for a radical change in patterns of ownership. Unlike the Jacobins and the petty bourgeoisie, he did not believe that it was possible to eradicate social conflicts of interest. Using his newspaper *The People's Tribunal* (*Le Tribun du peuple*) as a mouthpiece, he began in October 1795 to advocate the use of force to establish an egalitarian and communist society and to put an end, once and for all, to the hated rule of the bourgeoisie. In his '*Plebeians' Manifesto*', he demanded 'the introduction of communal administration, the abolition of private ownership, the right of the individual to do a job of his own choosing, the establishment of both community storage depots and an administrative authority whose task would be to allocate to each individual the foodstuffs and everything else necessary to meet his needs'. He also called for all land be taken into public ownership and worked co-operatively.

Babeuf believed that every private appropriation of agricultural and industrial property was theft, a criminal act, that the state was the source of all moral and social progress, and that all men had the same natural right to enjoy all goods. What was required was a 'Republic of Equals' based on the community of property, a notion which had its roots in the Enlightenment and in humanitarianism. This would enable man to discover his true nature, eradicate all social dependency, and guarantee social

7.9 Paul Barras (Count) in his official robes as a member of the Directory. Barras, who had voted for the execution of Louis XVI in the Convention and played a part in Robespierre's downfall, was a member of the Directory from 1795 to 1799. Bonaparte was his protégé.

LE TRIBUN DU PEUPLE,

O U

LE DÈFENSEUR

DFS DROITS DE L'HOMME;

EN CONTINUATION

DU JOURNAL DE LA LIBFRTÉ DE LA PRESSE.

Par Gracchus BABEUF.

Le but de la société est le bonheur commun. *Droits de l'homme*, art. Ier.

Du 17 *Vendémiaire*, l'an 3me. de la République.

Avis à la Convention.

Lors'qu'on aime passionnément sa patrie ; lorsqu'on a vu
pendant cinq ans un peuple généreux faire tous les genres
d'efforts et de sacrifices pour la rendre libre ; et lorsque
fixant le résultat on n'apperçoit que *l'Oppression*,......
il est difficile à l'homme courageux qui n'a pas fait en vain

7.11 The social revolutionary and communist François-Noël 'Gracchus' Babeuf defends himself before a tribunal in Vendôme in May 1797.

7.10 The issue of Babeuf's newspaper *The People's Tribune or the Defender of Human Rights* published on 17 vendémiaire of the Year III (8 October 1794). The newspaper's motto was Article 1 of the Declaration of Human Rights which appeared in the Jacobin Constitution of 1793, which itself never came into force. It reads, 'The goal of society is general welfare' ('Le but de la société est le bonheur commun').

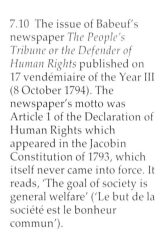

welfare for all, allowing every individual to develop his talents freely.

At the end of March 1796 Babeuf and his friends Buonarroti, Maréchal, Darthé, Lepeletier and Atonelle founded a 'secret directory of public welfare' whose tasks were to organize a popular uprising, establish links with the army and police, and lay in stocks of weapons. This working party of the 'Conspiracy of Equals' was the central cell of a revolutionary communist party. Although several hundred former supporters of Robespierre and Hébert were involved in the conspiracy, the conspirators chose not to initiate the disorientated and disarmed sansculottes, now living in abysmal poverty, into the details of the uprising. Babeuf and his fellow conspirators hoped to seize power and govern by means of a dictatorship until a communist order based on the community of property had

become established. The uprising was planned for 11 May 1796. On 10 May one of the conspirators, Grisel, betrayed the revolutionary plan to Carnot, a member of the Directory, and Babeuf and his supporters were arrested. In February 1797 proceedings were instituted against forty-seven defendants, and judgement was pronounced three months later. Babeuf and Darthé were condemned to death, five of the conspirators were deported and interned in an island fortress, and the others were acquitted. A generation later Buonarroti, who was released from prison in 1806, published his book *Babeuf's Conspiracy for Equality*, which revealed details of Babeuf's conspiratorial methods and communist doctrine. It was a book which greatly influenced the proleterian and revolutionary movements of the nineteenth century.

The Directory transformed France's defensive

7.13 Charles Maurice de Talleyrand-Perigord, the man 'who betrayed seven masters'. Although he was himself a bishop he suggested to the Constituent Assembly in 1789 that it should confiscate the Church's property for the benefit of the nation and swore an oath of allegiance on the Civil Constitution of the Clergy. He was abroad during Jacobin rule, but when he returned in 1797 he became the Directory's Foreign Minister. He helped Napoleon to seize power and remained Foreign Minister until 1809.

7.12 A cartoon mocking the *émigrés* who began to return to France in 1795 as a result of the fact that the royalists had become stronger. The Directory granted only a few *émigrés* the legal right to return. The *émigré* caricatured in the cartoon is returning illegally and risking persecution. Although he is poor and shabby, he has lost none of his arrogant pride.

war, which the Jacobin Committee of Public Safety had waged in order to secure the achievements of the Revolution and won, into a war of aggression. The west bank of the Rhine (with the exception of Mainz) had been under French occupation since the end of 1794, and on 1 October 1795 France annexed Belgium. Since the representatives of the bourgeoisie's economic interests were now participating directly or indirectly in the exercise of power, such expansionist tendencies served primarily to increase the economic strength of the new plutocracy. Heavy reparations were imposed on the conquered regions, and their wealth taken from them in order to fill France's empty state coffers. Part of the booty also found its way into the pockets of the rulers and their aides. There were many in the lower

7.14 The coup on 18 fructidor of the Year V (4 September 1797): General Augereau, who has forced his way into the Tuileries with his troops, arrests the royalist member of the Directory François Barthélémy (with the consent of three of the other members of the Directory, Barras, Reubell, and La Revellière).

ranks of the army who extorted money from the local population. Corrupt army suppliers and representatives lined their own pockets, stole public funds, and swindled the populations of the conquered lands. But although the Directory's utterances on the subject of freedom and equality were chiefly designed to disguise their aggressive aspirations, the occupation of neighbouring countries did also bring benefits for the local populations, since the French industrial and trading classes necessarily had to remove feudal restrictions on movement when they invaded neighbouring countries in order to create a market for the goods produced by their own profit-inspired social order. As had been the case in France itself, serfdom, statute-labour and tithes were abolished in Belgium and the

7.15 Napoleon Bonaparte as a young artillery officer.

7.16 Victory over the Austrians on the bridge at Arcola (15 November 1796). This battle took place during the Italian campaign and is considered one of Bonaparte's legendary acts of heroism. A tattered French standard in his hand, the young general charges towards the enemy at the head of his men.

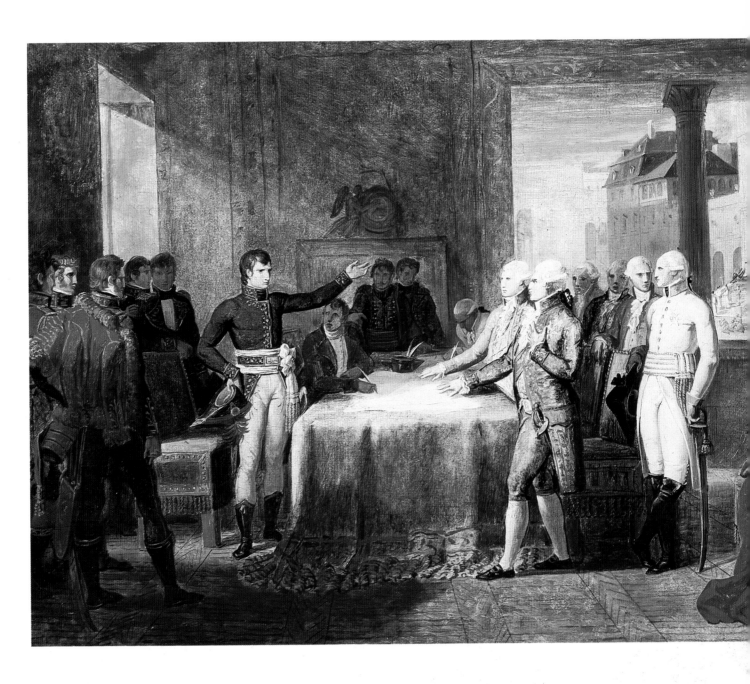

7.17 The preliminary peace negotiated at Leoben on 18 April 1797. Bonaparte, in a high-handedly triumphant pose, dictates his conditions to the Austrian negotiators General Meerveldt and the Earl of Gallo.

Rhineland without compensation, and land owned by the Church was sold. Freedom of trade was introduced, and the aristocratic legal system replaced by courts of assize and an independent system of free justice. Despite the corruption and mismanagement of the Directory, these anti-feudal reforms led to a considerable improvement in the lot of the conquered populations.

In February 1796 the *assignats* fell to a quarter per cent of their nominal value. The Directory abolished this worthless paper money and tried in vain to avert a financial catastrophe by means of compulsory loans and the introduction of a new brand of paper money known as *'mandats territoriaux'*.

The war of aggression begun in March 1796 by the Directory had two major purposes: firstly to solve France's economic crisis by exploiting its neighbouring countries and secondly to defeat the Habsburg Empire. The decision to solve the domestic cri-

sis by means of military aggression meant that the army began to maintain a constant presence in all spheres of public life, and that the Directory became increasingly dependent on victorious generals. Two armies under the command of Generals Jourdan and Moreau advanced into Germany without much success. Bonaparte, who had recently married a former mistress of Barras and widow of an executed general, Josephine Beauharnais, was given command of the Italian army. In his very first order he openly invited his soldiers to plunder 'the fertile plains of Italy'. His troops conquered Piedmont, Lombardy, Tuscany, Parma and Modena, and at the end of 1796, with the co-operation of Italian Jacobins, he set up the 'Cispadane Republic'. The huge war reparations which he imposed upon the conquered provinces were chiefly used to feather his own nest, although that part which had been paid in gold and silver was sent to Paris, where the booty helped to alleviate France's financial difficulties.

7.18 The Treaty of Campo Formio (near Udine) signed by France and the Habsburg Empire on 17 October 1797. Above, in the middle window are Napoleon (right) and the Austrian Foreign Minister Cobenzl. Two baroque angels trumpet *Laus Deo* – God be praised.

When Bonaparte's troops conquered the important Austrian stronghold at Mantua in February 1797 after a siege lasting several months, he signed the Treaty of Tolentino with the Pope and turned north. Within a few weeks his army had pushed into Styria, and Emperor Franz II's government was forced to conclude a preliminary peace in Leoben in order to prevent Vienna from coming under occupation.

The French elections in April 1797 strengthened the hand of monarchist right-wingers. One of their number was the new member of the Directory Barthélémy, who replaced the outgoing Letourneur. On the insistence of Barras, who wanted to reach an agreement with England, Talleyrand, a former deputy in the Constituent Assembly and a shrewd and experienced politician who had returned from exile in America, was appointed Foreign Minister. As a result of the subversive activities of English and Austrian agents, who had gained the support of

7.19 The triumphant French army under the command of General Berthier enters Rome on 27 pluviose of the Year VI (15 February 1798). The Roman Republic was proclaimed on this very day, and five days later the pope was deported to Siena.

7.20 Bonaparte addresses the army before the Battle of the Pyramids on 21 July 1798: 'Remember that from those monuments yonder forty centuries look down upon you!'

General Pichegru, the threat of a royalist revolution grew. Three members of the Directory (Barras, Reubell, and La Revellière) decided to organize a coup. Both the commander of the Rhine army (Hoche), and Bonaparte made troops available for the purposes of eliminating counter-revolutionary elements.

The *coup d'état* of 18 fructidor of the Year V (4 September 1797) passed off without bloodshed. Barthélemy and Pichegru were arrested, and Carnot, who had not wished to take part in a coup against the legally constituted parliament, escaped abroad. April's election results were declared null and void, and 177 deputies lost their seats. Since political clubs were once again permitted, neo-Jacobin 'constitutional circles' now sprang up in Paris, in certain

7.21 After his victory over the armies of the Mameluke Bonaparte rides into Cairo.

provincial towns such as Metz and Toulouse, and in the annexed Rhineland. They attempted to preserve their radical democratic heritage, condemned the corruption and tyranny of civil servants, called for the citizen to be consulted more on matters of public concern, and drafted programmes of social and politico-educational reform.

Although the coup of 18 fructidor saved the republican regime, it also meant that attempts to find a constitutional basis for the Directory had failed. The manipulation of election results became a fact of life for the 'lawyers' government' and so too did reliance on the army, without whose help it would have been impossible to thwart a series of attempted coups.

Under the Treaty of Campo-Formio (17 October 1797) Austria ceded Belgium and Lombardy to France. In return she received the Venetian Republic, which Bonaparte had conquered during the summer of 1797. In addition, Austria granted recognition to the three French satellite states: the Batavian, Ligurian, and Cisalpine Republics (the latter having developed out of an extension of the Cispadane Republic and a few provinces ceded by the Papal State). The final delimitation of the Rhine border and the reorganization of territorial arrangements on the east bank of the Rhine were left to a congress which convened in Rastatt at the end of 1797. The annexation of the Rhineland, which was divided into departments, and France's intervention in German affairs signified the beginning of the end for the thousand-year-old 'Holy Roman Empire of the German Nation'. During the Rastatt Congress France's diplomats pursued a policy of trading people and exchanging lands with the same enthusiasm as did the absolutist powers and ignored the principle of a nation's right to self-determination.

Until its inglorious end the Directory manoeuvred between royalism and Jacobinism. The democratic clubs which sprang up following the coup of 18 fructidor were stamped out again in May 1798. Despite a compulsory loan and reform of the taxation system the Government was unable to balance the budget, for the corruption of the civil service and the increasing influence exerted by speculators and fraudulent army suppliers frustrated every attempt to solve the economic crisis.

The easiest solution was for France to exploit its satellite states. The Directory did not regard the democratic patriots in such states as equal partners, but merely as instruments of an expansionist foreign policy. At the beginning of 1798 French troops marched into Switzerland. The Directory used the dissatisfaction of the rural population in the patrician, oligarchic Cantons of the confederation to transform Switzerland, with the help of bourgeois admirers of the Revolution, into the 'Helvetic Republic'. The bulging state coffers were taken from Bern to Paris in order to finance Bonaparte's Egyptian expedition. A French army also occupied the Papal State, which was renamed the 'Roman Republic', and Pope Pius VI was taken to Siena and later Valence, where he died.

After the Treaty of Campo-Formio England was the only country still at war with France. Since a landing in England was impracticable, Bonaparte announced his willingness to sail to Egypt at the

7.22 The murder of French envoys Raberjot and Bonnier on their departure from the Rastatt Congress on 9 floréal of the Year VII (28 April 1799).

7.23 The coup on 30 prairial of the Year VII (18 June 1799), following which two members of the Directory were changed. The coup resulted in a strengthening of the Left in the Council of Five Hundred.

head of an expedition designed to shake England's position of strength in the Mediterranean and India. France's merchant population, which was keen to trade in the Levant, hoped to transform Egypt into a valuable colony. The Directory provided money, ships and soldiers for the venture, since it recognized a threat to its own position of power in the popularity of the victorious general and was glad to be rid of him.

In May 1798 the expedition set sail with 350 ships and 30,000 men, conquered Malta, and landed in Egypt, where Bonaparte's army defeated the Mameluke armies in the Battle of the Pyramids. A few days later Britain's Admiral Nelson marooned the expeditionary force by destroying the French fleet. The Egyptian campaign signified a turning point in the history of the French Revolution: it no longer had anything to do with the national interest, but was much more an imperialist adventure. Despite its policy of plunder, France had liberated the populations of the annexed regions and its European satellite states from many feudal ills, but in Egypt Bonaparte behaved like a cruel conqueror and military dictator with no intention of introducing any social reform at all. After he had crushed an uprising

in Cairo with merciless force, he set off for Palestine at the head of his army. From there he planned to forge ahead to Constantinople via Syria and Asia Minor, but the campaign was halted outside the stronghold at Akko. Throughout the two-month siege the English Admiral Sidney Smith supplied the stronghold (by sea) with weapons and food, and Napoleon was unable to capture it. In May 1799 the French army, decimated by war losses and sickness, returned to Egypt.

The Egyptian campaign led to the formation of a new alliance against France. It was financed by England, and its members included Turkey, Russia, Austria, and several other states. On 12 March 1799, after the Austrians had granted Russian troops the right of passage through the country, the Directory declared war on Russia. An army commanded by the tsarist General Suvorov soon found its way to Italy and scored several victories over French troops. The Rastatt Congress broke up without achieving a settlement, and two French delegates were murdered by Austrian hussars as they departed.

In the course of a few short months the fruits of Napoleon's victories had been lost; the Italian satellite republics disappeared. The success of this new

Victoire d'Aboukir en Egypte, du 7 thér. an 7

7.24 The Battle of Abukir (in the Nile Delta, on the Egyptian coast) between the Turkish army under the command of Mustafa and French expeditionary troops led by Bonaparte, 25 July 1798. The Turkish army of 15,000 men was almost completely destroyed.

counter-revolutionary crusade forced France back onto the defensive. Having been unable to hold France's military conquests, to permanently anchor its republican institutions, to restore soundness to the economy, or to consolidate changes in ownership, the Directorial Government was on the verge of political bankruptcy. In April 1799 Sieyès, who even at the beginning of the Revolution had represented the interests of the upper middle classes, was elected to the Directory and began to suggest that the Constitution of the Year III be revised. The coup on 30 prairial of the Year VII (18 June 1799) brought about a new shift to the left, with both Councils imposing a compulsory loan of a hundred million *livres* on the wealthy. The Paris Jacobin Club re-

recognized that France needed a 'strong man' was the former terrorist Fouché, now the Minister of Police. In the middle of August he had the Paris Jacobin Club closed down again.

These three former priests, Sieyès, Talleyrand and Fouché undertook the task of finding a general who was covered in glory, capable, and to whom they could hand over political power. In this way they hoped to ensure that the economic command post remained all the more firmly in bourgeois hands. The first general to whom Sieyès turned was General Joubert. He declared himself willing but was ruled out when he fell on 15 August in the Battle of Novi against Suvorov. Bernadotte was out of the question since he had no wish to destroy the Republic, and Moreau hesitated and asked for time to think.

In the meantime news had filtered through to Napoleon in Egypt that as a result of France's vari-

7.24 The coup on 18 and 19 brumaire of the Year VIII (9 and 10 November 1799). Furious deputies from the Council of Five Hundred surround Bonaparte in a hall at the Château of Saint Cloud. They threaten to ostracize him because he wants to dissolve the two elected Councils and rescind the Constitution of the Year III. The President of the Council of Five Hundred, Lucien Bonaparte, is standing on the podium and attempting (successfully) to remove his brother from the room.

opened and demanded both that offices of state should be filled by genuine republicans and that speculators and royalists should be brought to trial. On 14 July 1799, the tenth anniversary of the storming of the Bastille, General Jourdan, victor at the Battles of Wattignies and Fleurus, who was a member of the Council of Five Hundred, proposed a toast to 'the resurrection of the pikes'. The pikes were the lower ranks, and by proposing such a toast Jourdan made it clear that the time had come for a new popular uprising. Sieyès came to the conclusion that only a military dictatorship could save France from the permanent threat posed by left-wing and right-wing rebels. Talleyrand, who left the sinking ship of the Directory and returned to his post as Foreign Minister, shared this view. The third politician who

7.25 A short time later: Bonaparte's grenadiers storm into the hall and use their bayonets to expel the deputies, who flee and jump out of the window.

ous defeats confusion and disruption was rampant at home. The Directory, it was said, was panic-stricken and hated by the people. He wasted no time in making his decision. He handed over supreme command of the expeditionary army to General Kleber and sailed from Egypt with the firm intention of seizing power. On 8 October he reached the French coast and eight days later he was in Paris. His charismatic personality aroused enthusiasm, and most people expected that the conqueror of Italy and Egypt would soon put an end to the corrupt regime and restore peace, calm and order. Talleyrand acquainted Bonaparte with Sieyès' plan to replace the Directory with a provisional executive of three consuls who could then draft a new constitution. Sieyès, who underestimated Bonaparte, hoped to be able to use the 30-year old general as a willing tool and control the fortunes of the nation himself. Fouché offered Bonaparte his services as Minister of Police.

Sieyès informed one of the members of the Directory, Roger Ducos, of his plan to stage a coup which would be organized in such a way as to retain a semblance of legality and make it appear as if the two Councils had appointed Bonaparte to his new position of power. On 18 brumaire of the Year VIII (9 November 1799) Bonaparte notified the officers of the Paris garrison that they should put their troops on the alert in order to 'save the Republic'. His friend spread rumours of a terrorist plot and moved in the Council of Ancients that Bonaparte should be named as commander of the troops stationed in Paris. They also moved that the sittings of the two Councils should be moved to St. Cloud, a small town not far from the capital, for although the sans-culottes' revolutionary verve had been extinguished, the conspirators feared that the dissolution of the two Councils might cause popular revolt.

When, on the next day, several deputies in the Council of Five Hundred protested against the breach of the Constitution and tried to offer resistance, grenadiers forced their way into the chamber and brought the obstreperous deputies to their senses with bayonets. On the evening of 10 November the Council of Ancients dismissed the Directory, and a three-man Consulate took its place. The coup of 18 brumaire, which reduced the legislative bodies to impotent and submissive instru-

ments of the executive and transferred all their power to the authoritarian government, stifled the spirit of the Revolution once and for all. The military despotism against which Robespierre had warned in his last speech could now take its hold.

On 13 December 1799 the provisional government proclaimed the hastily drafted Constitution of the Year VIII, which no longer contained any Declaration of Human Rights. As head of the state the all-powerful First Consul, Bonaparte, would exercise almost unlimited powers, appointing all ministers and all members of the Council of State, initiating all laws, and maintaining control over the budget. Bonaparte ditched Sieyès and Roger Ducos and named as Second and Third Consuls men whose areas of expertise were law and administration: Cambacérès and Lebrun. They were to have no political authority, only advisory roles. The Constitution provided for the establishment of three chambers (the Senate, the Tribunate, and the Legislative Body), but these imposing structures were to serve merely as a façade of legitimacy. In a communiqué accompanying the proclamation of the Constitution, Bonaparte announced laconically and with military conciseness:

'Citizens, the Revolution has now attained the goals which it set itself. It is over.'

7.26 On the evening of 10 November 1799, in one of the badly lit halls in the Château of Saint Cloud, the Council of Ancients gives its assent to a law transferring all powers exercised by the Republic to the Consuls Bonaparte, Sieyès and Roger Ducos.

Napoleon Bonaparte as Heir and Destroyer of the Revolution

Napoleon Bonaparte, who had set himself up as the ruler of France on 18 brumaire of the Year VIII, was as obsessed with legalistic scruples as with the internationalist dream of establishing an empire of nations founded on the principles of liberty, fraternity and equality. He ruled over France more absolutely than any of the previous kings had been able to do and regarded the state as his own personal property. He mocked the notions of popular sovereignty and parliamentarianism as the idle chit-chat of ideologues, and removed the population's hard-won revolutionary right to participate in the formulation of political objectives by replacing the principle of free elections with a system of referenda directed from above. In doing so, he showed the dictators of future generations how it was possible to distort the concept of democracy.

Although this usurper discarded those parts of the Revolution's intellectual armoury for which he could find no use, it has to be said that the form of government which he cultivated was nevertheless ideologically and politically rooted in

8.1 On 20 May 1800 the French army crosses the snow-fields of the Great St. Bernard Pass on its way to Italy. In the foreground there are soldiers dragging a gun-barrel which has been placed in a hollowed-out tree trunk.

the Revolution. Bonapartism borrowed several important concepts from Jacobinism, but reinterpreted them to suit the requirements of autocracy: national glory (*gloire nationale*), the revolutionary proprietary guarantee (*garantie révolutionnaire*), and the concentration of power (*principe d'autorité*).

To a large extent Napoleon depended on the army for the maintenance of his power, since it consisted chiefly of the now legally equal and personally free sons of the people. Having liberated France from the burdens of feudalism, the Jacobins had created this people's army in order to defend the country against its enemies. Under Napoleon it became an instrument of conquest. The Jacobins had sought to inspire every single warrior, by constantly reminding him that he was a member of the 'great nation' which had thrown off the joke of despotism by its own efforts. But whilst Jacobin patriotism linked national self-emancipation with a belief in democracy, Napoleonic patriotism was based on the

8.2 The Battle of Marengo (in Lombardy), during which troops under command of Napoleon were victorious over the Austrians led by Melas (14 June 1800).

8.3 Jacques-Louis David's idealized painting of Bonaparte the hero on the St. Bernard Pass. Written in the ground are the names of two other celebrated men who had crossed the Alps with their armies before him: Hannibal and Charlemagne.

notion that France's fame as a warrior nation, acquired through many magnificent victories, gave this 'great nation' the right both to rule the entire continent of Europe as a hegemonic power and to subjugate other peoples. Thus the concept of '*gloire nationale*' meant giving France's political and economic interests precedence over the needs of other countries. Since France's new social order, motivated as it was by performance and profit, found its neighbouring countries' class-based privileges irksome and superfluous, Napoleon introduced bourgeois reform wherever his army planted its victorious standard and whenever he imposed his will on other peoples and states. Although he had destroyed and ended the Revolution within France itself, he now extended its legacy beyond the borders of France and thus became the liberator as

8.4 A royalist assassination-attempt in the rue Saint-Nicaise on the evening of 24 December 1800: an explosive device exploded shortly after a carriage taking the First Consul from the Tuileries to the opera had passed. The attack left 22 dead and 56 injured, but Bonaparte was unhurt.

8.5 Joseph Fouché. During Jacobin rule this former monk gained notoriety as a result of his bloody terrorist outrages in Lyon. In 1799 he became the Minister of Police, helped to plan Bonaparte's coup, and held his post until 1810. He was also Minister of the Interior for a long time. He built up an elaborate network of agents and spies and played all political groupings off against each other.

Overleaf:
8.6 The Place de la Révolution, where the guillotine had stood, was renamed the Place de la Concorde. A market and various folk festivals were held there.

well as the oppressor of the peoples of Europe.

The proprietary guarantee anchored in Article 94 of the Constitution of the Year VIII confirmed that the changes in ownership which the Revolution had brought about were no longer reversible. Property which had once belonged to the Crown, emigrant aristocrats, and the Church, and which had been acquired by the bourgeoisie and the peasantry during the Revolution, would remain in the hands of its new owners. Essentially these changes in ownership had been implemented during Jacobin rule. By guaranteeing the sanctity and inviolability of ownership Napoleon was able to commit all of those who had materially benefited from the Revolution to his rule, on the grounds that his fall from power and the return of the Bourbons would pose a threat that such property might be re-expropriated.

The 'principe d'autorité', the basic principle by which all legislative and executive powers were to be concentrated in the person of the autocrat, was a complete negation of the revolutionary concepts of the separation of powers and popular sovereignty, and deprived the population of every opportunity to express its political views. Napoleon's system of prefectures created for the dictator a loyal administrative and legal bureaucracy which exercised wide powers even at the lower levels. Each prefect represented the 'principe d'autorité' within his own administrative unit. He was responsible for the administration of the law in his own particular department and regularly reported the political mood of the local population to headquarters in Paris. In this way Bonaparte was able to perfect the centralist tendencies of France's old absolutist

8.7 General Jean Victor Moreau, under whose command French troops scored victory over the Austrians at Hohenlinden on 3 December 1800. The battle decided the war of the second coalition in favour of France. Moreau, whose popularity Napoleon feared, was innocently dragged into a royalist plot involving Cadoudal and Pichegru. Napoleon had him deported to North America. He returned in 1813, entered the service of the Russians, and fell in the Battle of Dresden.

system. It would be a mistake, however, to equate Napoleon with the kings of the old regime, even though he consistently and systematically developed an absolutist model of the state and was consequently known as the last enlightened despot. Whereas the kings of the old regime had depended on the feudal, class-based social hierarchy handed down from the Middle Ages, with all its privileges and special customs, this new autocrat's subjects were equal in the eyes of the law. Social status was determined not by immutable factors such as birth and descent, but by the dynamic principle of ownership. As an all-powerful autocrat, Napoleon's political interests lay in consolidating France's hegemony. Luckily, the economic interests of the upper middle classes, the chief beneficiaries of the Revolution, which lay in developing France's trade and industry and making it more efficient, were entirely compatible with this. Thus the 'principe d'autorité' fitted in nicely with the wishes of those who had helped this brilliant upstart into the saddle.

After his rise to power the usurper felt the need to prove himself in many fields; as a general and diplo-mat, as an economist, and as a reformer and law-giver. Consequently, he set himself several tasks: to smash the alliance of the enemy powers with a series of military defeats and force them to recognize France's hegemony in central Europe; to extinguish the royalist fires being fanned by the English in the Vendée and Normandy; to silence the remnants of France's democratic opposition; to straighten out the national budget, restore economic soundness to the currency, and stimulate competition in the economy; to make peace with the papal Court; and to permanently secure and legally codify the bourgeoisie's social and political achievements.

During his five years as consul, Napoleon Bonaparte successfully accomplished all these tasks.

Immediately following the proclamation of the Constitution of the Year VIII, which came into force on Christmas Day 1799, Napoleon began to organize his dictatorship. There was no time to lose, for in the spring he was due to set off on a crucial campaign against the Austrians. Firstly, he had the Constitution legitimized by a plebiscite. Out of seven million citizens who were entitled to vote, four million abstained, something over three million voted for

8.8 The bourgeoisie, which had become rich through the Revolution, and the dignitaries of the Napoleonic regime regularly came together in the salons and at dinner parties.

the Constitution, and 1,562 voted against. The chief purpose of Napoleon's system of referenda, which was directed from above and which represented an odd mixture of pseudo-democracy and authority, was to depoliticize the masses. The simultaneous abolition of press freedom was intended to do the same job: in January 1800, sixty of France's seventy-three political newspapers were banned. In the course of the next few years a further nine ceased publication, and the four newspapers which remained in existence after 1802 refrained from all criticism of government policy and had a joint daily circulation of scarcely 10,000. The minister in charge of censorship was Fouché. In fact, his Ministry of Police exercised wide powers; the police force was

8.9 Jacques-Louis David's portrait of the Benedictine monk Barnaba Count Chiaramonti, who was elected as Pope Pius VII in March 1800.

8.10 Signing of the concordat between France and the papal Court on 15 July 1801. The concordat re-established relations between the two parties. From left to right: Joseph Bonaparte, who is handing his brother the quill; behind Napoleon, the Councillor of State Jean Etienne Portalis, who conducted the negotiations for the concordat; wearing the black soutane, the pope's representative, Cardinal Consalvi; on the extreme right, Emmanuel Cretet, the governor of the Bank of France.

omnipresent, and arbitrary arrests commonplace. Besides being responsible for the administration of the regular police force, Fouché also created a political secret service which deployed an army of agents and stool-pigeons to uncover plots being hatched by royalists and Jacobins. As a deputy in the Convention the Minister of Police had voted in favour of the king's execution and had also committed terrorist outrages in Lyon. He now had an interest in consolidating Bonaparte's dictatorship, for he feared the revenge of the Bourbons if they were ever to be restored to the French Throne.

In January 1800 the banking system was reorga- nized and the *livre* replaced by the *franc*. It was hoped that reorganization would encourage an upturn in the economy and at the same time act as a weapon against the dominance of the English economy. The newly-founded Bank of France was a limited company with a monopoly on the issuing of bank notes. In addition, it managed the national debt and arranged loans to finance the war. Napoleon's economic and fiscal policies were, in fact, all part of his efforts to strengthen France's modern industrial capitalist system and thereby commit the bourgeoisie materially and ideologically to his regime. The nation's main sources of income were

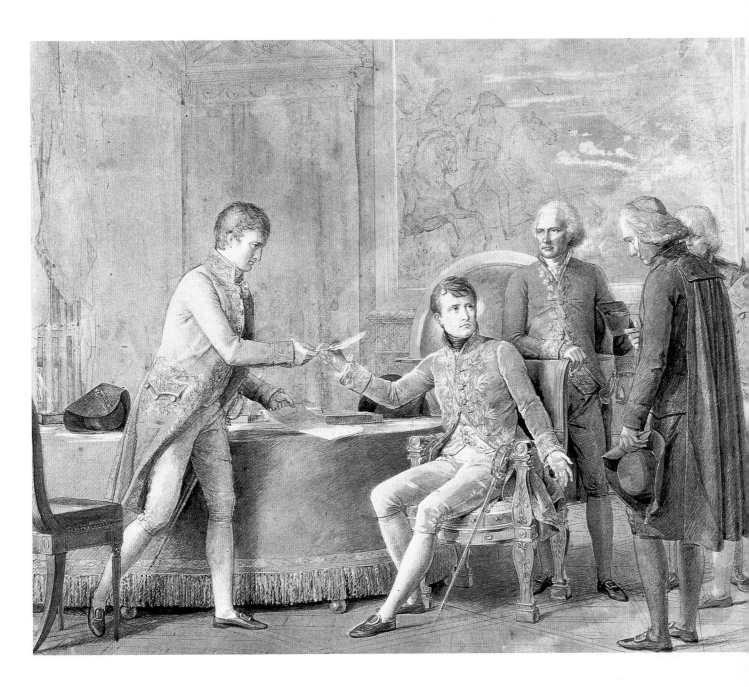

booty and reparations from the territories which it had conquered, but taxes also played a major part. These were mainly indirect and as such were looked upon favourably by the propertied classes. French production was safeguarded by a protectionist system of import tariffs.

Whereas the businessman's profits suffered no damage as a result of state interference, wage-earners were deprived of every opportunity to conduct a collective struggle against their exploitation. Whenever disputes arose over working conditions or wage levels the courts would only recognize depositions submitted by the employer, and the

ban on trade unions and other such organizations, which had been in force since 1791, was tightened by the introduction of a workman's pass which all new workers had to produce when taken on and which contained information about the worker's training, previous employment and, where relevant, prior convictions and political views. The proletariat was, in fact, a disenfranchised victim of police repression and entrepreneurial whim.

Napoleon knew that his ability to consolidate his regime depended on military success. In place of the terrorist outrages which had taken place on French soil during the Revolution, an integral part of the

8.12 Napoleon's triumph is celebrated in classical style on the victory carriage following the signing of the Treaty of Amiens with England in March 1802.

8.11 The three Consuls: Napoleon Bonaparte in the centre, on the left Jean-Jacques Cambacérès, and on the right Charles-François Lebrun. Below: Barthélémy hands Bonaparte a document naming him as a Consul for life (11 May 1802).

Napoleonic *modus operandi* was the perpetration of war outrages against other peoples. In May 1800 Napoleon set off with his army to northern Italy. Suvorov had ejected the French from this region in the previous year, and following Russia's retirement from the war the Austrian army under the command of General Mela had replaced his troops. Napoleon's unexpected crossing of the Alps via the St. Bernard Pass enabled him to surprise the enemy. Indeed, his victory at the Battle of Marengo (in Lombardy) on 14 June 1800 was crucial for the continuation of his rule. Had he lost, the English would undoubtedly have helped to restore the Bourbons to the French Throne. The war dragged on for several more months. Only after General Moreau had crushed the Austrians at Hohenlinden in Bavaria at the end of 1800 was Emperor Franz II willing to make peace.

The Treaty of Lunéville (9 February 1801) reaffirmed the agreements reached in the Treaty of Campo-Formio four years previously, namely that

France should retain its supremacy in Italy and that the Rhineland should remain annexed to France. The death knell had finally sounded for the thousand-year-old and increasingly decrepit Holy Roman Empire of the German Nation. Two years later the Regensburg Deputation of the German Estates sanctioned the secularization of the clergy and the mediatization of the princes temporal of the Empire. By ridding Germany of its archaic conditions, the heir of the Revolution was acting in the interests of social and political progress.

France's victory in the war of the second coalition enabled Napoleon to dismantle opposition at home. He attempted to bring about a reconciliation between his regime and aristocratic opponents of the Revolution and in October 1800 ordered the names of around 50,000 emigrant supporters of the Bourbons to be struck from the list of *émigrés*. However, the pretender to the Crown – the brother of the

8.13 The execution of the Duke of Enghien in the moat at the Château of Vincennes on the night of 20–21 March 1804. The duke, who had allegedly been involved in Cadoudal's royalist plot to murder Napoleon, was kidnapped from near Baden, and condemned to death by a war-court. He refused to be blindfolded before the shooting.

8.14 The trial of Georges Cadoudal, the leader of the Breton conspirators (Chouans), and 19 other royalists who had attempted to remove Napoleon and restore the Bourbon dynasty. They were sentenced to death on 9 June 1804, but Napoleon pardoned eight of them.

executed king – who requested permission to return to France, received a negative response. When royalist conspirators sought to dispose of the First Consul by means of an explosive device on 25 December 1800, Napoleon claimed that this attempt on his life had been perpetrated by Jacobins. Although Fouché had arrested the would-be assassins and was able to furnish evidence to the effect that the left-wing opposition had not been involved in the attempted murder, Napoleon ordered 130 actual and alleged Jacobins to be deported to Devil's Island in Guiana and to the Seychelles in the Indian Ocean, among them several former deputies from the Council of Five Hundred who had resisted his coup. In the spring of 1801 the English Prime Minister, Pitt, who had organized and financed the military alliance against France, fell from power. His successor, Addington, accepted Napoleon's offer of peace in the hope that England could reduce its huge national debt by exporting English industrial goods and groceries to France's sphere of influence. Negotiations dragged on for a year. In the Treaty of Amiens, signed at the end of March 1802, England agreed to withdraw its troops from Mediterranean bases in Malta, Minorca and Elba, whereas Napoleon adamantly refused to give up any territory still in French hands. The two great powers never really reached a fair settlement. Since France never opened its market up to English products, it soon became clear that the Treaty was nothing more than an armistice and that the resumption of war was simply a question of time.

For a few months it appeared that the powers of Europe would all recognize France's new position as a hegemony; the guns were silent for the first time in ten years. Napoleon was now at the peak of his popularity, and his term of office was extended by the Senate for the duration of his life. In the plebiscite to ratify this change in the Constitution over 3,500,000 voted for and 8,374 against the move. Those *émigrés* willing to swear an oath of allegiance were granted the right to return home, and some 140,000 of them did so. Only a few thousand were excluded from the amnesty. Many returning aristocrats were appointed to high-ranking offices of state and were even given back a proportion of any property which had once belonged to them and which had not been sold.

Just as Napoleon's reconciliation with the counter-revolutionaries had strengthened support for restoration and repressed notions of democracy, so the Concordat negotiated between France and the papal Court and proclaimed in April 1802 gave the Church the opportunity to exert more influence over the people of France. Napoleon had an interest in this, for although he was religiously indifferent himself, he recognized the role of religion as a stabilizing factor within the social order. 'Without fear of eternal damnation', he said, 'the poor would descend upon the rich and massacre them.'

The Concordat ended the battle between Church and state which had been raging since 1790. The French state recognized Catholicism as 'the religion of the majority of the French people' (though not as the official state religion), and in return the Pope relinquished all claims to the property which had been expropriated from the Church during the Revolution. He also recognized the establishment of registries empowered to record civil weddings and divorces, as well as the transfer of responsibility for recording births, deaths and marriages to the civil domain. Archbishops and bishops were to be appointed by Napoleon and only then consecrated by the Pope and raised to their new rank. The issue of papal bulls and other Church communiqués was to require permission from the state. In return, the state pledged to pay the salaries of the priests and to maintain the churches. The restrictions placed on the practice of the Catholic faith were lifted, and the celebration of the Sabbath and Christian festivals once again permitted. Numerous unsworn priests returned from exile, others were freed from prison. The revolutionary calendar would remain in use until 1 January 1806.

The compromise between revolution and restoration which the Concordat represented was also discernible in the Civil Code ('*Code Civil des Français*', later the '*Code Napoleon*') issued in March 1804. The code was the crowning glory of Napoleon's programme of reform and soon became the keystone of the legal systems both in France and in the countries conquered by the French. It was drafted by a board

8.15 Napoleon in his coronation robes, with the victor's laurels on his head.

of legal experts and thoroughly debated in the Council of State (*Conseil d'État*), an institution which comprised fifty talented and experienced lawyers selected and appointed by Napoleon and which was responsible for preparing decrees and legal text. The First Consul often took part in its sittings.

The Civil Code codified all of the secular and private-sector laws which had been enacted during the Revolution. It licked the bourgeoisie's victory over the old privileged order into legal shape and worked on the assumption that the bourgeois right to ownership was a natural law, the free-play, security and inviolability of which had to be protected if it was to be impervious to attack from both feudal and proletarian forces. The free choice of an occupation, freedom of movement and contract, and religious freedom were granted the status of legally sanctioned regulations. In the Napoleonic Code equality was understood to mean equal access to those civil rights guaranteed by law, but not equality of socio-economic conditions. The blacks in the French colonies, where slavery was reintroduced in 1802, were not even equal in the eyes of the law. Nor did the Civil Code commit the state to pay benefits of any kind to invalids, the unemployed, or patriots who had fallen on hard times. The family law was conservative, with a husband having the undisputed right to dispose of his wife's property as he saw fit, and a wife needing her husband's permission before she could transact business of any kind. Illegitimate children were at a great disadvantage when it came to claiming inheritances.

During 1802 it became clear that for Napoleon peace was merely a continuation of war by other means, since he demanded complete political and economic freedom of action. When English industrialists and merchants found not only the French but also the Dutch and Italian markets closed to them, even after the Treaty of Amiens had been signed, England's statesmen were unable to accept the situation any longer. When France annexed Piedmont and occupied Switzerland, and Napoleon brusquely rejected the English ambassador's interpellation, the London Government feared that the French dictator might be planniing to use his dominant position on the Continent to attack England. In May 1803 England declared war.

Whilst Napoleon began to prepare for his invasion of the British Isles by establishing an army camp on the coast near Boulogne, his enemies in London were concocting a violent plan to finish him off. In the war of the first coalition the English had attempted to topple the French Government by providing military and financial assistance to the rebels in the Vendée and the royalist Chouans in Brittany. The leader of the Chouans, Georges Cadoudal, who had fled to England, now announced that he was willing to kidnap and murder Napoleon. He landed in France in August 1803, hurried to Paris, and took refuge with people of like mind. One of the conspirators was General Pichegru. Having gone over to the royalists in 1797, he had been banished to Devil's Island, but had escaped. He attempted to persuade General Moreau to join the conspiracy. Moreau, who as the victor of the Battle of Hohenlinden enjoyed a good reputation, was a central figure in the republican opposition, for he rejected both the suppression of the freedom of speech and the restorative tendencies of the Consular regime. Although unprepared to lift a finger to help the royalists, he did not betray them and thereby became an ally, since they stood to gain from a successful assassination attempt.

In February and March 1804, having been informed by his agents of the conspirators' preparations, Fouché ordered the arrest of Pichegru, Cadoudal and more than forty others, including Moreau. His informers reported that one of the Bourbon princes was standing by to seize power. On the basis of some vague pointers the Duke of Enghien, who lived in Ettenheim near Baden, not far from the French border, and was a descendant of an offshoot of the French dynasty, came under suspicion. Fouché and Talleyrand advised Napoleon to have him kidnapped. On 20 March mounted French gendarmes raided Baden, arrested the duke, took him to Paris, and handed him over to a military court which then met during the night. He was accused of having been in the pay of the English and carrying arms against France and condemned to death as a traitor. At daybreak on 21 March he was shot in the moat of the fortress at Vincennes.

By executing a prince of royal blood Napoleon, who had been planning to establish a dynasty of his own ever since his appointment for life to the post of First Consul, illustrated his intention never to allow the Bourbons to return to power. The failure

8.16 Empress Josephine in
her coronation robes.

of the royalist plot was not the cause but rather an
excuse for transforming his position as consul into
that of hereditary emperor. Those who were bene-
fiting from Napoleon's authoritarian regime and
who were profiting from the codification of the
'revolutionary guarantee', the upturn in the economy, and France's hegemony in Europe,
demanded that Napoleon's rule be stabilized once
and for all.

    On 18 May 1804 the Senate voted to 'entrust the
government of the Republic to an emperor' and to
offer this office to the First Consul, who henceforth
became known as Napoleon I. Whilst the upstarts
from the Senate were paying homage to their new
imperial ruler, the royalist conspirators were standing trial. Pichegru had already been found strangled
in his cell at the beginning of April, and there was
some doubt as to whether he had committed suicide
or had been murdered at Napoleon's behest. At his

Overleaf:
8.17 Napoleon is crowned
'Emperor of the French' in
the Cathedral of Nôtre Dame
on 2 December 1804. Painting
by Jacques-Louis David.
Napoleon is crowning
himself. Pope Pius VII is
seated behind him. Before
him kneels the Empress
Josephine. In the centre of
the picture, on the large
throne, is Napoleon's mother
Laetitia, who in actual fact
was not present at the
coronation.

trial Moreau proudly confessed to being one of those *citoyens* who had always remained true to the Revolution's quest for liberation. The judges were unable to prove any involvement in the royalist plot and intended to acquit him, but when Napoleon learned of this he intervened. He was determined to rid himself of this potentially dangerous rival. He exerted so much pressure on the judges that they altered their verdicts and sentenced Moreau to two years imprisonment. Fouché advised Napoleon to banish the irksome fighter for freedom, and Moreau was duly despatched to the United States. Cadoudal and eleven of his fellow conspirators mounted the scaffold at the end of June 1804.

In the plebiscite held to ratify the establishment of an empire, over 3,500,000 votes were cast in favour and 2,569 against. One of those who voted against the proposal was Lazare Carnot, the 'organizer of the Revolution's victory' in that crucial year of 1793. As a member of the Tribunate, he protested strongly against the final destruction of the Republic. The overwhelming majority, however, acclaimed their new emperor. Napoleon did not wish to be regarded as a successor to the French kings, but rather as the heir to Charlemagne, who for his part had attempted to resuscitate the Roman Empire and had succeeded in uniting the countries of the West.

The Empire, the heir to the Revolution, made imperial princes and princesses of Bonaparte's family and elevated generals to the rank of imperial marshals, senior civil servants to the rank of high dignitaries. Napoleon was keen for Pope Pius VIII to attend the coronation in person, for the Pope's participation was important to him in his attempts to revive the rights and claims of Emperor Charlemagne.

On 2 December 1804 the imperial couple was ceremonially crowned in the very same cathedral (Nôtre Dame in Paris) in which the revolutionaries had paid homage to the Goddesses of Reason and Freedom during the dechristianization campaign eleven years before. It was a truly splendid occasion. The pope, the clergy, the new aristocracy, and the diplomatic corps were all present when Napoleon, wishing to demonstrate the fact that he owed his imperial power solely to his own abilities, set the crown on his own head.

Somewhere in the immense crowd which watched the sparkling coronation was Jean François Delmas. Once a deputy in the National Convention, Delmas had voted for the execution of King Louis XVI, had been a member of the Committee of Public Safety from April to June 1793, and had later fought as an officer in the Revolutionary Army. When asked how he was enjoying the ceremony, he cried,

'What a fancy-dress ball! Everyone has put in an appearance. No one is missing, no one except for the hundred thousand fighters who gave their lives to make such ceremonies impossible!'

Chronological Table of Events

1787

22 February The Assembly of Notables meets in Versailles for the purposes of solving France's financial crisis. The aristocracy is not willing to give up the privilege of exemption from taxation. Beginning of the 'Aristocratic Revolt' against the absolute monarchy.

9 April Dismissal of Finance Minister Calonne.

1 May Loménie de Brienne, Archbishop of Toulouse, is appointed as Finance Minister.

25 May Dissolution of the unsuccessful Assembly of Notables.

16 July Beginning of the Government's conflict with the Paris *parlement*, which rejects Brienne's reform edict and demands the convocation of the States-General.

19 November Huguenot Toleration Act.

1788

May Intensification of the conflict between the Crown and the *parlements*. Creation of the *Cour plenière*. Uprisings in Paris, Rennes, Dijon and seats of government.

7 June Street battles and stoning of the military in Grenoble (*jour des tuiles*).

June The clergy's General Assembly declares its opposition to the *Cour plenière*.

Summer Crop failures, rising food prices, the textile crisis and unemployment lead to an increase in mendicancy.

21 July Assembly in Vizille (Dauphiné). The three estates discuss the elections to the States-General.

8 August The king's Council of State agrees to convene the States-General on 1 May 1789. *Cour plenière* is suspended. Brienne is dismissed and Necker appointed as Finance Minister.

27 December Government agrees to double the number of the Third Estate's delegates to the States-General.

1789

24 January Elections to the States-General begin.

January Publication of the broadsheet *What is the Third Estate?* by Emmanuel Sieyès.

February to May A flood of broadsheets. Composition of electors' petitions (*cahiers de doléances*). Bread riots in various parts of the country.

28 April Workers in Paris revolt against the entrepreneur Réveillon.

30 April Founding in Versailles of the 'Breton Club' (precursor of the Jacobins) by deputies of the Third Estate.

5 May Opening of the States-General in Versailles.

17 June The States-General is converted into a National Assembly for the purposes of drafting a new Constitution.

20 June Tennis-Court Oath.

23 June The National Assembly, led by Mirabeau, successfully resists the king's command to dissolve itself and proclaims the immunity of its deputies.

9 July The National Assembly declares itself to be a Constituent Assembly.

11 July Necker is dismissed. The Court concentrates troops in order to attempt a counter-revolutionary coup against the National Assembly.

12 July Formation of a civil militia in Paris. Demonstrations against Necker's dismissal and street battles.

13 July The National Assembly declares its permanence. The troops leave Paris.

14 July Popular uprising; storming of the Bastille, the symbol of despotism.

15 July Necker is recalled. The aristocracy begins to emigrate. Bailly becomes mayor of Paris, Lafayette commander of the National Guard.

16 July to 4 August Peasants uprisings in the provinces: 'the Great Fear'. Formation of bourgeois National Guards and revolutionary municipal authorities throughout France.

4 August The aristocratic deputies in the National Assembly forgo some of their privileges.

11 August The National Assembly resolves to 'abolish feudalism'. The king refuses his assent.

26 August Declaration of the Rights of the Man and Citizens. The king refuses to ratify it.

September White plantation-owners agitate against the granting of human rights in the Colonies.

12 September First edition of Jean Paul Marat's the *People's Friend* (*Ami du peuple*).

5 October The women of Paris march on Versailles. Marat warns of a new counter-revolutionary coup attempt.

6 October The Court and the National Assembly move to Paris. The Breton Club takes up residence in the Friary of Saint Jacques.

2 November The National Assembly votes to expropriate ('nationalize') the Church's property (at the suggestion of Talleyrand) in order to repay the nation's debts.

9 November The Constituent Assembly meets for the first time in the Manège of the Tuileries.

19 November A law is passed authorizing the issue of *assignats* to defray the national debt (for the time being 400 million *livres*).

22 December France is divided into new departments (implementation date 26.2.1790). The Constituent Assembly adopts a property qualification and divides the population into 'active' and 'passive' citizens.

1790

13 February Closure of religious orders.

17 April The *assignats* become official currency.

22 May The Constituent Assembly pledges never to conduct a war of conquest.

4 June The 60 districts of Paris are converted into 48 sections.

12 June Revolution in the papal enclave of Avignon.

19 June Titles of hereditary nobility abolished.

12 July Civil Constitution of the Clergy.

14 July 'Federation Festival' on the anniversary of the storming of the Bastille.

16 August The aristocracy's administration of the legal system is abolished. Creation of justices of the peace.

6 September Abolition of the 13 class-based *parlements* (High Courts).

21 October The Tricolor becomes France's national flag.

October An attempted revolt by the coloureds in the French colony of Haiti is put down with armed force.

31 October Abolition of internal customs duties in France.

23 November General land-tax is introduced.

27 November Priests required to swear an oath of allegiance on the Civil Constitution of the Clergy.

14 December First note of protest from Emperor Leopold II because of the violation of the feudal rights of the estates of the Empire in Alsace.

1791

16 February Abolition of guilds and corporations. Introduction of freedom of trade.

10 March Pope Pius VI condemns the Civil Constitution of the Clergy.

2 April Death of Mirabeau.

15 May Robespierre, Abbot Grégoire, and other 'friends of the blacks' get a decree through the Constituent Assembly on the subject of equal rights for the free coloureds in the Colonies.

14 June Le Chapelier's Law: ban on friendly societies etc. and strikes.

20 June Flight of the royal family. The Earl of Provence, the king's brother and later King Louis XVIII, succeeds in escaping to Belgium.

21 June The king is recognized at Varennes, near the border, and taken back to Paris by deputies from the Constituent Assembly.

16 July The Jacobin Club splits for the first time. The monarchist constitutionalists leave the Jacobins and form the Feuillant Club.

17 July The radical Cordelier Club organizes a rally on the Champs de Mars to demand a republic. Lafayette orders his troops to fire on the republican petitioners. The National Guard carries out a massacre on the Champs de Mars.

22 August Large-scale uprising of negro slaves in the colony of Haiti.

27 August Counter-revolutionary Declaration of Pillnitz issued by Emperor Leopold II and King Frederick William II of Prussia. Threat of war.

3 September Completion and proclamation of the liberal monarchist Constitution.

14 September Louis XVI swears an oath of allegiance to the Constitution. Elections to the Legislative Assembly.

24 September The decree of 15 May, which granted equal rights to the free coloureds in the Colonies, is rescinded.

28 September Granting of full civil rights to France's Jews.

30 September Final sitting of the Constituent Assembly.

1 October Convocation of the Legislative Assembly, none of whose members are deputies in the Constituent Assembly. Out of 745 deputies in the Legislative Assembly, 264 are right-wing Feuillants, 345 independents (centre), and 136 left-wingers, divided between Girondins and radical Jacobins.

20 October Brissot, the spokesman for the Girondins, begins to agitate for war.

14 November The Girondin Pétion is elected as mayor of Paris.

3 December Louis XVI secretly asks the Prussians to intervene.

7 December A Feuillant government is appointed by the king.

1792

2 January Robespierre speaks out against war in the Jacobin Club.

14 January Talleyrand emigrates under the pretext of a diplomatic mission.

February/March Popular uprisings as a result of inflation and the hoarding of foodstuffs by speculators. Looting.

7 February Austro–Prussian military convention against France.

1 March Death of Emperor Leopold II. Franz II ascends the Throne (until 1806 as Emperor of the Holy Roman Empire, 1804–1835 as Emperor Franz I of Austria).

15 March Appointment of Girondist ministers (including Roland and Dumouriez).

20 April Legislative Assembly declares war on Austria.

25 April Captain Rouget de L'Isle composes and sings his *War-song of the Army of the Rhine* at the home of the mayor of Strasburg, Friedrich Dietrich. It is sung by volunteers from Marseille as they march into Paris (30.7.) and becomes known as the *Marseillaise*.

28 April The French army strikes back at the Austrians on the Belgian border. Formation of volunteer battalions.

27 May Decree against priests refusing to swear an oath of allegiance.

29 May The king's guard is disbanded.

11 June Louis XVI uses his veto against the decree concerning unsworn priests.

12 June The king dismisses his Girondist ministers.

20 June Organization of a mass demonstration against the king's obstructionism on the third aniversary of the Tennis-Court Oath. Petition of the Paris sections is presented to the Legislative Assembly and crowds invade the Tuileries.

3 July Eulogius Schneider, a German immigrant living in Alsace, begins publication of his newspaper *Argus or the Man with a Hundred Eyes* in Strasburg.

11 July State of emergency declared by the Legislative Assembly: *La Patrie en danger*.

25 July Counter-revolutionary manifesto issued before the beginning of armed intervention by the Duke of Brunswick, commander in chief of the allied troops.

3 August Speaking on behalf of 47 of the 48 sections of Paris, Mayor Pétion demands that the Legislative Assembly depose the king.

4 August The king summons the Swiss Guard to the Tuileries.

10 August The Paris sections establish an insurrectionary Commune, but the Legislative Assembly disputes their right to do so. Storming of the Tuileries. Deposition and imprisonment of the king. Formation of a Girondist cabinet. Danton is appointed as Minister of Justice. In the *People's Friend* Marat calls for a merciless struggle against the enemies of the Revolution.

11 August Legislative Assembly votes to elect a National Convention. Universal suffrage introduced for all men over the age of 21.

13 August The royal family is interned in the Temple.

17 August An extraordinary revolutionary tribunal is established.

19 August Prussia invades France. Lafayette goes over to the Austrians (imprisoned until 1797).

23 August The stronghold at Longwy surrenders.

26 August Eighteen foreign supporters of the Revolution are granted French citizenship by the Legislative Assembly and with elections imminent are urged to stand for election to the National Convention. They include the Germans Klopstock, Schiller, Campe, and Cloots, the Americans Washington, Hamilton, Madison, and Paine, the Englishmen Wilberforce, Priestley, and Bentham, the Swiss Pestalozzi, and the Pole Kosciousko. Only Paine and Cloots become members of the Convention.

2 September The stronghold at Verdun surrenders.

2–6 September September massacres. Around 1,100 prisoners held in Paris, including a number of unsworn priests, are murdered as royalist conspirators (many after hasty trials by 'Tribunals of People's Justice').

20 September Final sitting of the Legislative Assembly. Victory of the revolutionary army under the command of Generals Dumouriez and Kellermann in the cannonade at Valmy. Important turning point in the war. The allied armies begin to retreaat.

21 September Convocation of the National Assembly (750 deputies). The Gironde (around 180 members) forms the right wing, the Mountain (110 members) forms the left. The centre ('marsh' or 'plain') supports the Girondins until May 1793. Abolition of the monarchy and founding of a united and indivisible republic.

22 September Beginning of the Year I of the French Republic (introduction of the Revolutionary Calendar takes place on 5.10.1793).

27 September The revolutionary army is victorious in Savoy.

10 October The Jacobin Club splits for the second time. The Girondins (Brissot,

Vergniaud and others) are expelled.

October The Prussian army crosses the border back into France.

21 October Troops under the command of General Custine capture Mainz.

23 October Founding of the Mainz Jacobin Club (the 'Association of German Friends of Freedom and Equality') by the Jacobins Böhmer, Wedekind, Hofmann, and others.

6 November The revolutionary army under the command of General Dumouriez is victorious at Jemappes. France occupies Belgium until the middle of November.

19 November Decree passed by the National Convention on the subject of supporting other peoples wishing to free themselves from despotism.

20 November Discovery of secret papers belonging to Louis XVI in the Tuileries. Exposure of his links with the enemies of France.

27 November France annexes Savoy.

29 November The Revolutionary Tribunal of 17.8.1792 is dissolved.

30 November The Girondin Chambon is elected as the mayor of Paris.

11 December The trial of Louis XVI opens before the Convention.

16 December Aachen is captured by the revolutionary army.

1793

18 January Louis XVI is sentenced to death.

21 January The king is executed.

1 February The Convention declares war on England and the Netherlands.

7 February The Convention declares war on Spain.

14 February Pache becomes the mayor of Paris.

21 February The *enragé* Jacques Roux demands the death penalty for speculators.

24 February Decree conscripting 300,000 volunteers. Elections to the 'Rhenish–German National Convention' in the French-occupied Rhineland.

25 February Storming of Paris shops as a result of shortages.

10 March Revolutionary Tribunal established.

11 March Royalist revolt begins in the Vendée.

17 March Rhenish National Convention opens in Mainz. Proclamation of the first republic based on the sovereignty of the people ever to exist on German soil.

18 March The revolutionary army under the command of Dumouriez is defeated at Neerwinden in Belgium.

19 March Convention passes a decree on the subject of counter-revolutionary unrest (directed against the Vendée).

28 March Decree on the subject of punishing *émigrés*.

30 March Convention votes to meet the request of the Jacobin Georg Forster, sent to Paris by the Rhenish–German National Convention, and to annex the conquered left bank. Mainz surrounded by Prussian troops.

5 April General Dumouriez deserts to the Austrians.

6 April Committee of Public Safety established at the request of Danton.

11 April Controlled rates introduced for the *assignats* in order to check inflation.

13 April Convention resolves not to interfere in the affairs of foreign countries any more. Charges brought against Marat in the Convention at the insistence of the Gironde.

24 April Marat aquitted.

4 May Convention passes decree on the subject of the 'first' or 'small' maximum prices in order to guarantee the supply of foodstuffs.

10 May The 'Society of Revolutionary Republican Women' is founded by Claire Lacombe and Pauline Léon.

18 May A twelve-man committee is established by the Girondins in order to crush the radical Paris Commune.

20 May Convention passes a decree imposing a compulsory loan to the nation of a thousand million *livres*.

29 May An anti-Jacobin ('federalist') rebellion begins in Lyon.

31 May The Paris sansculottes rise up against the Gironde. The Commission of Twelve is dissolved.

2 June The uprising is successful. 29 leading Girondins are arrested. The beginning of 'authentic' Jacobin rule.

3 and 10 June Law passed to enable the sale of property belonging to *émigrés* and the sharing out of common land between the peasants.

13 June Escaped leaders of the Gironde meet in Caen (Normandy) and declare civil war. The war soon spreads to half of France.

24 June The Jacobin–republican Constitution is adopted by the Convention.

25 June Jacques Roux reads out the 'Manifesto of the *Enragés*' to the Convention on behalf of the Cordelier Club and the Paris sections Bonne Nouvelle and Gravilliers.

13 July Marat is murdered by Charlotte Corday. Roux continues to publish Marat's newspaper under the title *Publiciste de la République française*. Paris volunteer troops are victorious over the Girondist troops in Normandy.

17 July Final abolition of all feudal rights without compensation.

23 July The stronghold at Mainz surrenders after a siege lasting almost four months.

27 July Robespierre is elected to the Committee of Public Safety.

28 July Fall of Valenciennes.

4 August Plebiscite to ratify the Jacobin Constitution: 1,800,000 for, 18,000 against.

10 August Celebration of France's 'unity and indivisibility' on the anniversary of the overthrow of the monarchy. The result of the plebiscite on the new Constitution is made public.

23 August Decree of *levée en masse* (general conscription) introduces compulsory military service for all men between the ages of 18 and 25.

27 August Toulon is captured by the English.

28 August General Custine is executed.

5 September The sansculottes attempt a revolt against the Convention, which agrees to certain demands – such as the creation of a 'Revolutionary Army' to punish speculators. Jacques Roux, leader of the *enragés* is arrested.

8 September The army under the command of Houchard is victorious at Hondschoote in Belgium.

17 September Law of Suspects. The Terror begins.

29 September Convention passes a decree introducing a 'second' or 'large' maximum: ceiling prices are fixed for basic foodstuffs and vital commodities.

9 October Jacobin troops defeat the rebels in Lyon.

10 October A Revolutionary Government is established. The Committee of Public Safety is given far-reaching dictatorial powers. The Convention resolves only to enact the Constitution of 24 June 1793 after peace is concluded.

October The Society of Revolutionary Republican Women is disbanded.

16 October The army under the command of Jourdan is victorious at Wattigny in Belgium. Marie-Antoinette is executed.

17 October The rebel peasants in the Vendée are defeated.

31 October The leaders of the Gironde (Brissot, Vergniaud and others) are executed.

3 November Execution of the royalist feminist Olympe de Gouges.

8 November Execution of Madame Roland and Barnave.

10 November Climax of the dechristianization campaign led by left-wing Jacobins (Hébert). 'Festival of Reason' in Nôtre Dame. Large-scale closure of churches begins.

17 November Several supporters of Danton are arrested for their part in a financial scandal ('*Companie des Indes*').

18 November Robespierre speaks in the Convention on the political position of the Republic.

21 November Robespierre champions religious freedom and condemns the anti-Christian excesses of Hébert, Fouché, and others.

November Fouché and Collot d'Herbois carry out mass executions in Lyon.

22 November Danton launches his 'campaign for clemency'.

28 November Supporters of the *enragés* and Jacques Roux, the spokesman for the sansculottes, are arrested.

4 December A rigidly centralized Revolutionary government is appointed.

14 December Eulogius Schneider, public prosecutor to the Alsacian Revolutionary Tribunal, is arrested by officials of the Convention (Saint-Just and Lebas) in Strasburg.

15 December The third issue of the newspaper *Vieux Cordelier* is published and contains Desmoulin's attack on Robespierre.

19 December Toulon is recaptured.

20 December Introduction of compulsory education.

23 December The rebels in the Vendée are defeated. Carrier carries out mass executions in Nantes.

1794

10 January Georg Forster dies in Paris.

4 February Convention passes a decree abolishing slavery in the Colonies.

10 February Jacques Roux commits suicide in prison.

26 February and 3 March Saint-Just suggests the 'Decrees of Ventôse' and how they should be implemented. The decrees allow for property belonging to enemies of the Revolution to be confiscated and used to compensate the poor.

14 March Hébert and his supporters are arrested.

24 March Execution of Hébert and the left-wing of the Jacobin Club.

27 March The Revolutionary Army set up to punish speculators is disbanded.

28 March Condorcet commits suicide whilst in hiding.

30 March Danton and his supporters are arrested.

1 April Eulogius Schneider is executed.

5 April Execution of Danton, Desmoulins, the right-wing faction known as the *Indulgents*, and a number of speculators and spies.

13 April Execution of Chaumette and the former Archbishop of Paris, Gobel.

10 May The mayor of Paris, Pache, is arrested. His place is taken by the Robespierrist Fleuriot-Lescot.

8 June Festival of the 'Supreme Being'

under the chairmanship of Robespierre.

10 June Significant intensification of the Terror as the Law of 22 prairial of the Year II is adopted. Beginning of the Great Terror.

15 June Unsuccessful attempt on Robespierre's life.

26 June Revolutionary troops under the command of Jourdan score a decisive victory over the Austrians at Fleurus (in Belgium). The whole of Belgium is conquered and the troops advance on the German border.

23 July *Maximum des salaires* is introduced, and the workforce is angry over the freezing of wages.

26 July Robespierre's last speech to the Convention, in which he forecasts the military dictatorship.

27 July 9 thermidor: Robespierre falls from power and is arrested, along with his supporters Saint-Just, Lebas and Couthon.

28 July Robespierre is executed without trial. By the beginning of August over 100 of his supporters, including the members of the Revolutionary Tribunal and the Paris Commune, are guillotined. Beginning of Thermidorian rule.

5 August Revolutionary troops capture Trier.

24 August the Thermidorian Convention passes a decree to reorganize the government, the revolutionary committees and the Paris municipal authorities.

6 September Cologne and Coblenz are captured. By the end of October the Rhineland (except Mainz) is almost entirely occupied by French troops.

September The '*Jeunesse dorée*' commits outrages against the sansculottes and Jacobins. Beginning of the White Terror in Paris and the provinces.

5 October Babeuf's newspaper *Tribun du peuple* is published for the first time.

11 October The Paris Jacobin Club is closed down.

8 December Recall of those members of the Convention who had been expelled for their intervention on behalf of the Girondins.

24 December Abolition of price ceilings. Complete devaluation of the *assignats*, inflation and famine.

1795

5 January General Pichegru's troops invade the Netherlands.

6 January The Convention's resolution of 13 April 1793 not to interfere in the affair of foreign countries is rescinded.

19 February A peace treaty is concluded between France and Tuscany.

1 April 12 germinal: the sansculottes stage an unsuccessful bread riot against

the Convention.

5 April Peace concluded between France and Prussia in Basle. Prussia retires from the coalition.

7 May Fouquier-Tinville, public prosecutor under the Jacobins, is executed.

16 May Peace is concluded between France and the Netherlands in The Hague. Establishment of the Batavian Republic, a satellite state.

20–23 May The prairial uprising staged by the sansculottes is violently crushed. Several Jacobins are executed. Collot d'Herbois, Billaud-Varenne, and others are deported to Cayenne.

21 July Republican troops under the command of General Hoche are victorious over the *émigrés*, royalists and Chouans on the peninsula of Quiberon (Brittany).

22 July Peace is concluded with Spain in Basle.

22 August Proclamation of the Constitution of the Year III.

1 October France annexes Belgium.

5 October 13 vendémiaire: royalist uprising in Paris, which is put down by troops under the command of General Bonaparte.

31 October The National Convention is dissolved and a Directory inaugurated.

30 November Babeuf publishes his *Plebeian's Manifesto*.

1796

19 February Abolition of the *assignats*.

28 February The Pantheon club is closed. In the following weeks Babeuf's agitation for a 'Republic of Equals' and the installation of the Jacobin Constitution of 1793 reaches its peak.

30 March Napoleon Bonaparte begins his Italian campaign.

10 May Babeuf and his supporters are arrested one day before the planned uprising.

16 May Bonaparte enters Milan.

23 May Bonaparte negotiates a ceasefire with the Pope in Bologna.

31 December The Cispadane Republic (a satellite state) is founded.

1797

2 February Bonaparte's troops capture the Austrian stronghold of Mantua.

19 February Peace is concluded between France and the Papal State in Tolentino.

18 April A ceasefire is negotiated between France and Austria in Leoben.

27 May Babeuf and Darthé are executed. Others involved in the 'Conspiracy of Equals' are given prison sentences.

6 June Founding of the Ligurian Republic (a satellite state).

9 July Founding of the Cisalpine Republic (a satellite state formed out of the Cispadane Republic on 15.7.).
15 July Talleyrand is appointed as Foreign Minister.
4 September 18 fructidor: the Directory (Barras, Ruebell and Lerevellière-Lépaux) stage a coup against their colleagues Carnot and Barthélémy.
14 September Founding of the Cisrhenan Republic at the insistence of General Hoche. It is abolished a few days later.
19 September General Hoche dies in Wetzlar.
17 October A treaty is concluded between France and Austria in Campo-Formio, and the Rhine border is recognized. The war of the first coalition ends.
16 December The Congress of Rastatt meets to lay down conditions for peace between France and the German Empire.
29 December The stronghold at Mainz surrenders to the French.

1798

9 February Founding of the Helvetic Republic (a French satellite state).
15 February Founding of the Roman Republic (a French satellite state). Pope Pius VI is taken prisoner (dies 1799).
19 May General Bonaparte sets out on his Egyptian expedition.
21 July Battle of the Pyramids. Bonaparte's troops score victory over the Mamelukes.
12 September Turkey declares war on France when Bonaparte's army occupies Egypt.
24 December Alliance between Russia, Turkey, Great Britain, Austria, and the kingdoms of Naples and Portugal. The war of the second coalition begins.

1799

23 January King Ferdinand IV is driven out of Naples. Founding of the Parthenopean Republic (a French satellite state).
6 February Bonaparte's troops invade Palestine.
27 April Milan is captured by Austrian and Russian troops, and the Cisalpine Republic is dissolved.
28 April When the Rastatt Congress ends without result, two French delegates are murdered by Austrian hussars.
20 May Following their unsuccessful siege of the stronghold at Akko, Bonaparte's troops retreat and return to Egypt.
7 June The French army under the command of General Masséna is defeated by Archduke Charles at Zurich.
18 June Coup of 30 prairial. The Jaco-

bin Club is reopened (closed once and for all 13 August).
July Dissolution of the Roman and Parthenopean Republics.
15 August Defeat and death of General Joubert at Novi (in Northern Italy).
8 October Bonaparte returns to France.
22 October Russia retires from the coalition.
9 November 18 brumaire: Napoleon stages a coup (with the help of Sieyès, Fouché and Talleyrand). The Directory is dissolved.
10 November Formation of a provisional government consisting of the Consuls Bonaparte, Sieyès and Ducos.
13 December Proclamation of the Constitution of the Year VIII. Napoleon is First Consul, Cambacérès and Lebrun Second and Third Consuls.
15 December The military dictator Napoleon Bonaparte declares that the Revolution has been accomplished and is over.

1800

7 February Plebiscite to ratify the Constitution of the Year VIII.
13 February Founding of the Bank of France.
17 February Prefectures are established in the departments of France. Increased centralization.
14 March Pope Pius VII ascends the Throne of St. Peter.
May Bonaparte's troops cross the St. Bernard Pass.
14 June The French army under the command of Bonaparte is victorious at Marengo (Northern Italy).
3 December The French army under the command of General Moreau is victorious at Hohenlinden (Bavaria).

1801

5 January The Senate votes to deport 130 Jacobins to the Seychelles in the Indian Ocean.
7 February The black army commander Toussaint-Louverture, who has driven the English and Spaniards out of the French colony of Haiti, becomes Haiti's President for life.
9 February Peace is concluded between France and Austria in Lunéville. The Rhine is recognized as the border, and the Batavian, Helvetic, Cisalpine and Ligurian Republics are recognized. End of the war of the second coalition.
18 March Peace is concluded between France and the Kingdom of Naples.
9 May Toussaint-Louverture proclaims a constitution for Haiti.

9 July A concordat is signed by France and the papal Court (comes into force in 1802).
10 August The French army capitulates in Egypt.

1802

25 March Peace is concluded between France and England in Amiens.
26 April A general amnesty for royalist *émigrés* is declared.
19 May Founding of the Order of the Legion of Honour.
20 May Reintroduction of slavery in the Colonies. The blacks rebel.
7 June Toussaint-Louverture is arrested and deported to France (dies in the fortress prison of Fort Joux in 1803).
2 August After a plebiscite, Napoleon is made Consul for life.
4 August The Constitution of the Year X. The executive is strengthened at the expense of the legislature.
11 September France annexes Piedmont.

1803

25 February The Deputation of the German Estates meets in Regensburg and decides to compensate sovereign princes for the loss of territories. Most of the spiritual princes are secularized and the temporal princes mediatized.
7 April The Franc becomes France's new currency.
12 April The ban on workers' combinations etc. is tightened. Introduction of a workman's pass.
3 May The French colony of Louisiana is sold to the United States.
12 May Breach of the Treaty of Amiens. The Anglo–French war is resumed.

1804

20 March Final draft of the *Code civil*.
21 March Execution of the Duke of Enghien in Vincennes.
18 May Promulgation of an imperial constitution. The Senate votes to award Napoleon a hereditary emperorship.
5 June General Moreau is sentenced to two years imprisonment for alleged conspiracy. Later he is deported to the United States.
28 June Execution of Cadoudal and his royalist fellow-conspirators.
6 November Plebiscite on the subject of the imperial Constitution of the Year XII.
2 December Napoleon is crowned emperor in the church of Nôtre Dame in the presence of Pope Pius VII.

List of Illustrations

Chapter One

1.1 The coronation of Louis XVI in Reims Cathedral on 11 June 1775. The king swears always to obey the Catholic Church and persecute heretics.

1.2 An idealized painting of the 'Forest of Versailles', where the court nobility would often stroll. In the eighteenth century these grounds served as a model for the countless royal residences throughout the absolutist states of Europe.

1.3 King Louis XVI in his coronation robes. He ascended the French Throne in 1774 at the age of 20, after the death of his grandfather Louis XV, and had been married to the youngest daughter of Empress Maria Theresa, who lived in Vienna, since 1770.

1.5 Queen Marie-Antoinette in her bedroom at the Palace of Versailles. A painter portrays her as a harpist amid a group containing members of the high nobility, who were entitled to enter the royal chambers.

1.6 Queen Marie-Antoinette in her ceremonial court dress, around 1780. The lilies of the Bourbon standard are embroidered onto her purple robe in gold. Her intricate hair ornament consists of pearls, flowers and a bouquet of diamonds.

1.7 The *Comédie Française* during an opera performance before an aristocratic audience in the court theatre at Versailles.

1.8 In this idealized representation King Louis XVI is depicted as a benefactor of the people. In reality, he concerned himself little with the weal and woe of his subjects and spent his time either attending hunts and court festivities or in his locksmith's shop, where he made elaborate locks which he then showed off to visitors.

1.9 This is how a kitchen belonging to a serf or statute-labourer would have looked. They owned no land of their own and lived in abysmal poverty.

1.10 Anne Robert Jacques Turgot, Louis XVI's Finance Minister 1774–1776. He hailed from a wealthy, ennobled bourgeois family, and was a councillor in the Paris *parlement* and co-founder of the Physiocratic (liberal) school of economic thought. He tried in vain to reform the abuses of the old regime.

1.11 Jacques Necker, a protestant banker from Geneva, director general of King Louis XVI's finances from 1776 until 1781 and from 1788 until 1790.

1.12 Charles Alexandre de Calonne, Finance Minister to Louis XVI from 1783 until 1787. Like Necker, he was unable to restore financial soundness to the French budget.

1.13 The official opening of the Assembly of Notables on 22 February 1787 took place in the presence of King Louis XVI at the Palace of Versailles.

1.14 Caricature of the class-based privileged order. The peasant, whose stockings are torn and who wears clogs on his feet, carries the clergy and the aristocracy on his back. The receipts hanging from the pockets of the well-dressed members of the privileged classes show details of the clergy's prebends and pensions and the feudal dues and taxes which burden the peasants.

Chapter Two

2.1 The cavalry attacks employees of the carpet-manufacturer Reveillon in the Paris suburb of St. Antoine on 28 April 1789. During their rebellion they threw furniture from the factory from the windows and set fire to it.

2.2 Abbot Emmanuel Joseph Sieyès, whose broadsheet *What is the Third Estate?* contained the programme of the bourgeois Revolution. He was a member of both the Constituent Assembly and the Convention, voted for the king's death, but kept in the background during Jacobin rule. He was envoy to the Prussian Court 1798/99. He was then elected to the Directory and planned Bonaparte's coup on 18 brumaire (9 November 1799).

2.3 Opening of the States-General in the *'Salle des Menus Plaisirs'* at the Palace of Versailles on 5 May 1789.

2.4 A procession in the States-General at Versailles on 5 May 1789. The procession is in three columns, with the aristocracy on the right, the clergy in the centre, and the Third Estate (with twice as many delegates) on the left.

2.5 On 20 June 1789 the deputies of the Constituent National Assembly swear in the 'Tennis-Court Oath' to draft a constitution for France. The astronomer Bailly (later mayor of Paris) is speaking (on the table), in the foreground a regular clergyman (dom Gerle), a Catholic priest (Abbot Grégoire) and a Protestant pastor (Rabaut Saint-Etienne) embrace each other.

2.6 On 20 June 1789 the deputies of the newly-formed Constituent National Assembly, whose chamber has been locked on the instructions of King Louis XVI, go instead to the building in which the Versailles aristocracy used to play rackets (*Jeu de Paume*).

2.7 At a sitting of the Constituent National Assembly on 23 June 1789 Mirabeau calls out to the master of ceremonies, Dreux-Brézé, 'We are here by the will of the people and we will not stir from our seats unless forced to do by bayonets.'

2.8 Honoré Gabriel de Riqueti, Count Mirabeau, who was elected to the States-General as a Third Estate deputy despite being an aristocrat, tried in vain to achieve an English-style constitutional monarchy in France.

2.9 Camille Desmoulins, speaking in the gardens of the *Palais Royale* on 12 July 1789, appeals to the people of Paris to rebel.

2.10 On the night of 12–13 July crowds armed with guns, sabres, scythes and picks keep watch in Paris in order to prevent the town from coming under military occupation.

2.11 Having plundered the weapon store of the armoury (*Hôtel des Invalides*), crowds march to the Bastille with cannons and guns on the morning of 14 July 1789.

2.12 Storming of the Bastille on 14 July 1789. The assailants position the cannons.

2.13 The Bastille is demolished after its capture by the Paris crowds.

2.14 Marie-Joseph Motier, Marquis Lafayette, former comrade-in-arms of General Washington in the American War of Independence, as commander of the National Guard on the Paris Champs de Mars.

2.15 Patriots march triumphantly wearing sashes in the colours of the tricolor and red liberty caps. They carry a model of the stormed Bastille.

2.16 Night-time sitting of the Constituent National Assembly in Versailles on 4–5 August 1789. The sitting abolished feudal privileges.

2.17 The Declaration of the Rights of Man and Citizens adopted by the Constituent National Assembly on 26 August 1789 was later incorporated into the Constitution of 1791.

2.18 Allegory on the fact that the Declaration of Human Rights did not apply to the French colonies: a black slave demands that the Declaration's pledge that 'men are born free and with equal rights and remain so' be met. On the left stand four demons: the aristocracy, selfishness, injustice and revolt.

2.19 Painted medallion depicting the torso of a black slave woman who is wearing a liberty cap and demanding that the promises made in the Declaration of Human Rights be kept. The inscription reads, 'I (want to be) free too 1789'.

2.20 Headwear as a symbol of the Revolution: a young middle-class man sets a liberty cap on his head and throws his tricorn and wig to the ground.

2.21 The aristocrat and the clergyman are horrified when the citizen lying on the ground bursts his chains and seizes a weapon. In the background the Bastille is being demolished. Those who have just stormed the Bastille carry the heads of the commander of the stronghold, de Launay, and the merchant leader Flesselles on picks.

2.22 A banquet for the king's household troops in the opera hall at the Palace of Versailles on 1 October 1789, at which a tricolor was thrown to the ground and trodden on.

2.23 Parisian market women armed with stabbing weapons and a cannon march on Versailles on 5 October 1789. On the left is a noblewoman (wearing a trimmed hat), who does not join the procession.

2.24 On 6 October 1789 the demonstrators, joined by Lafayette's National Guard meet at Versailles. Soldiers fire their rifles in celebration as the king promises to transfer his residence to Paris.

2.25 Louis XVI and his family seated in a state coach drawn by eight horses. Under pressure from demonstrators, they have been forced to move their residence from Versailles to the Tuileries. The Parisian market women accompanying the procession joyfully wave sprigs of poplar.

Chapter Three

3.1 Following the closure of religious orders by the Constituent Assembly in February 1790, the monks and nuns move out of their cloisters.

3.2 A meeting of the Jacobin Club in the library of the former Friary of St. Jacques in the rue St. Honoré. After June 1791 the Jacobin Club met in the church itself since there was more room. On the left of the picture (standing) is the President, at the lectern on the right is a speaker.

3.3 Ordinary people dance around a tree decorated with a liberty cap and sing the revolutionary song *La Carmagnole. Ça ira, rejouissons nous, le bon temps viendra* – things will be fine, let us rejoice, good times are on the way.

3.4 The population of a provincial town in France plants a tree for freedom in the presence of the mayor and the National Guard. The National Guards wear sashes

in the colours of the tricolor. Young girls and children with garlands in their hair sing to the strains of a wind band.

3.6 The press freedom introduced by the Revolution created a new profession: newspaper sellers. Hundreds of newspapers and journals sprang up, many of them only short-lived. A newspaper seller shouts out details of the issue of *assignats*. The *'Patriote français'* is handed out by Brissot, the leader of the Gironde, on the left of the picture. The newspapers posted up next to Brissot, the *Journal du Soir* and the *Chronique de Paris*, were apolitical.

3.7 At the federation festivities in Paris on 14 July 1790 Louis XVI and Marie-Antoinette swear an oath of allegiance to the nation and the law.

3.8 The federation festivities on the Paris Champs de Mars on 14 July 1790, the first anniversary of the storming of the Bastille. In the centre is the newly-erected 'altar of the fatherland', from which a tricolor flies. The enthusiastic crowd swears an oath of allegiance to 'nation, law, and king'.

3.9 At the federation festivities on 14 July 1790 the Paris municipal authorities had wine and food distributed to the population on the Champs Élysées.

3.10 Soldiers of the National Guard on their way to the Palais Royal on the anniversary of the storming of the Bastille. They wear liberty caps to demonstrate their support for the Revolution and are surrounded by jubilant girls and children.

3.11 On 14 July 1790 a ceremony takes place on the spot where the demolished Bastille had once stood. The spot has been decorated for the occasion, but sections of the foundations walls of the Bastille are still visible to the left and right of the entrance.

3.12 At the federation festival on the site of the Bastille people dance and celebrate through the night in the glow of countless Japanese lanterns.

3.13 A coffee morning for patriotic women. The speaker reads from the *Moniteur* and the participants donate money for the nation.

3.14 The postmaster Drouet, who had recognized the king and thwarted his attempt to flee at Varennes on 22 June 1791 by barricading a road and thus stopping the carriage containing the royal family. He is dressed as a valet.

3.15 The royal family returns to Paris on 25 June 1791 under the watchful eye of the National Guard. On the left of the carriage sit Louis XVI, Marie-Antoinette, and the two children. On the right sit the king's sister Madame Elisabeth and a lady's maid. The deputies Barnave and Pétion, who are accompanying the car-

riage, are partly hidden.

3.16 The Constitution, drawn up by the Constituent Assembly, to be handed over to the king on 3 September 1791.

3.17 On the Champs de Mars on 17 July 1791 the National Guard carries out a massacre of republican petitioners at the orders of Lafayette.

3.18 On 14 September 1791 King Louis XVI swears an oath of allegiance to the Constitution drafted by the Constituent National Assembly.

3.19 A caricature of the king's points up his insincerity and two-facedness: he promises the deputies of the Constituent Assembly that he will uphold the Constitution at the same time as he is telling the priests that he will destroy it.

3.20 King Frederick William II of Prussia, Emperor Leopold II, and the Elector of Saxony, Frederick Augustus III, discuss their joint 'Declaration of Pillnitz' of 27 August 1791. It is regarded in France as a threat and the beginning of an anti-revolutionary crusade.

3.21 On 14 September 1791 the liberal-monarchist Constitution is proclaimed on the Paris marketplace *des Innocents*.

Chapter Four

4.1 The black slaves in Haiti revolt against the white plantation-owners, Autumn 1791.

4.2 Following the abolition of slavery in February 1794, the black slave François-Dominique Toussaint-L'Ouverture, cautious and talented leader of the revolts in Haiti, entered the service of the Republic. As a general, he successfully fought off the English invasion of Haiti and in 1800 declared the colony's independence. Expeditionary troops sent by the First Consul, Bonaparte, forced a surrender. He was deported to France and died in a fortress prison.

4.3 As a member of the Constituent Assembly the cleric Henri Gregoire drafted the Civil Constitution of the Clergy and later became the constitutional bishop of Blois. He was a leading champion of emancipation and equality for the Jews and of the abolition of slavery in the Colonies.

4.4 The cartoon depicts a meeting of the Paris Jacobin Club in January 1792 at the height of the fierce debate on the subject of war and peace with the allied forces of Austria and Prussia. The four speakers on the platform, clearly Girondins, are calling for war, but are opposed by the President of the Club (on the right). One member bares his behind, and in the centre stands a group of figures wearing boots and the clothing normally associated with the aristocracy. The figures either sport horns or have the heads of birds. Members of the public are seated on the balustrade above.

4.5 As a result of inflation and the economic crisis many craftsmen and owners of small workshops were unable to find their rent and were thrown out onto the streets by their landlords.

4.6 Pierre Victurnien Vergniaud, a lawyer from Bordeaux. Vergniaud was a member of the Legislative Assembly and the Convention and was a brilliant speaker for the Gironde. He was executed on 31 October 1793.

4.7 Jean-Marie Roland de la Platière. Roland was Minister of the Interior in Louis XVI's 'Gironde Government' from March until June 1792, and after the overthrow of the monarchy from 10 August 1792 until January 1793. He fled to Normandy after the overthrow of the Gironde and committed suicide when he heard news of his wife's execution.

4.8 The Legislative Assembly meets in the riding arena of the Tuileries. On the left is the President's table and chair, behind that a plaque quoting the Declaration of Human Rights, and on the right a speaker at his lectern. The public watches from the stands, and guards armed with pikes keep order.

4.9 On 25 April 1792 at the home of Mayor Friedrich Dietrich of Strasburg (seated on a chair in the centre) Captain Rouget de L'Isle sings his newly-composed *War-song of the Army of the Rhine* (*Marseillaise*).

4.10 Tens of thousands of copies of the sheet music of the *Marseille March* are printed and distributed among soldiers in the army and in the hinterland. The *Marseillaise* was translated into German six times during the Revolution.

4.11 Manon Roland (née Philipon), wife of the Minister of the Interior and twenty years his junior. Girondist deputies often met in Madame Roland's salon. She was a passionate opponent of the radical Jacobins and was executed on 8 November 1793.

4.12 General Theobald Dillon is murdered on 29 April 1792 in Lille. At the beginning of the war he had given the order to retreat and was accused of treason by his own troops.

4.13 The masses force their way into the Tuileries on 20 June 1792. They are protesting against both the dismissal of the Girondist ministers and the king's veto.

4.14 A crowd armed with picks, swords, scythes, and pitch forks carry placards saying 'Up with the sansculottes!' and 'Down with the veto!' into the royal chambers. One sansculotte has climbed onto a chair and is pointing at Louis and Marie-Antoinette. The king turns for help to the officers of the National Guard.

4.15 Volunteers leave for the front following the Constituent National Assembly's appeal on 11 July 1792, which claimed that the fatherland was in danger and that it was the duty of all citizens to defend their freedom.

4.16 Duke Charles William Ferdinand of Brunswick, the commander-in-chief of the allied Prussian and Austrian armies. On 25 July 1792 he issued a manifesto threatening Paris with destruction and on 19 August he invaded France. Following their defeat in the cannonade at Valmy he ordered his troops to withdraw.

4.17 Jerôme Pétion de Villeneuve, a member of the Constituent Assembly and mayor of Paris from November 1791 until November 1792. In the Convention he sided with the Gironde and after their fall from power fled to Normandy. Following the defeat of the federalist revolts he went underground and, when discovered in June 1794, committed suicide.

4.18 Louis XVI and his family retreat to the chamber of the Legislative Assembly, where it is decided to remove him from office. The battle between the rebels of 10 August and the Swiss Guard is visible in the background (right). The commander of the Swiss Guard has a rope tied around his ankles and is being dragged through the streets on his back.

4.19 Rebellious patriots storm the Tuileries on 10 August 1792 using artillery and cannon volleys.

4.20 One of the sansculottes who took part in the storming of the Tuileries on 10 August 1792. He is wearing the red liberty cap and long striped trousers (*pantalons*) in the national colours (red, white, and blue), not knee-breeches (*culottes*) such as those worn by the aristocracy. He is armed with both a sabre and a gun.

4.21 The Swiss Guards defending the Tuileries are mowed down on the evening of 10 August.

4.22 The 'Temple', formerly the meeting house of the Knights Templar, served as a state prison during the French Revolution. Louis XVI and his family were held prisoner here after 13 August 1792.

Chapter Five

5.1 Between 2–4 September 1792 many unsworn priests being held in the former monastic prison of the abbey (*l'Abbaye*) in the rue de Saint-Germain-des Prés were massacred as counter-revolutionaries. Here the crowd celebrates amid bodies which have been thrown out onto the street. One man carries the head of one of the victims on a pike.

5.2 A detainee, clearly identifiable by his clothes as an aristocrat, is brought before the 'Tribunal of People's Justice' which went into session in the abbey prison during the September Massacres of 1792.

5.3 The *Hôtel de la Force* (formerly a palace belonging to an aristocrat) in the rue du Roi de Sicile served as a prison during the Revolution. In September 1792 prisoners being held here are beaten and beheaded with hatchets and pick-axes.

5.4 The cannonade between the Prussian army under the command of the Duke of Brunswick and the revolutionary forces led by Generals Dumouriez and Kellermann at Valmy on 20 September 1792. There was no close combat, and on the next day the invading army began to retreat.

5.5 This poster from the autumn of 1792 bears the slogans of the Revolution. A fighter sits half-naked in a classical pose and with a huge liberty cap suspended above his head, a tricolor blowing in the wind on either side of him. He is leaning on a placard which reads 'Death to the tyrants', and beneath him is a stone block with the inscription 'Unity, Indivisibility of the Republic, Freedom, Equality, Fraternity, or Death'.

5.6 General Charles François Dumouriez, commander of the victorious revolutionary forces who fought at Valmy (20 September 1792) and Jemappes (6 November 1792). He lost the Battle of Neerwinden on 18 March 1793 and deserted to the Austrians three weeks later.

5.7 On 29 September 1792 the French army under the command of General Adam Philippe Custine attacked the town of Speyer. The picture shows an army division crossing the Rhine.

5.8 The 13,000-strong army under the command of Custine marches into the stronghold of Mainz, which surrendered without a fight on 22 October 1792.

5.9 The Battle of Jemappes (Belgium) on 6 November 1792, which saw the revolutionary forces under the command of General Dumouriez score a victory over Austrian troops led by Duke Albert of Saxe-Teschen.

5.10 A French cartoon mocks the defeat of the Prussian and Austrian troops in the autumn of 1792. The Austrian commander is saying, 'How these wretched sansculottes fight!' The Prussian King Frederick William II (who was present when his troops were defeated at Valmy) is answering, 'Who would have believed it!' The two are sitting back to front on their horses, and are being drawn by a double-headed eagle with the words 'News of new conquests' in its beak.

5.11 German peasant girls, priests and

French revolutionaries dance around a tree planted in the name of freedom and adorned with a liberty cap. A child holds high a flag bearing the words 'Freedom and Equality'. The scene was painted by an unknown artist during French occupation of the southern Rhineland (October 1792 – March 1793).

5.12 An advance party of the French Mosel army marches into the duchy of Zweibrücken on 10 February 1793. On the following day the troop planted a 'freedom tree' adorned with a liberty cap on the square in front of the duke's residence and promised to bring his subjects freedom and equality. The duke himself had fled to Mannheim.

5.13 A water-colour painted by Goethe in the autumn of 1792, during the French occupation of the Rhineland. From its position on the river bank the 'freedom tree', which has been decorated with a liberty cap and a tricolor, acts as a kind of border post and announces to those passing that the country all around is free.

5.14 On 11 December 1792 the king's trial opens before the Convention. The deputy Bertrand Barère (in the centre) presides over the sitting and is questioning the king, whom he addresses as 'Louis Capet' and who is visible in profile. The deputy Valazé (with his back to the onlookers) shows the king documents bearing his signature and upon which his crimes against the nation are based.

5.15 The king's second hearing on 26 December 1792. The deputy chairing the sitting is Defermon (on the right with a document in his hand). The king is standing in the background. On the left, at the table, are his three defence counsel Malesherbes, Tronchet, and De Sèze, who is summing up.

5.16 This handbill announcing the death sentence imposed upon King Louis XVI reads, 'Louis, traitor, read your sentence.' The hand breaking through the wall writes on the wall the words which the prophet Daniel (ch. 5, vv. 26 and 27) spoke to the Babylonian despot Belshazzar: 'God hath numbered thy kingdom and finished it. Thou art weighed in the balances and art found wanting.' Beneath the guillotine are the words 'Waiting for the guilty'.

5.17 Louis XVI on 18 January 1793, three days before his execution.

5.18 Louis XVI, accompanied by his confessor Abbot Edgeworth, glances back before climbing the steps to the guillotine.

5.19 A cartoon mocking 'the coalition of the kings or crowned villains against the French Republic' after England and Spain had entered the war early in 1793.

The animals are singing a 'dramatic potpourri'. No. 1: the fox, Pitt with an open purse on the table; No. 2: the turkey, George III of England (in a cage because his powers are limited); No. 3: the ostrich, Emperor Franz II; No. 4: the bitch, Catherine II (the Great) of Russia, at whose breast the emigrant brothers of the late king are suckling (the Tsarina provided them with money); No. 5: the toad, William V of Orange, stadhalter of the Netherlands; No. 6: the owl, King Frederick William II of Prussia; No. 7: the bat, William V's wife; No. 8: the pig, the Duke of Brunswick; No. 9: the horned billy-goat, King Charles IV of Spain (whose wife was the mistress of the Prime Minister Godoy); No. 10: the dachshund, King Ferdinand of Naples and Sicily; No. 11: the hare, Queen Maria I of Portugal; No. 12: Victor-Amadeus III, King of Piedmont and Sardinia; No. 13: the ass wearing the tiara on its head, Pope Pius VI.

5.20 A sansculotte on watch. The slogan on the tricolor reads 'Freedom or Death!' The folk-singer Chenard, who took part in the festival of freedom in Savoy on 14 October 1792, was the model.

5.21 William Pitt the Younger, English Prime Minister from 1783. He belonged to the Tory Party and had been financing the anti-French coalition ever since England had entered the war in February 1793. In the war of the second coalition (1798–1801) Pitt once again organized and financed the powers fighting the French.

5.22 A meeting at the working-class political club in one of the Paris sections. It was through these clubs that the sansculottes made their social and political demands in the years 1792–94.

5.23 Inhabitants of the Paris slums appease their hunger in the street, where the cook of an eating house provides hot meals.

5.24 An *assignat* to the value of 50 *sous* (two and a half *livres*).

5.25 *Nouveaux-riches* speculators and soldiers of fortune, for whom the devaluation of paper money is a source of enrichment, on their way to a banquet.

5.26 Several skirmishers from the revolutionary forces position a cannon. They fought, not in close formation, but in scattered skirmish lines.

5.27 In the summer of 1793 women also take part in the struggle to defend house and home.

5.28 A soldier of the Revolutionary Army in battle dress. He is armed with a gun and a sabre.

5.29 A meeting of the Paris 'Society of Revolutionary Republican Women' led by Pauline Léon and Claire Lacombe, which existed from May to October 1793.

5.30 Having invaded the town, royalist counter-revolutionaries in the Vendée tear up the tree planted in the name of freedom, chop it up, and burn the guillotine. In the background a procession led by clergymen and carrying a flag bearing a cross make their way to the church.

5.31 Rebellious peasants in the Vendée hide among the broom bushes. They are fighting revolutionary forces.

5.32 Camille Desmoulins, a journalist who had appealed to the masses to storm the Bastille. He was a deputy in the Convention and published the weekly newspaper *Le Vieux Cordelier*, which in December 1793 accused Robespierre of being a tyrant and demanded an end to the Terror.

5.33 Maximilien Robespierre, a deputy in the Constituent Assembly and the Convention, member of the Committee of Public Safety, head of the Jacobin Government from July 1793 until July 1794.

5.34 Georges Danton, founding member of the Cordelier Club, Minister of Justice after 10 August 1792, deputy in the Convention, member of the Committee of Public Safety from April to July 1793, leader of the *Indulgents* in the Jacobin Club from November 1793 until March 1794.

5.35 The radical democrat Thomas Paine, who lived in America from 1774 until 1787 and, as a journalist, played an important role in the War of Independence, was granted honorary French citizenship by the Legislative Assembly and became a member of the Convention. His book *The Rights of Man* (1791) became a gospel for republicans all over Europe. He objected to the execution of Louis XVI and was imprisoned from December 1793 until after the fall of the Jacobins.

5.36 Jean Paul Marat. He was originally a doctor, but did not practise after the outbreak of revolution. In his newspaper *L'Ami du peuple* (the *People's Friend*) he called for enemies of the Revolution to be fought relentlessly and correctly prophesied the king's treason, and that of Generals Lafayette and Dumouriez, and of the Gironde. As a deputy in the convention he resolutely spoke out on behalf of the sansculottes.

5.37 Louis Antoine de Saint-Just, deputy in the Convention, member of the Committee of Public Safety, friend of Robespierre, represented the Convention as a commissioner in Alsace and on the northern front.

5.38 Marat is acquitted by the Revolutionary Tribunal on 24 April 1793. The crowd decorates him with a citizen's crown.

Chapter Six

6.1 Jacques-Louis David's painting 'The Dead Marat' was commissioned by the Convention and hung in its chamber. The martyr of the Revolution lies dying in the bath, in which he sought relief from the pain caused by his skin disease. In his right hand he still holds a quill, his political weapon, which is contrasted with the murder weapon lying on the ground. In the left hand he holds the petition which his murderess used to gain access to his home.

6.2 Charlotte Corday is led away after having murdered Marat.

6.3 Charlotte Corday is led to the scaffold after having been sentenced by the Revolutionary Tribunal (17 July 1793).

6.4 On 16 July, his corpse having been embalmed, the murdered Marat lies in state on the deathbed of the Franciscan Friary in which the Cordelier Club met.

6.5 The executioner holds up the head of General Adam Philippe Custine, who was guillotined on 28 August 1793 for having surrendered the Rhineland (conquered by his troops in the autumn of 1792) and suffered various setbacks in Belgium. The sentence beneath the dripping blood reads, 'their impure blood should water our fields', a translation of the last line of the chorus of the Marseillaise, 'Son sang impure abreuva nos sillons'.

6.6 A Jacobin broadsheet denouncing the 'White Terror' in Lyon in the summer of 1793. The counter-revolutionary, the symbol of the anti-Jacobin 'Society of the Sun' on his chest, tramples the Constitution underfoot. His accomplices beat an unarmed worker.

6.7 Antoine Quentin Fouquier-Tinville, public prosecutor for the Paris Revolutionary Tribunal during Jacobin rule. His merciless severity was notorious. Even after the fall of Robespierre he attempted to retain his post, but was arrested and tried by the Thermidorians. He defended himself, unsuccessfully, with the argument that he had only been following orders, but was guillotined in May 1795.

6.8 The public prosecutor sums up during the Revolutionary Tribunal's trial of several aristocrats.

6.9 A local revolutionary committee in session during Jacobin rule. These committees were responsible for watching and interrogating citizens, as well as receiving their requests and accusations.

6.10 A Paris prison cell during the 'Great Terror' in the summer of 1794. A jailer, holding a list in his hands, calls out the names of 'suspects' to be taken before the Revolutionary Tribunal for trial.

6.11 The Revolutionary Tribunal tries Marie-Antoinette ('Widow Capet') on 14 and 15 October 1793.

6.12 Marie-Antoinette on the way to her execution, drawn by Jacques-Louis David on 16 October 1793 from a window in the home of the deputy Julien.

6.13 Marie-Antoinette on the scaffold. The drawing depicts an anecdote according to which she unintentionally trod on the executioner's foot and apologized to him before the executioner's assistants placed her head on the guillotine.

6.14 The sentence passed on Brissot and 20 other Girondins is read out in the Revolutionary Tribunal on 31 October 1793. The condemned men rise indignantly from their seats, and the deputy Valazě plunges a dagger into his chest.

6.15 The Girondins are loaded into two rack waggons with large wheels for transportation to their place of execution.

6.16 The courtyard of the Saint-Lazare prison, which housed 700 prisoners. This prison, in which numerous aristocrats were held, was known as a 'dandy's prison' (*prison des muscadins*) since the conditions were somewhat better than elsewhere: the prisoners were allowed to hire comfortable beds and keep servants. The picture shows several prisoners playing ball. No September Massacre took place at the Saint-Lazare prison, rue du Faubourg Saint-Denis.

6.17 A scene in Strasburg Minster, which was transformed into a 'Temple of Reason' during the dechristianization campaign led by the Jacobins Hébert and Chaumette in November 1793. In the foreground is the stone torso and arm of a toppled statue, probably of Saint Peter (there is still a key in the figure's hand). A Jacobin with a cap in his hand is preaching. In the background, on the altar, is an actress, who is meant to personify 'reason'.

6.18 The Church of *St. Jean en Grève* is pulled down during the dechristianization campaign.

6.19 Mass execution of royalists and other counter-revolutionaries in Lyon in December 1793. The shootings were ordered by the Jacobin commissioners Collot d'Herbois and Fouché.

6.20 The English fleet which landed in Toulon in the middle of August 1793 is driven out of France on 19 December. In the foreground (with the telescope) is the young artillery captain Napoleon Bonaparte, who headed the operation.

6.21 Lazare Carnot. Because of his outstanding military talents the Convention elected him to the Committee of Public Safety, where he acted, to all intents and purposes, as Minister of War. He organized the arming of the population, employed modern methods of mass warfare, and drew up, with great efficiency, operation plans for all fourteen of the revolutionary armies which defended France.

6.22 Bertrand Barère de Vieuzac, one of the best speakers in the Convention, was a member of the Committee of Public Safety. He composed communiqués to proclaim military victories and spoke out, along with Collot d'Herbois and Billaud-Varenne, for the Terror to be stepped up. In 1795 he was condemned to deportation to Devil's Island, but managed to escape. Given an amnesty by Bonaparte.

6.23 The 'Ultra-revolutionary' Jacques-René Hébert and his comrades in a rack waggon pulled by two horses on their way to the guillotine on 24 March 1794. On the right (in the background) is the entrance to the Jacobin Club with its inscription 'Equality, Freedom, or Death', in front of it a tree planted in the name of freedom.

6.24 The Festival of the Supreme Being on 20 prairial of the Year II (8 June 1794). The parade began at the Tuileries (left) and ended on the Champs de Mars, where a model of a mountain had been erected.

6.25 Camille Desmoulins embraces Georges Danton before their execution on 5 April 1794. The executioner's assistant grips Danton by the shoulder in order to lead him to the scaffold.

6.26 Citizens condemned by the Revolutionary Tribunal are transported to their place of execution in an open rack waggon. In the background (on the left) the outline of a guillotine is visible.

6.27 Victims of the Terror are loaded onto carts after their execution and taken to burial grounds.

6.28 The Battle of Fleurus (in Belgium) on 26 June 1794, in which the northern army under the command of General Jean Baptiste Jourdan defeated Austrian troops led by Josias of Saxe-Coburg.

6.29 The Place de Grève, in front of the Paris town hall, on the afternoon of 9 thermidor of the Year II (27 July 1794). Armed sansculottes from several sections assemble for the purposes of freeing Robespierre and his companions, who were arrested in the Convention.

6.30 In the early hours of 10 thermidor of the Year II (28 July 1794) the gendarmes sent by the Convention force their way into the 'Hall of Equality' in the Paris town hall in order to rearrest Robespierre and his companions. A gendarme by the name of Merda shoots at the seated Robespierre with his pistol and shatters his jaw-bone. In the foreground is the wounded Georges Couthon, who has fallen to the ground and is trying to fight off an assailant.

6.31 The morning of 28 July 1794. The seriously wounded Robespierre, whose head is resting on a wooden ammunition box, lies on a table in a meeting room used by the Committee of General Security.

6.32 The afternoon of 28 July 1794. 22 revolutionaries, including Maximilien Robespierre and his brother Augustin, Louis Antoine Saint-Just, and Georges Couthon, are driven to their execution on three rack waggons. The executioner is holding up the head of the first to be executed, and another is climbing the steps to the guillotine. Robespierre is the last to be beheaded. On the ground in front of the guillotine lies the deputy Philippe François Lebas, who had committed suicide when the gendarmes forced their way into the town hall. Several citizens celebrate the executions.

Chapter Seven

7.1 The Paris Jacobin Club in the rue Saint-Honoré is closed down on 11 November 1794 on the instructions of the Thermidorian Convention.

7.2 The French army under the command of General Pichegru enters Amsterdam on 19 January 1795. The town surrendered without a fight.

7.3 General Jean Charles Pichegru, conqueror of the Netherlands, 1794/95. He later went over to the side of the royalists, was deported to Guiana, fled to London, and took part in a royalist plot against Napoleon in 1804. He was arrested and found strangled in his cell.

7.4 The uprising on 1 prairial of the Year III (20 May 1795). The sansculottes force their way into the chamber of the Convention. One rebel carries the head of the murdered deputy Jean Feraud on a pike and holds it out towards the President of the Convention, Boissy d'Anglas.

7.5 Republican troops led by General Hoche are victorious over the royalist émigrés landed on the peninsula of Quiberon (Brittany) by English ships on 3 thermidor of the Year III (21 July 1795). After the capture of Fort Penthièvre (on the left of the picture), over which a tricolor is already flying, the royalists surrender. 748 captured émigrés and rebellious peasants were executed after the victory.

7.6 The royalist uprising of 13 vendémiaire of the Year IV (5 October 1795). Troops under the command of General Bonaparte respond with volleys of cannon fire and are carrying out a bloodbath on the steps of the Church of Saint Roche.

7.7 General Lazare Hoche. The son of a stableman, he rose to the rank of general during the Revolution, commanded the

Mosel army in 1793, and despite being innocent, spent several months in prison after having been denounced by General Pichegru. In 1795 he defeated the corps of émigrés which landed at Quiberon and fought the rebels in the Vendée. In 1797 he promoted the establishment of a republic on the German left bank of the Rhine, which would be set up with the help of Jacobins from the Rhineland. He died in Wetzlar at the age of 29.

7.8 During the rule of the Directory the extravagantly and fashionably dressed beneficiaries of the Revolution would meet at the 'Galerie de Bois'. In the centre is a spruced-up dandy (muscadin) wearing a high necktie, tightly-fitting frock coat with long tails, and soft pointed boots.

7.9 Paul Barras (Count) in his official robes as a member of the Directory. Barras, who had voted for the execution of Louis XVI in the Convention and played a part in Robespierre's downfall, was a member of the Directory from 1795 to 1799. Bonaparte was his protégé.

7.10 The issue of Babeuf's newspaper The People's Tribune or the Defender of Human Rights published on 17 vendémiaire of the Year III (8 October 1794). The newspaper's motto was Article 1 of the Declaration of Human Rights which appeared in the Jacobin Constitution of 1793, which itself never came into force. It reads, 'The goal of society is general welfare' ('Le but de la société est le bonheur commun').

7.11 The social revolutionary and communist François-Noël 'Gracchus' Babeuf defends himself before a tribunal in Vendôme in May 1797.

7.12 A cartoon mocking the émigrés who began to return to France in 1795 as a result of the fact that the royalists had become stronger. The Directory granted only a few émigrés the legal right to return. The émigré caricatured in the cartoon is returning illegally and risking persecution. Although he is poor and shabby, he has lost none of his arrogant pride.

7.13 Charles Maurice de Talleyrand-Perigord, the man 'who betrayed seven masters'. Although he was himself a bishop he suggested to the Constituent Assembly in 1789 that it should confiscate the Church's property for the benefit of the nation and swore an oath of allegiance on the Civil Constitution of the Clergy. He was abroad during Jacobin rule, but when he returned in 1797 he became the Directory's Foreign Minister. He helped Napoleon to seize power and remained Foreign Minister until 1809.

7.14 The coup on 18 fructidor of the Year V (4 September 1797): General Auger-

eau, who has forced his way into the Tuileries with his troops, arrests the royalist member of the Directory François Barthélémy (with the consent of three of the other members of the Directory, Barras, Reubell, and La Revellière).

7.15 Napoleon Bonaparte as a young artillery officer.

7.16 Victory over the Austrians on the bridge at Arcola (15 November 1796). This battle took place during the Italian campaign and is considered one of Bonaparte's legendary acts of heroism. A tattered French standard in his hand, the young general charges towards the enemy at the head of his men.

7.17 The preliminary peace negotiated at Leoben on 18 April 1797. Bonaparte, in a high-handedly triumphant pose, dictates his conditions to the Austrian negotiators General Meerveldt and the Earl of Gallo.

7.18 The Treaty of Campo Formio (near Udine) signed by France and the Habsburg Empire on 17 October 1797. Above, in the middle window are Napoleon (right) and the Austrian Foreign Minister Cobenzl. Two baroque angels trumpet Laus Deo – God be praised.

7.19 The triumphant French army under the command of General Berthier enters Rome on 27 pluviose of the Year VI (15 February 1798). The Roman Republic was proclaimed on this very day, and five days later the pope was deported to Siena.

7.20 Bonaparte addresses the army before the Battle of the Pyramids on 21 July 1798: 'Remember that from those monuments yonder forty centuries look down upon you!'

7.21 After his victory over the armies of the Mameluke Bonaparte rides into Cairo.

7.22 The murder of French envoys Raberjot and Bonnier on their departure from the Rastatt Congress on 9 floréal of the Year VII (28 April 1799).

7.23 The coup on 30 prairial of the Year VII (18 June 1799), following which two members of the Directory were changed. The coup resulted in a strengthening of the Left in the Council of Five Hundred.

7.24 The Battle of Abukir (in the Nile Delta, on the Egyptian coast) between the Turkish army under the command of Mustafa and French expeditionary troops led by Bonaparte, 25 July 1798. The Turkish army of 15,000 men was almost completely destroyed.

7.24 The coup on 18 and 19 brumaire of the Year VIII (9 and 10 November 1799). Furious deputies from the Council of Five Hundred surround Bonaparte in a hall at the Château of Saint Cloud. They threaten to ostracize him because he wants to dissolve the two elected Councils and rescind the Constitution of the Year III. The President of the Council of Five Hundred, Lucien Bonaparte, is standing on the podium and attempting (successfully) to remove his brother from the room.

7.25 A short time later: Bonaparte's grenadiers storm into the hall and use their bayonets to expel the deputies, who flee and jump out of the window.

7.26 On the evening of 10 November 1799, in one of the badly lit halls in the Château of Saint Cloud, the Council of Ancients gives its assent to a law transferring all powers exercised by the Republic to the Consuls Bonaparte, Sieyès and Roger Ducos.

Chapter Eight

8.1 On 20 May 1800 the French army crosses the snow-fields of the Great St. Bernard Pass on its way to Italy In the foreground there are soldiers dragging a gun-barrel which has been placed in a hollowed-out tree trunk.

8.2 The Battle of Marengo (in Lombardy), during which troops under command of Napoleon were victorious over the Austrians led by Melas (14 June 1800).

8.3 Jacques-Louis David's idealized painting of Bonaparte the hero on the St. Bernard Pass. Written in the ground are the names of two other celebrated men who had crossed the Alps with their armies before him: Hannibal and Charlemagne.

8.4 A royalist assassination-attempt in the rue Saint-Nicaise on the evening of 24 December 1800: an explosive device exploded shortly after a carriage taking the First Consul from the Tuileries to the opera had passed. The attack left 22 dead and 56 injured, but Bonaparte was unhurt.

8.5 Joseph Fouché. During Jacobin rule this former monk gained notoriety as a result of his bloody terrorist outrages in Lyon. In 1799 he became the Minister of Police, helped to plan Bonaparte's coup, and held his post until 1810. He was also Minister of the Interior for a long time. He built up an elaborate network of agents and spies and played all political groupings off against each other.

8.6 The Place de la Révolution, where the guillotine had stood, was renamed the Place de la Concorde. A market and various folk festivals were held there.

8.7 General Jean Victor Moreau, under whose command French troops scored victory over the Austrians at Hohenlinden on 3 December 1800. The battle decided the war of the second coalition in favour of France. Moreau, whose popularity Napoleon feared, was innocently dragged into a royalist plot involving Cadoudal and Pichegru. Napoleon had him deported to North America. He returned in 1813, entered the service of the Russians, and fell in the Battle of Dresden.

8.8 The bourgeoisie, which had become rich through the Revolution, and the dignitaries of the Napoleonic regime regularly came together in the salons and at dinner parties.

8.9 Jacques-Louis David's portrait of the Benedictine monk Barnaba Count Chiaramonti, who was elected as Pope Pius VII in March 1800.

8.10 Signing of the concordat between France and the papal Court on 15 July 1801. The concordat re-established relations between the two parties. From left to right: Joseph Bonaparte, who is handing his brother the quill; behind Napoleon, the Councillor of State Jean Etienne Portalis, who conducted the negotiations for the concordat; wearing the

black soutane, the pope's representative, Cardinal Consalvi; on the extreme right, Emmanuel Cretet, the governor of the Bank of France.

8.11 The three Consuls: Napoleon Bonaparte in the centre, on the left Jean-Jacques Cambacérès, and on the right Charles-François Lebrun. Below: Barthélémy hands Bonaparte a document naming him as a Consul for life (11 May 1802).

8.12 Napoleon's triumph is celebrated in classical style on the victory carriage following the signing of the Treaty of Amiens with England in March 1802.

8.13 The execution of the Duke of Enghien in the moat at the Château of Vincennes on the night of 20–21 March 1804. The duke, who had allegedly been involved in Cadoudal's royalist plot to murder Napoleon, was kidnapped from near Baden, and condemned to death by a war-court. He refused to be blindfolded before the shooting.

8.14 The trial of Georges Cadoudal, the leader of the Breton conspirators (Chouans), and 19 other royalists who had attempted to remove Napoleon and restore the Bourbon dynasty. They were sentenced to death on 9 June 1804, but Napoleon pardoned eight of them.

8.15 Napoleon in his coronation robes, with the victor's laurels on his head.

8.16 Empress Josephine in her coronation robes.

8.17 Napoleon is crowned 'Emperor of the French' in the Cathedral of Nôtre Dame on 2 December 1804. Painting by Jacques-Louis David. Napoleon is crowning himself. Pope Pius VII is seated behind him. Before him kneels the Empress Josephine. In the centre of the picture, on the large throne, is Napoleon's mother Laetitia, who in actual fact was not present at the coronation.

Selected Bibliography

The literature which has been published on the subject of the French Revolution is endless. This bibliography has been weighted in favour of the most notable works produced by historians of the nineteenth and twentieth centuries which have been written in or translated into English. Articles published in journals are not included at all.

Brinton, Crane, *A Decade of Revolution, 1789–1799*. New York and London, 1934, new edition 1964.

Cobban, Alfred, *Aspects of the French Revolution*. London, 1968.

Furet, François and Richet, Denis, *La Révolution. Des Etats Généraux aux 18 Brumaire*. 2 vols. Paris, 1965–67. English translation by Stephen Hardman: *The French Revolution*. London, 1970.

Furet, François, *Penser la révolution française*. Paris, 1978. English translation by Elborg Forster, *Interpreting the French Revolution*. Cambridge, 1981.

Gershoy, Leo, *The French Revolution and Napoleon*. New York, 1966.

Greer, Daniel, *The Incidence of the Emigration during the French Revolution. A Statistical Interpretation*. Cambridge (Massachusetts), 1951.

Greer, Daniel, *The Incidence of the Terror during the French Revolution. A Statistical Interpretation*. Cambridge (Massachusetts), 1967.

Guérin, Daniel, *Bourgeois et bras nus 1793–1795*. Paris, 1973. English translation by Ian Patterson, *Class Struggle in the First French Republic*. Pluto Press, 1977.

Lefebvre, Georges, *La Révolution française*. Paris, 1968. English translation in two vols.: *The French Revolution*. Vol. 1 by Elizabeth Moss Evanson. London, 1962. Vol. 2 by John Hall Stewart and James Friguglietti. London, 1964.

Mathiez, Albert, *La Révolution française*. 3 vols., Paris, 1922–27. English translation by Catherine Alison Phillips, *The French Revolution*. London, 1928.

Michelet, Jules, *Histoire de la revolution française*. 7 vols., Paris, 1847–1853. Numerous new editions. English translation by Charles Cocks (ed.), *History of the French Revolution*. Chicago, 1967.

Palmer, R.R., *Twelve who Ruled. The Committee of Public Safety*. New York, 1965.

Rose, R.B., *The Enragés: Socialists of the French Revolution?* Melbourne, 1965.

Rose, R.B., *Gracchus Babeuf. The First Revolutionary Communist*. Stanford, California, 1978.

Rudé, George F. *The Crowd in the French Revolution*. London, 1967.

Soboul, Albert, *Précis d'histoire de la révolution française*. Paris, 1971. English translation by Geoffrey Symcox, *A Short History of the French Revolution*. California, 1977.

Talmon, Jacob, L., *The Origins of Totalitarian Democracy*. London, 1952.

Thompson, James Matthew, *The French Revolution*. Oxford, 1959.

Thompson, James Matthew, *Leaders of the French Revolution*. New York, 1967.

Tilly, Charles, *The Vendée*. Cambridge (Massachusetts), 1964.

Tocqueville, Alexis de, *L'Ancien Régime et la révolution*. Paris, 1856. English translation by Stuart Gilbert, *The Ancien Régime and the French Revolution*. London, 1966.

Vovelle, Michel, *La Chute de la monarchie, 1787–1792*. Paris, 1972. English translation by Susan Burke, *The Fall of the French Monarchy, 1787–1792*. Cambridge, 1984.

Woloch, Isser, *Jacobin Legacy. The Democratic Movement under the Directory*. Princeton, 1970.

Woronoff, Denis, *La République bourgeoise. De Thermidor à Brumaire*. Paris, 1972.

Index of Place Names

Aachen 225
Abukir *197*
Akko 196, 227
Alsace 223
Amiens *213*, 216, 218, 227
Amsterdam *176*
Angers 160
Arcola *188*
Arras 54, 160
Athens 105
Avignon 67, 74, 223

Basle 178, 179, 226
Bayonne 74
Berlin 83, 91
Bern 195
Bologna 226
Bordeaux 74, *134*, 143, 160
Boulogne 218

Caen 143, 225
Cairo 194, 196
Cambrai 148
Campo-Formio 179, *190*, 195, 214, 227
Cayenne, Devil's Island in French Guiana 104, 159, 177, 183, 215, 218, 226
Chambéry 115
Coblenz 83, 85, 226
Cologne 226
Condé (Northern France) 148

Dauphiné 32
Devil's Island, see Cayenne
Dijon 223

Elba 216
Ettenheim 218

Fleurus *167*, 173, 198, 226

Geneva 29
Grenoble 32, 143, 223

Haiti *81*, 82, *82*, 223, 224, 227
Hohenlinden *208*, 213, 218, 227
Hondschoote 159, 225

Jemappes *109*, *111*, 112

Leoben *189*, 191, 226
Limoges 143
Loire 160, 177
London 218
Longwy 105, 224
Louisiana 227
Lunéville 213, 227
Lyon 133, *134*, 143, 144, *156*, 160, 176, 210, 225, 226

Mainz *110*, 112, 130, 148, 186, 225, 226, 227
Malta 196, 216
Mantua 191, 226
Marengo 202, 213, 227
Marseille 133, *134*, 143, 160, 176
Metz 79, 195
Milan 226, 227
Minorca 216

Nantes *134*, 160, 226
Neerwinden *109*, 129, 225

Novi 198, 227

Olmütz 104

Palestine 227
Paris *15*, *33*, 40, 41, *41*ff, 49, 60, 61, 65, 73, *75*, 77, 79, 80, 94, 97, 99, 102, 104, 112, 116, 123, *124*, *125*, 127, *128*, 133, 135, 144, 150, 158, 166, 172, 174, 176, 190, 195, 199, 223ff
Piedmont 227
Pillnitz 79, 83, 224

Quiberon (Brittany) *179*, 180, *181*, 226

Rastatt 195, *195*, 196, 227
Regensburg 214, 227
Reims *17*, 166
Rennes 160, 223
St. Antoine (suburb of Paris) *33*, 40, 98
Saint Bernard 201, *202*, 213, 227
Saint Cloud *198*, 199
Saint Marceau (suburb of Paris) 98
Savoy 224, 225
Seychelles 215, 227
Siena *191*, 195
Speyer *109*, 112
Strasburg *154*, 166, 224, 226

The Hague 226
Tolentino 191, 226
Toulon 143, 144, *157*, 160, 176, 225, 226
Toulouse 143, 195
Trier 226
Tuscany 226

Udine *190*

Valence 195
Valenciennes 148, 225
Valmy *96*, *105*, *109*, 112, *112*, 224
Varennes 74, 79, 98, 224
Vendée 125, *130*, *131*, 145, 160, *181*, 208, 218, 225
Verdun 105, 112, 224
Versailles *18*, *19*, 22, *22*, 24–5, *30*, *34*, 35, 55, *56*, *57*, 58, 60, 223
Vienna *18*, 83, 191
Vincennes 227
Vizille 32, 223

Wattignies 160, 198, 225
Wetzlar *181*, 227
Worms 112

Zurich 227
Zweibrücken *115*

Index of Names

Names referred to in captions have been set in italics.

Addington, Henry 216
Albert, Duke of Saxe-Teschen *111*
Antonelle, Pierre-Antoine, Marquis of 185
Artois, Charles Philippe de Bourbon, Earl of (later Charles X, King of France 1824–30) 50
Augereau, Pierre-François-Charles *187*

Babeuf, François-Noël, called Gracchus 183, *184*, 185, *185*, 226
Bailly, Jean-Sylvain *35*, 49, 84, 160, 223
Barère de Vieuzac, Bertrand 110, *116*, 123, 131, 149, *159*, 177
Barnave, Antoine-Joseph 43, 60, 61, *75*, 79, 80, 84, 160, 225
Barras, Paul-François-Jean-Nicholas, Earl of 174, 182, 183, *183*, *187*, 190, 191, 194, 227
Barthélémy, François *187*, 191, 194, *213*, 227
Beauharnais, Josephine 190, *219*
Belshazzar *119*
Bentham, Jeremy 224
Bernadotte, Jean Baptiste 198
Berthier, Louis-Alexandre *191*
Beurnonville, Pierre, Marquis of 129
Billaud-Varenne, Jean Nicolas 110, 149, 150, *159*, 177, 183, 226
Biron, Armand-Louis, Duke of Lauzun 93
Böhmer, Georg Wilhelm 225
Boissy d'Anglas, François-Antoine *178*
Bonaparte, Laetitia *219*
Bonaparte, Lucien *198*
Bonaparte, Napoleon (until 1796 Buonaparte) *34*, *82*, 129, *157*, *159*, 174, *177*, *180*, 182, *183*, *186*, *188*, *189*, 190, *190*, 191, *191*, 194, *194*, 195, 196, *197*, 198, *198*, 199, 200, *200*, 201, 202, *202*, 204, *204*, 205, *205*, 208, *208*, 210, *210*, 211, 213, *213*, 214, *214*, 215, *215*, 216, 218, 219, *219*, 222, 226, 227
Bonnier, Louis Antoine *195*
Bouchotte, Jean-Baptiste-Noel 131
Bouillé, François-Claude de 79
Breteuil, Louis-Auguste Le Tonnelier, Baron of 49
Brienne, see Loménie
Brissot de Warville, Jean-Pierre 65, 80, 85, 86, 90, 99, 112, 114, 123, 130, 131, 136, *151*, 160, 177, 224, 225
Brunswick, Duke of, see Charles William Ferdinand
Buonarroti, Filippo Michele 185

Cadoudal, Georges *208*, *214*, 215, 218, 222, 227
Calonne, Charles-Alexandre de *29*, 30ff, 223
Cambacérès, Jean-Jacques de 200, *213*, 227
Cambon, Joseph 110, 131

Campe, Joachim Heinrich 105, 224
Carnot, Lazare 85, 149, *158*, 159, 160, 183, 185, 194, 222, 227
Carrier, Jean Baptiste 160, 174, 177
Catherine II, Tsarina of Russia *122*
Chalier, Marie-Joseph 134, 148
Charlemagne, Emperor *202*, 222
Charles IV, King of Spain *122*
Charles, Archduke of Austria 227
Charles William Ferdinand, Duke of Brunswick and Lüneburg 91, *96*, 99, 105, *105*, 112, *122*, 224
Chaumette, Pierre Gaspard, called Anaxagoras 61, 135, 153, *154*, 165, 168, 171, 226
Chenard (folk singer) *123*
Chiaramonti, Barnaba, see Pius VII
Clavière, Etienne 91, 103, 136, 160
Clermont-Tonnerre, Stanislas, Earl of 42, 75
Cloots, Jean Baptiste, Baron of Val de Grace, called Anacharsis 105, 110, 131, 169, 224
Coblenz, Johann Ludwig, Earl of *190*
Coburg, Duke of, see Saxe-Coburg 127, 129, 148
Collot d'Herbois, Jean Marie 110, 149, *156*, *159*, 160, 172, 177, 183, 226
Condé, Louis-Joseph de Bourbon, Prince of 50, 99
Condorcet, Antoine-Nicolas Caritat, Marquis of 28, 156, 160, 226
Consalvi, Ercole, Cardinal *210*
Corday d'Armont, Marie Charlotte *139*, 144, 145, 225
Couthon, Georges 85, 140, 148, 160, 170, *172*, *173*, 174, 226
Cretet, Emmanuel *210*
Custine, Adam Philippe, Earl of *109*, *110*, 112, 114, 115, 130, *141*, 160, 225

Daniel, (Old Testament prophet) *119*
Danton, Georges-Jacquese 61, 80, 99, 105, 108, 110, 127, 131, *133*, 148, 153, *164*, 167, 168, 170, 224, 225, 226
Darthé, Augustin-Alexandre-Joseph 185, 226
David, Jacques-Louis *137*, *149*, 172, *202*, *210*, *219*
Davout, Louis-Nicolas 129
Defermon 117
Delacroix, Jacques-Vincent 131
Delmas, Jean François 222
De Sèze (Desèze), Romain *117*
Desmoulins, Camille *40*, 49, 61, 110, *132*, *164*, 167, 168, 170, 171, 226
Dietrich, Friedrich *87*, 93, 224
Dillon, Theobald *92*, 93
Dreux-Brézé, Henri-Evrard, Marquis of *39*
Drouet, Jean-Baptiste *74*, 79
Dubarry, Jeanne Bécu, Countess 160
Ducos, Pierre-Roger 199, 200, *200*, 227

Dumouriez, Charles-François 91, *105*, *109*, *111*, 112, 114, 127, 129, 130, *134*, 135, 159, 224, 225

Edgeworth de Firmont, Henri-Essex *119*
Elisabeth, Madame, sister of Louis XVI 75
Enghien, Louis-Antoine de Bourbon-Condé, Duke of *214*, 218, 227

Fabre d'Eglantine, Philippe-François-Nazaire 165, 168
Feraud, Jean *178*
Ferdinand IV of Naples (Ferdinand I of the Two Sicilies) *122*, 227
Fersen, Hans Axel, Earl of 78
Flesselles, Jacques of *52*
Fleuriot-Lescot, Jean Baptiste Edouard 172, 174, 226
Forster, Georg 119, 225, 226
Fouché, Joseph *156*, 160, 174, 198, 199, *205*, 209, 210, 215, 218, 222, 226, 227
Fouquier-Tinville, Antoine-Quentin *143*, 159, 160, 169, 172, 177, 226
Franz I, see Franz II
Franz II, Emperor of the Holy Roman Empéror 91, *122*, 191, *213*, 224
Frederick Augustus III, Elector of Saxony 79
Frederick William II, King of Prussia 65, *79*, 83, 91, *112*, *122*, 224
Fréron, Stanislas-Louis-Marie 174

Gallo, Marzio Mastrilli, Earl of *189*
Garat, Dominique-Joseph 131
Gensonné, Armand 85, 136, 160
George III, King of England *122*
Gerle, Christophe-Antoine dom, Carthusian friar 35
Gobel, Jean Baptiste Joseph, Bishop of Paris 165, 171, 226
Godoy, Manuel de *122*
Goethe, Johann Wolfgang 112, *115*
Gouges, Olympe de 225
Grégoire, Henri, Abbot *35*, 43, 74, *83*, 111, 224
Grisel, Jacques Charles Georges 185
Guadet, Marguerite Elie 85, 131, 136

Hamilton, Alexander 224
Hannibal *202*
Hanriot, François 136, 174
Hébert, Jacques-René 123, 135, 136, 145, *154*, 158, *161*, 166, 168, 169, 171, 185, 225, 226
Hegel 10
Hérault de Sechelles, Marie-Jean 140, 149, 170
Hoche, Louis Lazare 160, *179*, *181*, 194, 226, 227
Hofmann, Andreas 225
Houchard, Jean-Nicolas 159, 160, 225

Isnard, Henri-Maximin 86, 136

Jeanbon, Saint-André 148, 149
Jefferson, Thomas 53, 108
Joubert, Barthélémy 198, 227
Jourdan, Jean-Baptiste 160, *167*, 173, 190, 198, 226
Julien, Marc-Antoine *149*

Kellermann, François-Joseph *105*, 112, 224
Kléber, Jean-Baptiste 173, 199
Klopstock, Friedrich Gottlieb 105, 119, 224
Kosciouszko, Tadeusz 224

Lacombe, Claire *128*, 135, 154, 225
Lacroix, Sébastien 171
Lafayette, Marie-Joseph, Mothier, Marquis of 32, 42, *46*, 49, 58, 61, 77, *77*, 79, 80, 84, 85, 91, 93, 104, 129, *134*, 223, 224
Lameth, Theodor 84
La Reveillière-Lépeaux, Louis-Maris 183, *187*, 194
La Rochefouocault, Louis-Alexandre, Duke of 42
Launay, Bernard-René-Jordan, Marquis of 49, *52*
Lebas, Philippe-François 161, *172*, 174, 226
Lebrun, Charles François (Third Consul) 200, *213*, 227
Lebrun-Tondu, Pierre Henri (Foreign Minister) 104, 136
Le Chapelier, Isaac-René-Guy 43, 70, 71, 72, 172, 224
Leclerc d'Oze, Theophile 145, 154
Léon, Pauline *128*, 154, 225
Leopold II, Emperor of the Holy Roman Empire 65, 78, *79*, 83, 85, 90, 91, 223, 224
Lepeletier de Saint-Fargeau, Felix (friend of Babeuf) 185
Lepeletier de Saint-Fargeau, Louis-Michel 157, 158
Lerevellière'Lépaux 227
Letourneur, Charles-Louis-François-Honoré 183, 191
Lindet, Robert 85, 131, 149
Locke, John 75
Loménie de Brienne, Etienne Charles 31ff, 223
Louis Philippe d'Orleans, King of the French 1830–48 130
Louis XI, King of France 17
Louis XIV, King of France 17, *18*
Louis XV, King of France *18*, 160
Louis XVI (Louis Capet), King of France 17, *17*, *18*, 26, 28, 30, 32, 38, 49, 56, 58, 61, 65, *66*, *75*, 78, 79, 80, 83, 85, *87*, *92*, *95*, 97, 98, 99, *102*, 116, 117, 119, *119*, 123, 129, *133*, 183, *183*, 222, 224, 225
Louis XVIII, King of France 1814(15)–24, Earl of Provence 79, 224
Luckner, Nicolas 93

Madison, James 224
Malesherbes, Chrétien-Guillaume de Lamoignon de *117*
Marat, Jean Paul 57, 61, 71, 80, 99, 110, 113, 114, 123, 129, 130, 131, 132, *134*, 135, *135*, 136, *137*, *141*, 144, 145, 223, 225
Marceau, François Severin 173
Maréchal, Pierre Sylvain 185
Maria I, Queen of Portugal *122*
Maria Theresa, Archduchess of Austria, Empress of the Holy Roman Empire *18*
Marie-Antoinette, Queen of France 17, *22*, *23*, 65, *66*, *75*, 85, *95*, 99, *149*, *150*, 160, 225
Masséna, André 227
Meerveldt (Austrian general) *189*
Melas, Michael, Baron of *202*
Mercy d'Argenteau, Florimund, Earl of 99
Merda, Charles André 170
Mirabeau, Honoré Gabriel de Riqueti, Count *39*, 43, 49, 61, 64, 65, 84, 223, 224
Montesquieu, Charles de Secondat, Baron of 35, 75
Moreau, Jean Victor 190, 198, *208*, 213, 218, 222, 227
Mustafa Pasha *197*

Napoleon, see Bonaparte
Necker, Jacques 29, *29*, 32, 49, 65, 223
Nelson 196
Noailles, Louis Marie, Viscount of 42, 51
Novalis, see Hardenberg

Orléans, Louis Philippe Joseph, Duke of, called Philippe Égalité 110, 129, 160

Pache, Jean Nicolas 153, 172, 225, 226
Paine, Thomas 110, *133*, 224
Pestalozzi, Johann Heinrich 224
Pétion de Villeneuve, Jerôme *75*, 79, 80, 84, *96*, 99, 132, 136, 160, 224
Philippe Égalité, see Orleans
Pichegru, Charles 160, *176*, 177, *177*, *181*, 194, *208*, 218, 219, 226
Pitt, William the Younger, Earl of Chatham *122*, *124*, 215
Pius VI, Pope (Gianangelo Count Braschi) 67, *122*, 195, 224, 227
Pius VII, Pope (Barnaba Count Chiaramonti) *210*, 227
Pius VIII, Pope 222
Polignac, Armand-Jules-Marie-Heraclius, Duke of 50
Portalis, Jean Etienne Marie *210*
Priestley, Joseph 224
Prieur de Côté d'Or, Claude Antoine 149
Prieur de la Marne, Pierre-Louis 148
Provence, Earl of, see Louis XVIII

Raberjot, Claude 195

Rabaut St. Etienne, Jean Paul *35*
Reubell, Jean-François 183, *187*, 194, 227
Reveillon, Jean-Baptiste *33*
Robespierre, Augustin *172*, 174
Robespierre, Maximilien-Marie-Isidore 43, 54, 57, 70, 79, 80, 85, 90, 93, 99, 110, 113, 114, 117, 123, 130, 132, *132*, 133, *134*, 135, *143*, 148, 151, 157, 158, 164, 166, 167, 168, *169*, 170, *170*, 171, *171*, 172, *172*, 173, 174, 175, 176, 177, 183, *183*, 185, 200, 223, 224, 225, 226
Rochambeau, Jean-Baptiste-Donatien de Vimeur, Marquis of 93
Roland de la Platière, Jean-Marie *87*, 91, 103, 119, 131, 136, 224
Roland, Jeanne-Manon, née Philipon *91*, 136, 160, 225
Romme, Charles-Gilbert 164
Ronsin, Charles-Philippe-Henri 169
Rouget de L'Isle (Lisle), Claude Joseph *87*, 93, 224
Rousseau, Jean Jacques 3, *3*, *5*, *8*, 35, 61, 75
Roux, Jacques 96, 123, 141, 145, 154, 169, 225, 226
Ruebell, Jean-François 183, *187*, 194, 227

Saint-Just, Louis-Antoine-Léon de 117, *134*, 140, 148, 157, 160, 161, 168, 170, 172, *172*, 174, *174*, 226
Saxe-Coburg, Duke Josias of *167*
Schiller, Friedrich 105, 119, 224
Schneider, Eulogius 160, 161, 224, 226
Servan, Joseph-Michel-Antoine 91, 103
Sieyès, Emmanuel Joseph, Abbot *34*, 35, 43, 197, 198, 199, 200, *200*, 223, 227
Smith, Sir William Sidney 196
Solon (Athenian lawgiver) 105
Suvorov, Alexander 196, 198, 213

Talleyrand-Perigord, Charles-Maurice de 43, 65, 67, 77, *186*, 191, 198, 199, 218, 223, 224, 227
Tallien, Jean Lambert 174
Toussaint L'Ouverture, François-Dominique 82, *82*, 227
Tronchet, François-Denis *117*
Turgot, Anne-Robert-Jacques 28ff, *28*

Valazé, Charles-Eleonor *116*, *151*
Varlet, Jean-François 154
Vergniaud, Pierre-Victurnien 85, *86*, 136, 160, 225
Victor-Amadeus III, King of Piedmont and Sardinia *122*
Voltaire, François-Marie Arouet de 28

Washington, George 108, 224
Wedekind, Georg 225
Wilberforce, William 224
William V of Orange, stadholder of the Netherlands *122*

York, John David Louis, Duke of 159